SOUTH FLORIDA
**HOME
BOOK**

D0453521

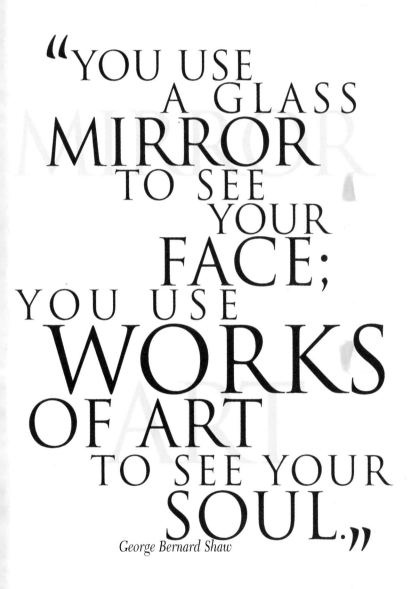

"YOU USE
A GLASS
MIRROR
TO SEE
YOUR
FACE;
YOU USE
WORKS
OF ART
TO SEE YOUR
SOUL."

George Bernard Shaw

SOUTH FLORIDA
HOME
BOOK

**A COMPREHENSIVE HANDS-ON DESIGN SOURCEBOOK
TO BUILDING, REMODELING, DECORATING,
FURNISHING AND LANDSCAPING A LUXURY HOME
IN SOUTH EAST AND SOUTHWEST FLORIDA**

Photo courtesy of:
SGA Architects Inc.

PUBLISHED BY
The
Ashley
Group

Chicago   New York   Los Angeles

Las Vegas   Philadelphia   Atlanta   Detroit

Phoenix   South Florida   Washington D.C.   Denver

San Francisco   Raleigh   Dallas

SOUTH FLORIDA
HOME
BOOK

Published By
The Ashley Group
3440 Hollywood Blvd., Suite 460
Hollywood, Florida 33021
954-985-8955 FAX 954-981-3728
www.southfloridahomebook.com

Cahners
Cahners Business Information
A Division of Reed Elsevier Inc

ISBN 1-58862-009-3

SOUTH FLORIDA HOME BOOK

Publisher *Mike Ruskin*

Editor-in-Chief *Dana Felmly*

Managing Editor *David Jackson*

Writers *Agnes Ash, Al Alschuler, Lois Prunner*

Office Manager *Margaret Wagner*

Account Executives *Jeffrey A. Sattler, Carmen A. Carrizales, Reese Cordisco*

Group Production Director *Steve Perlstein*

Production Director *Catherine Wajer*

Creative Director *Maura Gonsalves*

Production Managers *Anna Dronjak, Cory Ottenwess, Amie Smith*

Production Assistants *Jola Krysztopa, Karen Mages,
Kent Giacomozzi, Kirsten Hansen*

Graphic Designers *Sheri Bolliger, Ronda Farina, Kent Giacomozzi, Theodore
Hahn, Kirsten Hansen, Dona Kight, Dorit Paryzerband, Scott Piers*

Director of Marketing *Maria Bronzovich*

Public Relations Manager *Adam Miezio*

Prepress *Cahners Prepress, Lehigh Press Colortronics*

Printed in Hong Kong by *C&C Offset Printing Company*

THE ASHLEY GROUP

Group Publisher *Paul A. Casper*

Director of Publications *N. David Shiba*

Regional Director *J.D. Webster*

Director of Finance *Patricia Lavigne*

Group Administration *Nicole Port, Kim Spizzirri*

CAHNERS BUSINESS INFORMATION

Chief Executive Officer *Marc Teren*

Chief Financial Officer *John Poulin*

Executive Vice President *Ronald C. Andriani*

Vice President, Finance *David Lench*

Front Cover *Interior Designer Marc-Michaels Interior Design
Photo by Kim Sargent/Sargent Architectural Photography*

Back Cover *Custom Builder Miller Construction Company*

Editor's Note

This premier edition of *The South Florida Home Book* was created like most other successful products and brands—out of need. The *Home Book* concept was originally conceived by Paul Casper, currently Group Publisher of the Ashley Group. Paul, a resident of the North Shore, near Chicago, at one time was planning the design of his home. However, he quickly discovered problems locating credible professionals to help his dream become a reality. Well, Paul's dream did become a reality—it just happens to be a different dream now! Instead of Paul simply finishing his new home, he foresaw the need by consumers nationwide to have a complete home resource guide at their disposal.
Thus, Paul created the distinct *Home Book* to fulfill the consumer need for reliable and accessible home improvement information in the Chicago area.

After three years of successful publishing, the *Chicago Home Book* gained exposure and credibility, and drew the attention of Cahners Business Information. It proved to be attractive enough for Cahners, and in April 1999, Cahners purchased it. Since then, the *Home Book* network has grown rapidly. In addition to South Florida and Chicago, *Home Books* are also available in Washington D.C. and Los Angeles. Before the end of 2001, the *Home Book* will also be published in New York, Dallas, Denver, Detroit and Atlanta.

Public demand for high quality, home improvement services is still increasing. The Ashley Group recognizes this trend, and continues the challenging task of providing information about the finest and most experienced professionals to consumers. We exact the same amount of dedication and hard work out of ourselves as we expect from our *Home Book* clients. We sincerely hope our hard work rewards you with the quality craftsmanship you deserve, turning that dream house of yours into reality.

Congratulations on purchasing a *Home Book*. Now reward yourself by kicking back and delving through its pages. I hope you enjoy the inspiring ideas within!

Thank you very much, from myself and The Ashley Group.

Dana Felmly *Editor-in-Chief*

Why You Should Use This Book

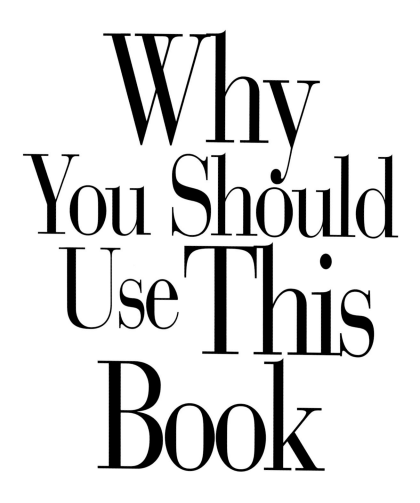

Why You'll Want to Use the South Florida Home Book

At times, in this high-speed information-driven culture, we can easily become lost and disoriented. Where we find information, how we find it, and how credible this information is, has become critical to consumers everywhere.

The *South Florida Home Book* recognizes and addresses these concerns, and provides ease of use and comfort to consumers looking to build, renovate or enhance their home. As a consumer, the anxiety of searching for trustworthy, experienced housing professionals can be overwhelming.

Relief is in Sight

The *South Florida Home Book* puts an end to this stress. It offers you, the reader, a comprehensive, hands-on guide to building, remodeling, decorating, furnishing and landscaping a home in South Florida and the surrounding area. The book also offers readers convenience and comfort.

Convenience

The *South Florida Home Book* compiles the area's top home service providers with easy-to-read listings by trade. It also dissuades readers' fears of unreliable service providers by featuring many of the finest professionals available, specialists who rank among the top 10 of their respective fields in South Florida and the surrounding area. Their outstanding work has netted them many awards in their fields. The other listings are recommendations made by these advertisers.

The goal of the *South Florida Home Book* creators is to provide a high quality product that goes well beyond the scope of mere Yellow Pages. Its focus is to provide consumers with credible, reliable, and experienced professionals, accompanied by photographic examples of their work.

This crucial resource was unavailable to the founders of the *South Florida Home Book* when they were working on their own home improvement projects. This lack of information spurred them on to create the book, and to assist other consumers in finding the proper professionals that suit their specific needs. Now, thanks to the team's entrepreneurial spirit, you have the *South Florida Home Book* at your fingertips, to guide you on your home enhancement journey.

Comfort

Embrace this book, enjoy it and relish it, because at one time it didn't exist; but now, someone has done your homework for you. Instead of running all over town, you'll find in these pages:

* More than 700 listings of professionals, specializing in 40 different trades.

* Instructional information for choosing and working with architects, contractors, landscapers and interior designers.

* More than 1,000 photos inspiring innovative interior and exterior modeling ideas.

*A compilation of the area's top home enhancement service providers with easy-to-read listings by trade.

Excitement... The *South Florida Home Book* can turn your dream into a reality!

Michael Ruskin, *Publisher*

The premier resource provider for the luxury home market

About the Front Cover:
A sumptuous South Floridian home interior, expertly decorated by Marc-Michaels Interior Design.

Contents

Continued

185

146

640

365

Contents

636

218

154

585

312

How To Use

TABLE OF CONTENTS

Start here for an at-a-glance guide to the 12 tabbed categories and numerous subcategories. The book is organized for quick, easy access to the information you want, when you want it. The Table of Contents provides an introduction to the comprehensive selection of information.

DESIGN UPDATE

Read what top home industry professionals think are the most exciting new styles, future trends and best ideas in their fields as we begin the new century. See even more inspiring photos of some of the South Florida's most beautiful, up-to-date luxury homes and landscapes. It's a visual feast, full of great ideas.

HOT DISTRICTS

An easy guide to a day of shopping in six of our city's hottest districts - West Palm Beach, Coral Gables, Palm Beach's Worth Avenue, the Miami Design District, Naples' Trade Center Way and the Bird Road Art District. Use the Hot District maps and information to plan weekend shopping sprees to some of the liveliest centers for furniture, fabrics, accessories, art, antiques and more.

"HOW-TO" ARTICLES

Each tabbed section begins with a locally researched article on how to achieve the best possible result in your home building, remodeling, decorating or landscape project. These pages help take the fear and trepidation out of the process by giving you the kind of information you need to communicate effectively with professionals and how to be prepared for the nature of the process. You'll have a step by step guide, aiding you in finding the materials you need in the order you'll need them.

FOCUS ON...

What's it like to live in the Palm Beach, Miami/Broward or Naples areas? These pages are filled with beautiful visuals that showcase the special atmosphere of these three well-known residential areas and their current design trends.

18

This Book

19

DIVIDER TABS

Use the sturdy tabs to go directly to the section of the book you're interested in. A table of contents for each section's sub-categories is printed on the front of each tab. Quick, easy, convenient.

LISTINGS

Culled from current, comprehensive data and qualified through careful local research, the listings are a valuable resource as you assemble the team of experts and top quality suppliers for your home project. We have included references to their ad pages throughout the book.

GREAT FEATURES!

From Interior Design Spotlight to New in the Showroom, we've devoted more attention to specific areas within the various sections. We've also gone in-depth, with feature articles in the Architects and Custom Builders sections.

ESSAYS

When home design, builders and landscape professionals get the chance to speak directly to their future clients, what do they have to say? Find out by reading the South Florida Home Book's Professional Essay Series. Their knowledge and unique viewpoints will entertain, enlighten and educate you. See the Table of Contents for the Essay pages.

BEAUTIFUL VISUALS

The most beautiful, inspiring and comprehensive collections of homes and materials of distinction in the South Florida area. On these pages, our advertisers present exceptional examples of their finest work. Use these visuals for ideas as well as resources.

INDEXES

This extensive cross reference system allows easy access to the information on the pages of the book. You can check by alphabetical order or individual profession.

The

A

Grou

THE ASHLEY GROUP

The Ashley Group is the largest provider of home
quality designing, building, and decorating information and
For more information on the many products of **The Ashley**
Cahners Business Information (www.cahners.com)
U.S. provider of business information to 16
manufacturing and retail. Cahners' rich content portfolio
Publishers Weekly, Design News and 152 other

ashley

RESOURCE COLLECTION

visual resource images, and strives to provide the highest
resources available, to upscale consumers and professionals.
Group, visit our website at www.ashleygroup@cahners.com.
a member of the Reed Elsevier plc group, is a leading
vertical markets, including entertainment,
encompasses more than 140 Web sites as well as *Variety*,
market-leading business-to-business magazines

Design

Kraton Gallery
USA, Inc.

Jacquie Macleod:
"Exotic and highly prized, Indonesian furniture, arts and crafts express a delightful mixture of Asian and European styles."

22

Update

23

SOUTH DADE
LIGHTING, INC.

Kathy Held: "There is currently a resurgence of interest in the concept of track lighting. Today's interest, however, is not in the traditional 'bare bones' ceiling mounted rigid track with the same old cylinder or square shaped fixtures available in black, white, chrome and bronze. The new track systems offer a broad range of choices in mounting options and fixtures. The track can be surface-mounted on the ceiling or dropped down on stems or cables. And it gets better. The sleek design of the newer track allows it to bend or curve above furniture settings and seating groups. Art displayed on curved walls can have the light source following the flow of convex or concave surfaces. Whimsical loops or graceful curves can be created with the track for a sculptural effect. Color, beyond the black and white of traditional track lighting systems, is now being introduced to coordinate or contrast with existing schemes. A surprising detail that can elevate a room to extraordinary is the wide variety of pendants and accessories available for track lighting. Cable hung lighting systems are ideal for small spaces or areas with low ceilings. Small rooms or tight spaces seem larger when illuminated with this unobtrusive system. The new track systems allow for the freedom in personal taste and statements that reflect a unique style of living."

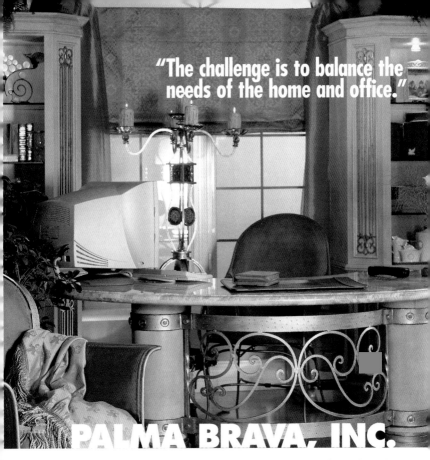

"The challenge is to balance the needs of the home and office."

PALMA BRAVA, INC.

Mila Nabor-Lee: "Whether you have a home-based business, work at home occasionally or are a full-time telecommuter, the home office is commanding a lot of attention these days. We are attempting to alleviate the frenetic pace dictated by our life choices and other members of our household with equally demanding schedules. Working individuals are increasingly dedicating their work time to a room or space in the home — one that is slightly 'softer' than a rigid carbon copy of a workstation, but still functional and practical. The challenge is to balance the needs of the home and office into designs that will meet this growing demand."

JOHANSON HOMES, INC.

Charlie Johanson: "The environment and sometimes harsh weather of South Florida has changed the way we build and created a host of new products and materials to make homes safer, less expensive to maintain and more comfortable. Our new homes have non-ventilated attic spaces to reduce air conditioning loads to save money and prevent moist, salt-laden air from entering living areas. Today's roofs use Gunite or concrete to provide better hurricane wind protection. Impact-tested windows have virtually eliminated hurricane panels and shutters."

GLOBAL FURNITURE

Therese Carreon: "The casual lifestyle is a very strong and important trend that is ultimately here to stay. Many shoppers are looking for more natural materials for their home, and regardless of style, the use of anything earthy like bamboo, wicker and rattan adds warmth and comfort to a room."

THE WORKSHOPS OF DAVID SMITH

Fran and John Markiewicz: "The kitchen is once again an integral part of the main family living space. It must function not only for food preparation, but also as a center for study, communications, or entertainment with the accompanying TV, fax, desk and computer workstation. Many choose to abandon the flush, fitted kitchen for one that has a homey feel of a collection of furniture. Cupboards, sideboards, desks and other elements put together at varying heights and depths form the basis of the look. Another key is an assortment of finishes, both painted and natural, with countertops possibly having several choices. Of course, while looking like furniture on the outside, the inside has all the functional options of today's living, including drawer glides, pantry pullouts, hidden appliances, task lighting, etc. The result is a kitchen specific to the client's needs and home style."

CERTIFIED POOL MECHANIC INC.

Grant Wilbanks: "Many clients now are requesting very naturalistic pool environments, utilizing elements such as rock and boulder waterfalls, lots of planter space, and a very random, free-form design philosophy. For those clients with larger sites, animatronics and theming with materials such as rock, bamboo and thatch are becoming quite popular. Beach entries and negative edges remain in great demand, as well as classically influenced designs. However, the hottest trend is mosaic tile patterns. These tiny glass or marble tiles can be used to create spectacular, three-dimensional effects that can transform the interior of a swimming pool or spa into a seemingly living, moving entity. For the homeowner who has limited space for an intricate pool design, this is a dynamic way to add 'punch'. This can also be said of other 'upgrade' materials such as marble, granite, slates, and other natural stone products that will greatly enhance the beauty of any swimming pool."

INTERNATIONAL STONE CONCEPTS, INC., *Lou Luzniak:* **"The most outstanding new trend we have observed in the stone industry is the use of lightweight natural marble and granite. New products have been introduced to allow application on ceilings, walls and wainscot without the liability of weight or stress cracks."**

Photo by J. D. Jaramillo

PAMI EXPORT-IMPORT, INC.

"The long history of decorating luxury residences with hand-painted ceramic tiles continues and shows no sign of slowing. It's not surprising. Today's artisans offer a wide choice of colors and patterns in both modern and traditional styles. To enhance any setting, fine ceramic tile is one of the most versatile decorating choices you can make."

DAN ALLEN LANDSCAPE LIGHTING

Dan Allen: "In the past few years, there has been a dramatic change in the landscape lighting industry. Quality 12-volt low-voltage systems are increasingly becoming the standard vs. 120-volt line voltage systems. Though line voltage systems have a place in some landscape lighting designs, low-voltage systems have more advantages, including no chance of electrical shock, pinpoint accuracy of light sources, energy efficiency, and the fixtures can be raised or moved as the ever-changing landscape in South Florida matures. And, because of low-voltage systems, today's landscape lighting designers can create magical views from interior spaces, lanais, gardens and the front lawn."

ROBERT CORDISCO STUDIO, *Robert Cordisco:* "Representative, two-dimensional art on the wall has given way to welcoming, tactile, three-dimensional sculptures in the foyer or in the garden. Whether whimsical or intense, in bright colors or muted metal tones, sculpture provides a positive escape and allows for personal reflection."

27

POLO HOMES
OF PALM BEACH, INC.

Misbah Ahdab: "We have been observing a very exciting trend toward new homes that not only are based on authentic architecture of the past, but also incorporate materials and processes used at the time. This has resulted in numerous floors, doors, fireplaces and other artifacts being transplanted from their homes of origin in Europe, the Middle East and Central America to the new homes locally. In addition, a limited, yet obvious rebirth of artisanship has been occurring in particular in the fields of plastering, creative painting and wrought iron woodworking."

"Function and style become one in today's kitchens and baths."

ELEGANT
HARDWARE

Gene Alonso: "Function and style become one in today's kitchens and baths. Your kitchen is where you create, as well as entertain. It's the home's nucleus. New semi-professional kitchen faucets and pot fillers provide a new look, and kitchen sinks come in many different configurations to fit any need. In the bath, there are endless ways to create a luxurious and private environment that reflects individual personality and lifestyle. Bathroom sinks can be mounted in many different ways and come in an array of materials, shapes and colors. They can be mounted on top of a counter or just half way in. They can be used on top of a variety of tables, such as glass or a piece of furniture."

WERNER DIETEL AND ASSOCIATES

Werner Dietel: "Due to the exciting selection of excellent outdoor lighting products, landscape lighting has become an art. Knowledgeable landscape lighting designers are able to 'paint' the nightscape by carefully selecting from an extensive palette of lighting materials. The result is a variety of lighting sources that illuminate and emphasize different landscape characteristics in a delicate yet dramatic manner."

LA MAISON FLEURIE, INC.

Annick Presles: "Recently, the soft palette of beige and white is less in favor with the public, and the general trend is moving toward warm, bright and vivid colors. There is a return to the Old World feeling with the use of antique furniture and artifacts in simplified and comfortable interiors. The contemporary style, while very modern and minimalist, is not as cold as in the past and uses warm, bright colors."

Photo by Johann Napp

STUDIO GALLERY NAPP

Gudrun Napp: "We have noticed a growing trend in the preference of works on canvas over works on paper in the selection of fine art. In many cases, colors seem to be of higher importance than subjects. Also, unique, handmade accessories are favored in all sizes, and custom designed contemporary items made to suit individual tastes are popular."

31

Photo by Robert Brantley

DENNIS CONNEL
INTERIORS

Dennis Connel

"We have discovered that more and more clients want their interior design to be personal, a reflection of their lifestyle, tastes and personalities. Whether it's a cutting edge media room or a living space designed around a favorite painting or oriental rug, we believe that the art of design consists of creating decorative elements that support this desire for self-expression."

33

Photo by George Lambros

SGA ARCHITECTS, INC.

ENVIROSCAPES, INC., *Mark Drew Martin:* "The task at hand is to find the alchemy of a landscape design. In combining my client's tastes, budget, needs and the existing architecture, these elements are transformed into a cohesive theme that will read aesthetically. By listening and communicating, the ideas are blended into textures, colors, smells and sounds, creating a garden environment that becomes art. The art lives; it is dynamic and offers my clients years of pleasure and enjoyment."

Spencer Goliger: "The exterior of a home should signal the character of its interior and reflect the overall architectural style. We see a trend toward multiple entrances, more detailing and the use of a variety of materials on the facades of today's custom homes. The use of more materials, particularly natural materials like stone for medallions, columns, and balustrades, coupled with multiple textures and bold colors, add depth and the result is a richer, more elegant feel."

NAPLES LUMBER AND SUPPLY CO.

Catherine Tebbe: "Today's kitchens and bathrooms are being designed in an Old World style. Homeowners want their kitchen and baths to look more like fine furniture with detailed crown moldings, fluted columns, turned posts and bracket feet. They are looking for more architectural detail. Warmer wood tones and creamy glazes are the most popular look of the new millennium. Inset doors are very popular, followed by the shaker look. More appliances are being paneled to 'melt' into the layout for that true custom look. Kitchens are looked at as the heart of the home where family and friends gather. Bathrooms are treated as a private retreat to go to relax and unwind."

Photo by Quality Custom Cabinetry

36

DISTINCTIVE INTERIORS

"Our customers want us to use exciting materials. Remaining a refreshingly simple, results-driven company, we are dedicated to extraordinary craftsmanship and good design. Believing our product must represent unequivocal and enduring value, our company is defined by our singular focus on the challenging realities of creating interiors."

AGOSTINO'S DESIGN GROUP

Kit Mathews: "Clients are leaning towards classic, timeless design in both traditional and contemporary spaces. The use of rich colors is very important. An eclectic combination of old and new allows for designs that are both casual and elegant."

Photo by Oscar Thompson

LAND DESIGN SOUTH, *R. Bradford Swanzy:* **"The environment and climate in South Florida have always been a strong factor in the quality of life. The environments we create for our clients vary from Florida casual to Palm Beach journal with all the lifestyles in between. The most recent trend has been toward specialty water features highlighted with unique tropical planting. This creates a truly personal space."**

Ⓐ INTERIOR MARKETPLACE, INC.

Alleen Lascala: "There is a resurgence in the quest for fine consignment furnishings, art and accessories that are vintage or new, and with expert craftsmanship will continue for generations to come. In this fast-paced age of mass production, it is reassuring to know that the quality of our decisions are preserved and remain timeless."

EVELYN S. POOLE, LTD.

Evelyn Poole: "The new trend in antiques is focused toward the Art Deco period — the fabulous designs of the early 20th century. The most important and beautiful furniture and accessories came from France during the 1920's and 1930's. 'L'Exposition and Internationale des Arts Decoratifs et Industriels Modernes' held in Paris in 1925 played an influential and crucial role in bringing the Art Deco designs to the attention of the public. Some of the most prominent designers of the period were Emile-Jacques Ruhlmann, Jules Leleu, Dominque, Edgar Brandt and Rene Lalique. The designs of the furniture, walls, floors, carpets, lighting and accessories, down to the last ashtray, contributed to the high style of the period."

SHOWROOM 84

A *Albert J. Herbert:* "The home exterior has become a prime category when a design budget is established on a project. No longer are outdoor furnishings left to the end of the job. Internationally renowned designers, like Larry Laslo for Veneman and Kip Stewart for Tropitone, are creating furniture collections for the outdoor market. They bring exciting new looks that are fresh, reflecting comfort and design. Partnering with the outdoor fabric mills, new collections have been introduced that mimic the jacquards and damasks that have endured in interior design for hundreds of years. We have seen the growth in this market increase substantially year after year and its importance grow to where we now see designers including the title of 'Exterior Designer' on their letterhead and business cards. The exterior of homes designed today pay closer attention to the melding of the exterior and interior square footage. These exterior living spaces must extend the home's ambiance and functionality as a place for entertaining and relaxation."

A

ONYX

Maria Flores: "Today's lifestyles are hectic and the outside world is cluttered. As a result, the trend is toward furniture that is comfortable and interiors that are serene and simple. We found that combining comfy, custom designed furniture covered in soft or silky fabrics with Oriental or Eastern touches is the key. Clients are also very personally involved with the decorating process; in most cases, a sofa or chair is not accepted until it perfectly matches the client's personal comfort level."

MARK MCCREE ARCHITECT

Mark McCree: "The resurgence of Old Florida and Mizner vernacular, coupled with the traditional neighborhood community planning movement, has made it imperative that the architect is a master of these mediums. The original creators of these concepts were seasoned craftsmen. Years of construction experience, coupled with 20 years of designing indigenous vernacular, has allowed my product to reflect a time-honored tradition."

Photo by Liz Ordonez

SIPURE DESIGN

Michelle Billet: "More and more concerned by the concept of their space, customers are looking for new contemporary interpretations of their home according to their own life styles and personalities. They became very selective in their choices. The demand is growing for quality design and high-end manufacturing incorporating the finest fabrics and materials. They know those demands make for vibrant, expressive spaces."

GULFCOAST MARBLE & GRANITE

Liz Ordonez: "Natural stone, because of its elegant beauty and durability, is the trend of the new millennium for new homebuilders. Today's natural stone products such as marble, granite, limestone and travertine offer a gamut of colors and finishes that allow architects and interior designers a great deal of flexibility for design and décor. Architectural stone elements bring an added dimension to the room."

CHRISTOPHER PEACOCK CABINETRY

Felton Perrier: "Of all the spaces designed for homes, the most challenging and rewarding has to be the kitchen. This room needs to perform very specific functions while providing an environment that is pleasing to the eye and expresses a personal aesthetic. As the kitchen has become more integral to the overall home plan, we often view it from one or more rooms. For this reason, cabinetry needs to be viewed as furniture. This furniture feel is achieved in many ways: the use of warm woods and hand-painted finishes; 'dresser' units that sit on worktops; housing appliances in cabinetry; open or glazed cabinets for storage and display; and leaving blank wall space for art. What's more, this attention to aesthetic has not overshadowed the increased functionality of the kitchen. Today's kitchens are boasting their purposeful nature with the use of professional-style ranges, refrigerators and other state-of-the-art appliances. The great design principle that form follows function is fundamental to good kitchen design. The challenge lies in marrying the two."

Photo by Eric Laignel

KURISU INTERNATIONAL

Michiko Kurisu: "Since ancient times, nature has been a balm for the pressures of daily life. These days, in the midst of an increasingly complex technological society, it is clear that our age-old ties to nature have become even more vital; people are discovering that, ultimately, material affluence and technological prowess alone do not satisfy. A balance needs to be struck, and people are rediscovering gardens as therapeutic spaces for inspiration and insight. Gardens link us to the eternal cycles of change and regeneration, reminding us of where we have come from, where we are going, and how living can truly be a sustainable joyous act of invigoration."

44

GULFSHORE HOMES

Steve Watt: "Increasingly, South Florida builders of custom estate homes are guided by two predominant themes: the strong influence of Mediterranean architecture and the prevailing practice that more is unquestionably better. Outdoor spaces have evolved into open-air living and dining rooms, complete with fireplaces, kitchens and furnishings. Water features are now integral elements of the architecture, and pools have grown both larger and more elaborate, with such elements as disappearing edges that eliminate lines of demarcation and create visual sheets of water. Indoors, virtually every facet of today's custom home is deeper, richer and more complex, from ornately detailed wall niches to intricately inlaid floors and inventive mingling of materials. And, fully integrated electronic technology continues to strengthen its role in these new homes with dedicated media centers accepted as the norm. For these homeowners, the standards are high and escalating, and that's a challenge we're happy to accept."

Ⓐ ARTE CERAMICA

John Fariello:
"The soulless influence of technology has left a void that is being filled by a ground swell of interest in high-touch things that provide comfort. Through the craft of the artisan, these single objects of contemplation are physical reminders of the world as it was before so many electronic snares. The best artisans work in the simplest materials — fabric, wood or clay. Some work in glass or metal. The medium is unimportant. That the object was made by hand and polished, painted, woven, or glazed by one person is the point. The finishes, colors and textures are a spot of consolation in our nanosecond-measured everyday pace."

46

Photo by Ronald Rosenzweig

WESSEL ASSOCIATES

Susan Bardin: "In today's hectic world, our clients are seeking personal spaces that calm and soothe. Yesterday's open spaces have given way to more intimate, framed vistas. Relaxing wood paneled libraries of warm cherry wood and leather are no longer the exception but the rule. Throughout the homes, decorative lighting sets the mood while grand scale indoor/outdoor spaces invite clients to live life to the fullest."

Ⓐ

Photo by John Fariello

INTERIORS BY STEVEN G., INC.

Steven Gurowitz: "Today's interior design is an extension of the client's personality. The use of straightforward materials such as stone and wood, combined with texture and color, add warmth, comfort, and elegance to an interior. Old World atmosphere combined with contemporary sophistication inspire today's great designs."

> ## "Modern architecture is a classic."

MITCHELL O'NEIL, AIA ARCHITECT

48

Mitchell O'Neil: "Today, modernism takes its place as a historic style in its own right, worthy of contemporary interpretation and implementation. Whether building a new home or renovating an existing structure, my clients are requesting the refined, aesthetically simple and uncluttered aspects of modern design. Even those who are drawn to Mediterranean, Bermuda Colonial or other traditional styles desire a design edited from a modern perspective. Formal and elegant, or casual and relaxed, the understated refinement of modern design enhances any lifestyle. Modern architecture is a classic."

Photo by
LouverDrape

MODERN VENETIAN BLIND CORP.

Cynthia Hall Othus: "It seems that all design trends go in cycles. South Florida is experiencing a desire to return to a more traditional look. We find that our customers are looking for interior window treatments that were in style in the 1950's. In addition, many of our clients are in the process of renovating historic homes and desire to hold to the integrity of the period in which their homes were built. Bamboo and matchstick Roman shades and two-inch wood venetian blinds have made an incredible comeback. People want products that are more natural with the beautiful variations of wood."

Photo by Brantley Photography

TAMARA TENNANT INTERIOR DESIGN

Tamara Tennant: "After two trips to Paris and another to Rome this year, it is apparent that clothing designers and people in general are turning their interests to styles that are simple and casual, but have an elegant quality about them. In talking with Lee Jofa about their line of fabrics, I found that they also are gearing their fabrics in this casual, elegant fashion with interesting patterns in Chenille, great silks and linens. The colors also are wonderful with the use of neutrals, tomato soup red, golds, blue-green, browns and grays. To see this wonderful range of color, refer to the Farrow & Ball Color Car."

RAY BARROWS WOOD FLOORS, INC., *Ray Barrows:* "We are seeing clients asking for various species of wood, such as Oak, bamboo or imported exotics in various finishes that are being used in homes and offices. Handcrafted wood inlays of exotic designs or logos, as well as artistic hand-paintings are also being asked for to provide a personal touch."

BOSS
PAVING

Philip Joseph: "Involved in many upscale projects, I have noticed a trend toward European design. Within this broad spectrum, one common thread seems to be prevalent: the aesthetic value of brick design becomes an integral part of the landscape. Brick shapes, colors and design features should express the client's unique personal needs."

51

Photo by Walter Webber

L.M. SILKWORTH

L.M. Silkworth: "The primary interest and desire of our clients is to have designed a Florida residence that accommodates their active schedule while allowing them to relax and enjoy a casual and understated, yet refined lifestyle. This directs us to tailoring their residence like a suit. They want to receive guests either formally or casually and have their home be comfortable on both occasions."

PACIFIC BEACH LANDSCAPING INC.

"The sound of water that tickles the ears and the sinuous sway of bamboo that treats the eyes are elements that have been added to today's vibrant, delightfully scented tropical landscaping. Put them all together and today's homeowner can come home to an exotic tropical paradise that treats all the senses."

53

MANTLE MAGIC

Victoria Digiulian: "Amateur and professional designers alike can enjoy a myriad of options to embellish homes today. Custom accents, fireplaces and columns make a dramatic or subtle statement in any room. Now, even master bedroom suites often feature fireplaces. Traditional architectural styles, though continuing to be the prevailing trend, are being given a contemporary flair. Despite the scientific and technological advances of our modern era, the human spirit still longs for the warmth of the hearth! The sense of warmth and familiarity of stone reminds people of a time when the world moved at a slower pace. The emphasis is on outstanding quality and craftsmanship. Longevity is a vital aspect of our creations; enduring qualities are essential."

Photo by Jim Harris

A'VARE DESIGN GROUP

Gloria Tian: "A tropical island look and mood has become an important part of our architectural and design creations. This elegant Loggia foyer epitomizes the trend. By combining the marble-topped plantation fluted console table, the sea grass wrapped circular mirror, and the painted banana leaf over the door, we have created an indoor island paradise."

54

Photo by Brantley Photography

NASRALLAH FINE ARCHITECTURAL DESIGN

Gloria Capozzi: "As the lifestyle demands of time and technology impact the home, the kitchen area grows in size and function. This major gathering place has become more than a room where meals are shared primarily due to advances in appliance innovation and client-craving conveniences. We see evidence of larger rooms with grand workspaces as well as wall-less openings to adjacent rooms to create its claim as the homes' centerpiece."

PALM BEACH LIGHTING & FAN CO.

"Lighting can be used for its basic function or offer ambiance, shadowing, or focus on the lighting fixture as a work of art. With the evolution of the bulbs using krypton, zenon and halogen, today's lighting makes for more versatility and brilliance than ever before."

LAVELLE CONSTRUCTION & DEVELOPMENT CORP.

Ronald J. Palladino:

"Over the past few years, the luxury home trend for our clients has turned away from the typical wide-open South Florida floor plans and gone back toward the more traditional separate room layout. Clients seem to be looking for more comfortable, livable quarters with defined spaces. Stone and wood floors, along with a variety of wood trim, help soften the appearance of each individual room. People want the ability to entertain clients and friends, but more importantly, they want the ability to have their families visit and stay comfortably under one roof. Even in vacation homes, our clients want to provide room for their children as well as their grandchildren. Four to six bedrooms, separate family and living rooms, libraries, game rooms, and exercise rooms are some of the standard features found in South Florida's newest luxury custom homes."

Photo by Steve Karafyllakis

"Stone and wood floors, along with a variety of wood trim, help soften the appearance of each individual room."

Ⓐ

CVRZON DESIGNS

Grenville Pullen: "We have found a major change in design trends over the last few years. Gone are the days of the bland South Florida style of the 1980's when everything was expressed in the name of Mizner or Mediterranean. Today's clients, whilst still enjoying an eclectic approach to English, French and Italian, are also expressing great interest in Art Deco and contemporary styles. This is an exhilarating trend which has generated a renewed interest in the best design of the 1920's and 1930's."

QUINCY JOHNSON ARCHITECTS

Ⓐ *Quincy Johnson:* "The most popular architectural trend in South Florida today pays homage to the design heritage of Addison Mizner. Known for architectural wonders like the Miami Biltmore, his unique blend of details from the south of France, the south of Spain and northern Italy has set trends that should continue long into the future. Our Mizner homes blend heritage with rooms to accommodate the very latest in entertainment and computer age technology."

JOHN PRINSTER ART DECO

John Prinster: "The number of people searching for the finest examples in craftsmanship and artistry have been progressively growing larger and larger over the years. The public is well informed and realizes the importance of surrounding themselves with furnishings that they love. It may be a piece of furniture used as a focal point, an exotic piece of pottery, a translucent form in glass, or a sleek and graceful lighting fixture. Today's collector knows treasures such as these, not only enrich their lives with style and elegance, but help to create a home that is a sanctuary."

THE AMERICAS COLLECTION

Carla Ortiz de Martinez: "We are noticing a growing demand for art from Latin America. This is true not only for the seasoned collector but also for the art-loving neophyte. Art is an essential element in any well designed home. Good art work is an investment in the quality of life, enriching our experience and enjoyment. The process of choice of art for the home should be an enjoyable adventure."

ABC
CARPET
&HOME

ABC CARPET & HOME

Matt Field: "The most popular styles in broadloom continue to be "wool sisals". Although traditional vegetable dyed, handmade oriental carpets continue to be strong sellers, contemporary carpets are definitely increasing in popularity."

BERRY'S BARBELL & EQUITMENT, INC.

Mike Howard: "The most exciting new trend we've experienced is the desire for club quality equipment for the home. Our customers want us to deliver that level of quality and feel for their homes. The typical home gym includes a multi-gym, one or two pieces of cardiovascular equipment, dumbbells, and a stretching machine."

BLAKELY & ASSOCIATES, LANDSCAPE ARCHITECTS & PLANNERS, INC.

Jeff Blakely: "Landscape architecture uses the constructed landscape to provide a balance between nature and culture. Today's clients desire a refuge from the demands of modern life that blends its comforts and aesthetics with that of the garden. The imaginative use of hardscape in the designed space, using old as well as new materials to complement and enhance planting is seen in the private as well as commercial project."

Photo by Jeff Blakely

BORROTO ARCHITECTS

Wilfredo Borroto: "Florida architecture is inspired by our wonderful climate. The trend is toward interiors that are open to the natural beauty outside with windows that frame colorful views and rooms that are informal yet elegant. Great architecture commands a search for the inner soul of each project and the soul of a South Florida home is found in the beauty of nature."

Photo by Otto Z. Borroto

Photo by Roy Quesada

S & B INTERIORS, INC.

Sandi Samole: "The audio/visual room is fast becoming one of the most important places in the home. Not only is it imperative that the sound and viewing be perfect, but the ambiance created by the furnishings is extremely important. We have seen media rooms go from being the smallest room in the house to becoming the largest, most important room. While theatre style seating has become popular, the more traditional leather sectional sofa is still one of our favorites."

PATRICIA CLOUTIER ART GALLERY

Patricia Cloutier: "In the 21 years that I have been in the art gallery business, I've watched the print medium undergo vast changes. The use of computers in producing the giclee or digital print make the printing process faster and more cost effective than the hand done fine art printing of serigraphs, lithographs and etchings. I personally feel the quality and time-honored tradition of the artist creating his own original print along with a team of craftsmen, gives us rich, unique and enduring images in their purist form. The revered etchings of Rembrandt, linocuts of Picasso or engravings of Durer set very high standards for contemporary artist-turned-printmakers. Handwork is bound up with art and original execution as opposed to the photo-mechanical and computer processes. Should the collector buy a giclee? The market for them is growing at more than 60 percent a year, so they are certainly capturing an increasing share of art sales."

FENG SHUI DESIGNS

Elyse M. Santoro: "The 'cocooning' lifestyle has been cultivated for several years. People have become more aware of how their environment effects them and are searching for ways to create a sanctuary for their souls. The art of Feng Shui is enlightened design. Nature's energy offers an infinity of joy; it evokes a universal connection, incorporating essential elements that bring balance and harmony to your environment. Utilizing the principles of Feng Shui will enhance any design process and is an alternative way of approaching traditional home design."

CHARLES H. PAWLEY ARCHITECT, P.A.

Charles H. Pawley, "Despite the geographic tie that the name 'tropical architecture' evokes, tropical elements can be used anywhere in the world, in any architectural style the client may prefer. What are these elements? High ceilings, big overhangs and tall (eight to nine feet) French doors are typical. The essence of this architecture is romantic with lots of natural light, a feeling of airiness, and a flow between indoor and outdoor spaces. Yet, these same romantic components also typify the elements of low maintenance, which appeals to everyone's pragmatic side. Forces of nature are kept away from direct contact with walls and windows, so the building is protected from attacks of any kind of weather. Proper site orientation maximizes the benefits and minimizes the disadvantages of the environment, allowing for cost-efficient energy use. Without actually using the word 'tropical,' this is what the recent generation of homeowners ask for: airiness and easy flow between living spaces, the perception of bringing the outdoors in, energy efficiency, low maintenance, and a structure's graceful blending into its environment over time. This has always been the tropical solution without a tropical location. It produces a house built for the millennium in any environment and any architectural style."

Photo by Dan Forer

RAINBOW TILE

Paul Young: "The trend in tiles and stone is definitely moving toward Old World looks. Clients are seeking materials that resemble centuries old stones, mosaics and tiles. The ability for limitless design patterns and color combinations has broadened the imaginations of designers, architects and homeowners."

SWEET ART AND DESIGN, INC.

Brad Conrad: "Homeowners are becoming more sophisticated and discriminating in their tastes. We have experienced a growing desire to blend various styles, techniques and mediums to our decorative wall finishes. Attention to detail and quality are both important. Clients are amazed how faux finishes, murals and trompe l'oeli create a comfortable and warm ambience in their home."

INTERNATIONAL INTERIORS

Rebecca Tedder: "The ultimate trend in design today comes from an renewed appreciation and use of natural materials. The rich beauty of a hand-carved cedar and polished black granite coffee table, the elegance of a custom-carved cedar sliding screen and the comfort of cedar-backed couches, make this contemporary room as pleasing to the eye as it is a refuge for the soul."

EXCEL AUDIO VIDEO

Rob McManus: "Consumers' appetites for surround sound has increased beyond our expectations. Many customers will convert a guestroom or study into a home theatre with amazing results. Now, even music CD's are being mixed in 5.1 channel audio. The technology, when properly installed and programmed; can provide a great escape and endless entertainment without leaving home. We will see more channels of audio (7.1) and HD video provide a greater sense of realism."

FIORELLI ANTIQUES

Ⓐ *Nino Pernetti:* "Ironically, Art Deco, which experienced its creative pinnacle in the 1920's, is the style of the future. With its simple lines, somewhat a variant of Cubism, Art Deco is full of intensity. The age experienced an explosion of great artists who were rebelling against classicism and therefore expressed themselves with an incredible freedom of design. The uniqueness of these antique pieces is that they harmonize with any home, blend with any decorative style, and yet, are not as pretentious as pieces from, for instance, the Rococo or Renaissance periods. In Miami, our gallery is something quite new. All pieces are costly, but entirely unique, not at all replicable and never again available."

Ⓐ

ROSS DESIGN ASSOCIATES, INC. *Anne Ross and Jerry Grissom:* "We are committed to the philosophy that the personality of a space belongs exclusively to the owner. We believe that good design should always focus on the client's heart and soul. Our priority is to understand what is meaningful to our clients, then create the space that will give comfort, embrace their friends and family, and inspire a feeling of pride and joy each time they enter the front door. For this reason, our designs are personal and timeless."

71

"Whether it is classical or ultra modern in design, today's custom library has the appeal for being a sanctuary in large-scale residences."

72

Photo by Robert Brantly

HANSEN L.C.

Denise Reyna: "The most exciting residential projects today contain handcrafted libraries in rich wood veneers and other natural materials. With homes becoming larger and larger in size and scope, interior architects and designers are incorporating living spaces that are not only warm and comfortable, but are also functional. We are seeing a great deal of interest in rare and exotic veneers, combined in the most part with a hand-polished or highly polished surface. Whether it is classical or ultra modern in design, today's custom library has the appeal for being a sanctuary in large-scale residences. Thus leading to the increase of architects and designers incorporating this special retreat into floor plans and interior design alike."

MOSAICA

James Crosfield: "We've seen a resurgence of interest in the art of mosaic. Highly popular in the 1950's, today, this intricate and durable art form is seen on dining and coffee tables, mirrors, wall plaques, floor medallions—even grandfather clocks and birdbaths."

Ⓐ

FLORENCE GALLERY

Amy Gasbarro: "Paintings with a comical edge add interest and conversation to any room. Dogs dressed in suits, monkeys drinking martinis, or rather large ladies undressing and serving cocktails certainly add a great presence of life and humor to all decors. From the most traditional to the ultra contemporary, these paintings are a great decorating trend that leaves everyone with a smile."

ROSE DE PARIS & PROVENCE

Ⓐ *Joëlle Rosanno:* "It is interesting to combine the charm of the antique with the contemporary style of the new wave of French designers. The result is an atmosphere that exudes a sophisticated French style while conserving a natural warmth and intimacy. The eclectic mix offers treasures for everyone from the newest francophile convert to the most seasoned French design aficionado."

SUB-ZERO DISTRIBUTORS, INC.

"'Fitted' kitchens tuck laundry and kitchen appliances into custom made cabinetry and dove-tailed drawers to match the interior design. From Old World provincial or country heartland to urban contemporary or ultra modern, the fitted kitchen utilizes craftsmanship, design and ergonomics to create a sophistication, comfort and sense of style."

MILLER CONSTRUCTION COMPANY

Grey Marker: "Today's high-end custom homebuyers are redefining outdoor living, with new design ideas and technology adding an exciting dimension to homes. For example, swimming pools frequently resemble water theme parks with grottos, bridges, rockscaping, waterfalls, spas and in-pool bars. Popular new approaches adding to year-round livability of outdoor spaces include elaborate covered lanai or loggia areas that integrate teak, cypress and other natural woods with marine-grade materials to protect against Florida's climate. These 'outdoor rooms' with marble or stone flooring now feature full-scale kitchens, bars, barbecues, fireplaces and seating, while cabanas and gazebos further extend the outdoor living space. Computer-driven sound, lighting and visual effects throughout lanais, pool areas and landscaping allow homeowners to custom-design ambience from dramatic to tranquil."

STEPHEN MULDOON STUDIO

Stephen Muldoon: "Because the traditional classical style is so popular in estate architecture, I'm seeing a corresponding resurgence in Renaissance mural art as an enhancement to interior room design. Today, I'm creating Renaissance murals on living and dining room walls, in foyers, within recessed arches and on domed ceilings. This is an artistic trend I see continuing."

GRATE FIREPLACE & STONE SHOPPE

Helyn Stasko: "An exciting, new trend in South Florida is the realistic electric fireplace that can operate with or without heat. They can incorporate glass doors and look like a working gas fireplace without the gas line or chimney. The fireplace can be surrounded with stone or wood in any style that matches the decor."

Ⓐ PLAYNATION, *Allen Blenden:* "Today's customers are demanding quality. They want play sets that are durable, strong and stable, even if adults decide to enjoy them. They are also looking for safety. Steps and rails must be of sturdy construction."

ⒶSNAIDERO USA

Dott. Dario Snaidero: "The kitchen is no longer simply a room in a house where one cooks a meal. It is a reflection of the homeowner's personality. Therefore, we see kitchens that excite the eye, stimulate the mind and arouse the spirit. We've seen an explosion of interest in contemporary kitchens that blend nostalgia with modernism. With sweeping curves, unusual angles, bold colors and non-traditional materials, these kitchens fulfill the traditional needs of the home with cutting-edge design and technologies, while reflecting a passion for life."

Ⓐ

MARC-MICHAELS INTERIOR DESIGN

Mark Thee: "In interior design, 'the rules are…there are no rules'. Today's client looks for architectural treatments as well as decorative design solutions to create a seamless fusion between design and technology. In the recent absence of pattern, our perspective on innovative design trends includes the integration of luxurious hues and varying textures with architectural design and functionality. The emergence of 'moment' are complemented by rich, natural materials such as precious stone or exotic woods drawn from the earth to highlight the beauty in simplicity and focus on space."

Ⓐ STRAUSS & WASSNER, INC.

H. ALLEN HOLMES,
H. Allen Holmes: "Our current portfolio runs the gamut from 'a little bit of country' to 'a little bit of rock & roll.' We see this trend as a reflection of the customer's desire for individuality in both style and comfort. Enhancing our wide palate of diversity in design is the increasing use of exciting new materials and technology."

Madelyn Strauss: "We are seeing a change in the types of woods used in Florida homes. Traditional libraries and media rooms abound, using cherry and mahogany in lieu of pickled oak and ash. The warm color palette of crimson, gold and moss helps achieve a classic, timeless look."

AZHAR'S ORIENTAL RUGS

Azhar Said: "Past and future merge as we enter this millennium with a renewed focus on the most traditional of Oriental rugs—those in hand-spun wool with a depth of texture and complex colors achieved by natural vegetable dyes. In the most venerable traditions of rug weaving, when natural vegetable dyes are applied to hand-spun wool, a distinctive patina and texture is created. It's a texture most associated with antique and heirloom Oriental rugs. After all, machine-spun wool and chromium dyes have only been in use during the past 100 years. There is a resurgence of natural vegetable dyes that create an intense, multi-faceted strength of color, particularly in the jewel tones of ruby and wine red, rich blues, and antique gold. Okra green is a popular color that showcases natural vegetable dyes. The best examples of these new rugs that embody ancient techniques and classic materials are from Afghanistan, Pakistan and Iran."

Photo by Barry Grossman

BELLISSIMO MARBLE DESIGN

Frank Esposito: "The use of marble and granite in any project is far from a trend or new style. The application on the other hand is where the new creativity comes into play. Some of the new ways we are seeing it used are for driveways, walkways, pool decks, walls and fountains. The mosaic style is also quite popular."

SOUND PLUS WOOD, INC. *Michael S. Moran:* "Currently, we are experiencing strong continuing interest in natural materials as the basis for our furniture designs. This interest appears equally strong in both the contemporary and traditional design arenas. Natural woods, wood veneers and stone products have replaced past standards such as plastic laminates. Additionally, the European style of furniture construction continues to make important inroads into all areas of furniture design, including kitchens, baths and media cabinets. This style incorporates engineered solutions to functional hardware such as door hinges and drawer elements."

Photo by Photographers II

ART GLASS ENVIRONMENTS, INC.

Bill Klug: "What we've noticed in the past few years is the resurgence of attention to detail from clients asking their architects and interior designers to seek out craftsmen who know how to design glass in specific period styles. Decorative glass entryways, privacy bathroom treatments and lighted ceilings (i.e., domes and back-lighted glass elements) may be used in any interior location."

AVAKIAN'S ORIENTAL RUGS

Paul Avakian: "Fall will see heightened interest in Oriental rugs as the preferred floor covering. The addition, in many homes, of wood, marble and tile floors has resulted in greater demand for hand-knotted rugs to create warmth and excitement in decor. Traditional designs woven in China, India and Pakistan are complimented by the contemporary appeal of deep pile Tibetan collections. The most exciting single thing to happen in 2000, however, is the reopening of trade with Iran, which allows true Persian rugs to be imported again. These wonderful rugs have become client favorites."

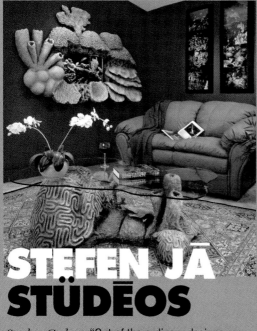

STEFEN JĀ STÜDĒOS

Stephen Gerhart: "Out of the ordinary designs are competing for high-impart spaces as eco-themes become the trend. Clients are looking for unique solutions for making not only their design statement but also their life statement. Realism is the test of quality in these artistic recreations as they reflect the magnificent beauty of the coral seas."

RESOURCEASIA *Susan Retz:* "South Floridians are seeking to create a respite from their hectic lives by being in touch with nature and the innate beauty of simple materials such as teak wood, bamboo and rattan. More and more, Eastern ideals and sensibilities are melding with tropical Western lifestyles in an expression of individuality, adventure and understated richness. In response, we are seeing clients select furnishings from Bali and Java that combine simple designs with the elegantly crafted accents that appeal to both wandering spirit and sensibilities. As consumers step away from the anonymity of mass production, pieces that incorporate fine woods, unique designs and engaging details will increasingly be in demand to make distinctive personal statements in Florida homes and offices."

ARTISTRY IN GLASS/OCEAN TRADING INATIONAL CORP., *Sergio Siqueira:* "Today, we are moving beyond ordinary (mere) windows. Decorative glass treatments are becoming important architectural elements. In many cases, we are designing original glassworks for new residences while they are still in the blueprint stage. A true work of art when created by an artisan, creatively designed glass is coming into its own."

86

BOUGHTON ARCHITECTS, INC.

Michelle Boughton: "More and more of our clients are seeking architectural designs that draw on traditional South Florida styles. Old Florida designs are highly sought after as are Mediterranean, Bahamian and Classical. Within these current design parameters, the final design also reflects our client's choice of lifestyle and function as well as taking advantage of the natural features of the property."

"Old Florida designs are highly sought after as are Mediterranean, Bahamian and Classical."

87

GENERAL CONTRACTOR SERVICES, INC., *Philip Modenos:* "In today's demanding South Florida market, the emphasis on custom waterfront homes has shifted from size to quality, finishes and amenities. To achieve true quality, a builder must guide a team consisting of the client, architect, designer, sub-contractors, material suppliers and individual craftsperson. Each project needs to be designed site specific to ensure maximization of a property for useable living spaces both inside and out while maintaining proper views, exposure, finishes and fulfilling the clients' lifestyle requirements. Builders offering this type of complete customer support in planning, coordination and teamwork turn homes into dream homes."

CAST IN STONE INTERNATIONAL

Lesley Vandemark: "We are seeing a trend toward people wanting natural elements (i.e., stone and water). Fountains with early European styling are becoming more popular for the soothing effect they can have on hectic lifestyles."

FERGUSON BATH &KITCHEN GALLERIES

Karen Campenella: "There's a growing trend toward therapeutic bathing. And, more and more homeowners are creating personal spas in their homes — relaxing retreats where they can go to unwind and rejuvenate after a long day. Custom whirlpools, luxury shower systems, brighter colors and vanities make up some of today's most popular items used to create havens of relaxation."

Ⓐ CM INTERIORS

"Whether my client's motivating passion is traditional, contemporary, Asian, Mediterranean, island flair, or special theme, they will receive guidance and creativity to bring out the presence of their individuality, each of us has a very special story that needs to be told through our surroundings. I want to always bring out my client's motivating passion so they will be heard."

DYEHOUSE GESHAY & COMERIATO

John Dyehouse: "Today's clients know what they want in a luxury residence. They expect a new home that is totally unique, with elements that reflect their personalities rather than copy outdated styles. They want creative and new ways to express a lifestyle, a feeling or drama. We integrate our clients' overall goals within a well designed residence."

Ⓑ

Ⓑ QUIET TIME, INC.

Stuart Surfer: "Tastes are always changing. The warmth and richness of wood is increasingly being used in South Florida interiors. Combined with glass, stone, metals and textiles, the home or office is becoming a more inviting place to be."

89

GREENBROOK POOLS

Ira Grabow: "An 'infinity' or negative-edge pool allows the water line to reach the top edge of the pool and actually wash lightly over the side. According to a viewer's location, the effect of an infinite water line is created between the pool and the adjoining ocean or waterfront area. The contemporary design evolved from coastal and mountain lake resorts in France and later grew up in California. It's particularly adaptable to South Florida's waterfront custom homes. When an infinity pool is placed visually adjoining the ocean or another waterfront, the effect is stunning."

GEOMANTIC DESIGNS, INC.

Robert Parsley: "After a brief detour into jungle landscaping, the formal garden is back with a tropical accent. We're seeing the use of new varieties of succulents including Crown of Thorns. Imported Thai hybrids, new varieties of espalier and different techniques of formal pruning are also gaining popularity in today's formal gardens."

ELLEMAR ENTERPRISES *Mark Rothenberg:* "The popularity of Chinese feng shui coupled with the natural splendor of Florida's lush flora has created a desire for luxury residences that bring the outside into the residence itself. Clients want atriums and interior green space, natural boulders in the foyer, and grand windows framing vibrant outdoor gardens. Water has become an integral part of today's designs as well, with waterfalls gracing indoor entranceways and peaceful, indoor reflecting pools creating a peaceful refuge."

RENAISSANCE
PLASTER USA, LLC

Nicholas Evans: "More frequently, discerning clients are seeking an alternative to standard moldings and trim that are commonly used. A desire to mix individuality with quality of craftsmanship has created a perfect environment for the resurgence of plaster trim work and finishes. Clients are able to design their own or select and adapt traditional designs to finish their walls and ceilings. Crown molding, arches, barrel and groin vault ceilings, columns, panel trim, and niches all give the client the opportunity to fully customize their home using a product that has been shown to stand the test of time."

TECNO WOOD

Roger Ahmadi: "We have found a new trend in custom cabinetry — children's bedrooms. Apparently, in the new information age, there seems to be a new teen-ager. Today, many kids' rooms are overloaded with computer equipment, TV, VCR, DVD player, video games and CDs. The combination of a fun and creative bedroom along with an adequate workspace that can enhance a child's study habits seems to be the best solution. Nowadays, most kids have a lot of homework assignments involving work with computers and research on the Internet. Our goal is to create a functional yet fun environment for children to enjoy. Many homeowners work with a designer to create an elegant living room, foyer, dining room or den; however, they sometimes overlook children's bedrooms."

PERLA LICHI DESIGN *Perla Lichi:* "We are finding that many clients are asking us to create a rich, neoclassical ambiance. But, they want texture, not color; opulence, not glitz. This can be achieved by masterfully combining natural elements such as marble, alabaster, crackle finishes, woods and leafing."

JACKSON POOLS, INC.

Cary Brown-Jesse: " The prevailing trend in swimming pool construction is to turn ordinary yards into extraordinary private retreats with the use of bridges, rock gardens, multiple waterfalls, bronze statues, Koi ponds, and natural and hand-carved rock. These natural swimming pool environments stimulate a new dimension of relaxation."

COLETTE DESIGN

"American clientele are changing their taste and leaning toward an open and airy design that accentuates sleek and contemporary furnishings. There is detailed attention being paid to the function and style of space that conveys a fresh and exciting contemporary style and look. The ease of mobility in this style of bedroom furnishings is popular in Europe. This style is quickly becoming a trend in the American home."

CELEBRATION HOMES *Richard Greco:* "Like clothing, I see a house as a fashion statement. The prevailing fashion trend among today's South Florida homebuyers is authentic Italian. They want houses that are built in true Italian style — floors that gleam with imported Italian marble and stone, walls that are decorated with hand-painted Italian tiles, kitchens that are enlivened with Italian cabinetry, and bathrooms that gleam with luxurious imported plumbing fixtures. We see the buyers' desire for the opulence of an authentic Italian Palazzo as a continuing trend."

HOUSE OF HIGH FIDELITY
Pamela Futch: "No one wants to look at speakers, yet we all want sound that perfectly fills the room. New speakers are being built into designer furniture. The perfect balance can be struck between decorating needs and true, high quality sound reproduction. High-end subwoofers can be found in designer end tables for better vocal placement, the center channel speaker is tucked inside a handsome coffee table or sofa table."

95

SARUSKI DESIGN

Michael Saruski: "Today we're seeing many more eclectic mixtures of furniture styles and unique combinations of textures as couples blend their furnishings, tastes and styles. In this case, the wife's traditional pieces and the husband's more modern furniture coexist beautifully."

SouthFlorida

Tour Guide to Your Dream Home

Tired of being lost? Feel that you don't know
where you're going without a map? Can't find useful information
regarding home improvement? The *South Florida Home Book*
Web site (www.floridahomebook.com) provides you
with a full-color atlas of information to
map out the home of your dreams.

www.floridahomebook.com

HomeBook.com

YOU WANT IT, WE'LL FIND IT

The *South Florida Home Book* Web site (www.floridahomebook.com) was officially launched in July of 2000. It covers a full range of resources for building, remodeling, decorating, furnishing and landscaping projects. Just log on at www.floridahomebook.com. It also provides the user with unique, functional features designed to locate all of the necessary information regarding the interior and exterior design of your luxury home.

YOUR RESEARCH SOURCE

The site enables the user to research the latest trends in luxury design and home enhancement through its current editorial segments and interviews with industry experts. Users can also search for professionals under a wide variety of criteria, including by location.

THE PERFECT PAIR

The *South Florida Home Book* Web site is best used when complemented by a copy of the **South *Florida* Home Book**. The Web site picks up where the book leaves off, providing regular updates to ensure that consumers have the most well timed and detailed information possible. Together, the two work in unison to provide consumers the most up-to-date and timely information regarding their most prized investment—their home.

WE'RE ONLY A FEW CLICKS AWAY

If you are planning to design or renovate your home, please don't hesitate to consult (www.floridahomebook.com) today. Allow us to be your road map, and we will gladly lead you to your final destination. There is only one premier resource provider for the luxury design and home enhancement market—the *South Florida Home Book*. Thank you from everyone at the *South Florida Home Book*, and we all hope to see you online!

The Internet domain seems as vast as outer space at times, especially when searching for home improvement, renovation, and remodeling information. The *South Florida Home Book* minimizes this complexity by acting as your guide to the stars. There is no doubt that consumer's will find the *South Florida Home Book* to be star packed.

There is only one premier resource provider for the luxury design and home enhancement market- the *South Florida Home Book*!

STUART: ARTSY & UNPRETENTIOUS

The main traffic circle in the picturesque seaside village of Stuart, Florida, is colloquially titled "Confusion Corner." Everything else in this city of 17,000 permanent residents is operated in an orderly fashion, thanks to a group of thoughtful civic leaders who preserved the small town ambience of the business district.

Symbolizing the midriff bulge on Florida's East Coast money belt, Stuart is located 40 miles from Vero Beach to the North, and equidistant from Palm Beach to the South. On the opposite side of The Inland Waterway is Hobe Sound, and Jupiter Island is the winter quarters for the founding families of America's basic industries. Among the newly arrived rich émigrés are Perry Como and Dan Marino.

The Florida "cracker house" is Stuart's indigenous architecture. A cracker house is a farmhouse style adapted to the climate by pineapple growers who came to the area in 1893 from Potsdam, Germany. The typical cracker house has a tin, or shingle roof, clapboard siding, and is raised on stubby pilings to permit airflow under the house.

Residents of Stuart were, from the beginning, and, for the most part, still are independent and devoted to an unpretentious lifestyle,

The interior of this home, designed by Kenneth Miller, has a streamlined simplicity to it. Miller who describes his style as "pluralistic," creates homes for Stuart residents that reflect their lack of pretension and independent-minded natures.

disdaining stratified society. Despite the city's marketing pitch, "Sailfish Capital of the World," that was adopted by the Chamber of Commerce, Stuart is almost stubbornly supportive of all art forms. The Lyric Theatre, The Stuart Heritage Museum, private art galleries and antique shops indicate that the city offers more than a good day's catch. The Chamber, however, has fortified the slogan by breaking ground for a public marina, The Anchorage, designed with 69 slips and full service accommodations.

Growth to the West is rapid, limited only by the Federally protected Everglades. Palm City, on the edge of the Everglades, is growing rapidly and has already outdistanced Stuart in population.

Thriving professionally in this environment is one of the South's most distinguished architects, Kenneth R. Miller, AIA, NCARB. Miller has been designing Florida homes for more than 40 years, usually sited on exclusive bits of land.

Soon after graduating from Pennsylvania State University with a professional degree in Architecture, Miller opened an office in Coconut Grove, a woodsy artist's colony just south of downtown Miami. He moved North to Jupiter Island 20 years ago and recently completed the house published on these pages.

Miller's trek North with his wife and three daughters, paralleled the population movement on Florida's shorelines. He notes, "I have observed the constant attraction of the water. Small communities along the shoreline have grown so rapidly — the Gulfstream provides such great climate, but only a narrow band of land between the Ocean and the Everglades is open for development. It's filling up quickly."

Miller has designed homes in North Carolina, Loblolly Pines and Palm Beach Gardens. He avoids putting a label on his style, but when pressed describes it as "pluralistic."

"The best work results when the client is open minded, free to consider ideas and suggestions. Architecture is an art form, and we try to prove that in our work," Miller said. "There are so many restrictions already imposed by building codes and zoning — it's extremely difficult to achieve a fresh approach to classic form. It's hard to be pure because technological advances in materials and comforts aren't recorded in history." ■

--Agnes Ash

PALM BEACH: CLASSY & HISTORIC

For more than a century, the three causeways linking the barrier island of Palm Beach with West Palm Beach, were little more than service roads providing mainland tradesmen access to wealthy clients—a proper Palm Beacher crossed Lake Worth only by airport limousine or ambulance.

It was just about 10 years ago when the island's insular social life experienced a sea change, and West Palm Beach began to evolve into the thriving metropolitan city it is today. Now Palm Beachers eagerly cross the bridges to mix with young working professionals crowding Clematis Street on balmy tropical evenings, to enjoy the sidewalk cafes, restaurants and art galleries.

West Palm Beach can easily match the cultural opportunities represented by Palm Beach's Society of the Four Arts and the Poinciana Playhouse. A restored downtown area is the anchored "CityPlace," a retail, restaurant and residential complex. And, newly dedicated in time for the winter season is the "Palladium," a European-style urban shopping mall within CityPlace. It was constructed at a cost of $500 million and contains 50 stores, the largest being Macy's. The Italianate-style Paladium, along with the nearby Kravis Center for the Performing Arts, is drawing shoppers and day trippers from all over South Florida .

The Island of Palm Beach is seven miles long and a half-mile wide. The year-round population is about 10,000, and it swells to 23,000 in the winter. Lining the lakefront and the ocean shore are mansions still identified by the names of original owners—Phipps, Sanford, Munn, duPont, Hitchcock, Armour, Pulitzer, Maddock, Matthews,

The Seagull Cottage is one of the landmarked houses recently restored by Tom Eastwood's firm, Worth Builders. The frame, a Queen Anne Revival building, was the first Palm Beach home of Henry Morrison Flagler, a founding partner of Standard Oil. Eastwood built an addition to the rear expansion, which now houses a library.

Reynolds, Guest, Woolworth, Post, Widener, Pierrepont and other recognizable names on the Dow Jones Industrial list.

While West Palm Beach is becoming a well-planned urban sprawl, bordered by the Everglades on the West, Broward County on the South and Martin County on the North, there is still ample agricultural land available to be developed into gated, golf course communities. This is in direct contrast to Palm Beach, where there isn't a single empty lot available, and landmarked houses are in the process of being restored. The interiors are being rebuilt as extensively as the Town's fanatically strict Architectural Review Board will permit. The unmarked, undistinguished houses on the small streets that link lake to ocean are being demolished to make way for more elaborate residences.

One contractor who is thriving in this confrontational architectural environment is Tom Eastwood, president of Worth Builders.

Eastwood has restored buildings on exclusive Jupiter Island as well as in Palm Beach, where he recently completed an addition to South Florida's oldest house, The Seagull Cottage. The frame, a Queen Anne Revival building was the first Palm Beach home of Henry Morrison Flagler, a founding partner of Standard Oil. Flagler built the railroad that is responsible for opening Florida's East Coast to development.

Many builders refuse to work on landmarked buildings, because inspections and restrictions frequently cause expensive construction delays. While Eastwood acknowledges that it is extremely difficult to obtain permits for restoration projects, he says that fact doesn't worry him one bit. "I let the architect take care of the politics and I do the work, which is very exacting, but always interesting. (The Architect for the Seagull expansion was Michael J. Johnson.) I am backed up by an experienced staff and local craftsmen who supply salvaged materials, or replicated doors and window frames that are no longer available."

Last year, Worth Builders was awarded the restoration contract for an addition to the Seagull Cottage. In keeping with the original structure, Eastwood's crew built an addition to the rear expansion, which now houses a library. "I have worked on more substantial jobs—restoring a Mizner of 28,000 square feet, but this project was special—we moved a staircase, added a room and tied in the new gabled roof, duplicating the original shingles," said Eastwood.

Eastwood claims that he hasn't seen much of the building boom in West Palm Beach, a rapidly growing city of a million and a half. He isn't bidding on mainland jobs there because The Palm Beach Preservation Society has already landmarked more than 200 buildings on the island. Eastwood believes that before he gets around to those he hasn't already given a skin peel, more will be added to the list for his company to restore. ■

–Agnes Ash

SEQUESTERED ENCLAVES

Almost four million South Floridians live in the Miami-Dade and Broward counties, a contiguous region whose balanced economy is based on a salutary blend of light manufacturing, investment services and commerce — often with international implications — as well as tourism and agriculture.

According to David Dabby, senior vice president of Miami-based Appraisal and Real Estate Economics Associates (AREEA), the concept of living and doing business in a semi-tropical, yet cosmopolitan area is a huge draw, and the region dominated by Greater Miami and Greater Fort Lauderdale continues to prevail as one of this country's "hot spots" for premium residential property, Shoreline properties are especially prized, but since so little beachfront is available, older estates are often purchased for six-figure prices and leveled, so that new multi-million-dollar houses can be built.

"Luxury residences now average eight to ten thousand square feet of enclosed space, some 40 percent larger than those just built a few years ago," says Toby Zack, a leading interior designer who maintains a Fort Lauderdale showroom, and services clients in both counties. "Today's economy has given rise to a variety of buyers with excess funds to invest in their dream house," states Robert D. Krieff, Breakstone Homes' chief operating officer. "And while new thoroughfares link workers living in western Dade and Broward to commercial and cultural centers nearer the coast, an easterly move is currently underway as many of these homeowners become more affluent," he adds.

This lovely home features a backyard area complete with pool to enjoy the sunny skies and warm temperatures experienced in Miami-Dade counties.

BAL HARBOUR VILLAGE

Equidistant between Miami and Fort Lauderdale is Bal Harbour Village. Once a large area of swampland, it is now an elegant oceanfront enclave, and boasts one of the toniest malls in the U.S., the Bal Harbour Shops. The opposite side of Collins Avenue is bordered by luxury high-rise condominiums, whose lofty towers increasingly punctuate Florida's southeast coastline. Beyond this area, and buffered by dunes, is the village's semi-secluded beach.

BAY HARBOR ISLANDS

Several small suburban municipalities are situated between Haulover Park and Miami Beach, including Indian Creek Village, whose sequestered island province is off-limits to uninvited visitors. But the neighboring Town of Bay Harbor Islands is a thriving city of primarily single-family homes with exceptional schools, convenient shopping along 96th Street – its principal thoroughfare – and the Atlantic Ocean a short distance to the east. The Miami mainland, due west, is readily accessible via the Broad Causeway for commuters.

While a present-day population of 4,700 occupies the less than one square kilometer of land area, a considerable stretch of realty borders the Intracoastal Waterway and one of its ancillary canals. Architectural styles are eclectic and the older homes here, and in neighboring Surfside, are still relatively affordable. Prices are rising, however, advises J. C. Herran, director of sales for Breakstone Homes, due to the accelerating demand by young professionals and executives for the felicitous, family-oriented lifestyle that can be found on these secure, manicured tracts.

GOLDEN BEACH

North of Haulover Cut, a navigable waterway connecting the Intracoastal and Atlantic, is Sunny Isles Beach, whose 1950's-era motels are now being supplanted by condominiums. And to its north, straddling both sides of State Road A1A for more than a mile to Broward's county line, is Golden Beach, formerly a quiet, low-rise city of some 300 single-family homes that began as a resort community. But according to Harold Kronstadt, a householder and chronicler for several decades of Golden Beach, this city's demographics have substantially changed in the past several years. Most seasonal residents and retirees have been replaced by affluent homeowners, who appreciate its guard-gated security and its strategic suburban setting, less than an hour from two international airports.

Properties anywhere in Golden Beach, a city with a population of some 900 that is 500 yards wide at most between the Intracoastal and its private beach on the Atlantic, now command top dollar whenever they come on the market.

An oceanfront lot, 75 feet wide by 150 feet deep, can cost $800,000, twice the price of a similar site on a canal, advises Bob Krieff, whose firm now has an "inventory" of 20 or so waterfront properties designated most likely to be razed and rebuilt. ■

–Al Alschuler

106

FORT LAUDERDALE: COSMOPOLITAN SETTING

Fort Lauderdale and its environs may lay claim to more than 300 miles of inland waterways, but Broward County offers fewer waterfront opportunities than neighboring Miami-Dade County, says Dan Lindblade, former executive vice president of the Greater Fort Lauderdale Realtor Association. He explains, "When it comes to supply and demand, our only drawback is the absence of available land." In spite of this, smaller houses are being razed and replaced with much larger ones, and often on combined lots. Significant "rehab" construction is also on the upswing.

While migration from Miami-Dade to Broward has decreased over the past few years, many families continue to move from congested urban areas to master-planned recreational communities in the western suburbs of both counties. Here too, leisure-minded retirees are converting their vacation homes to permanent residences.

According to Lindblade, an easterly move is also underway and the city proper is once again an appropriate venue, the result of considerable commercial construction and civic revitalization. Las Olas Boulevard, Fort Lauderdale's picturesque "main street," now features an eclectic array of boutiques, bookstores, bistros and coffee houses. Farther north, yet readily accessible, is the Galleria Mall, a chic alternative to the Bal Harbour Shops and Aventura in northern Miami-Dade County and similar sophisticated shopping centers in downtown Boca Raton and Palm Beach. Merely minutes away too are the Greater Fort

This lovely space uses open architecture to invite the bright South Florida sun into the room, creating a warm inviting environment.

Photo courtesy of Miller Construction Company

Lauderdale/Broward County Convention Center and Fort Lauderdale/ Hollywood International Airport.

While luxurious oceanfront high-rise condominium complexes cater to seasonal, as well as permanent residents, certain neighborhoods closer in location to Fort Lauderdale's central sector are attracting young executives, dual-income professionals and businesspeople, and moneyed Miamians with primarily local interests.

Reo Vista, a cosmopolitan setting increasingly favored by family-oriented city folks, is nestled just south of downtown below the New River, north of the 17th Street Causeway, in the midst of a somewhat amorphous area between U.S. 1 and the Intracoastal Waterway.

Relatively few multi-family homes can be found in Reo Vista, whose several hundred single-family residences range from older, relatively modest Cracker and Cape Cod houses to more elaborate Georgian and Mediterranean Revival architectural styles and assorted contemporary structures. Some are sizeable waterfront estates occupying wooded property along the Intracoastal New River, or along some ancillary canal. Many of the "sea-faring" owners belong to the Fort Lauderdale Yacht Club, one of the few non-residential enterprises in this neighborhood. One drawback of Reo Vista is its lack of public schools; most students attend private schools in a neighboring sector. But the quiet, and, to many observers, quaint, centrally-situated, yet essentially suburban-like setting apparently more than makes up for their absence.■

–Al Alschuler

PORT ROYAL:
A CHANGE OF FACE

In Naples, on the Southwest coast of Florida, the most symbiotic time of day is sunset when colonists and newcomers gather on porches, balconies, beaches and the historic 1,000-foot fishing pier to watch the sun sink into the Gulf of Mexico.

There is plenty to do, however, before the spectacular light show ends the day. After golf and fishing, shopping is the leading diversion. Alluring shops along 13th Avenue South and the original retail district along Fifth Avenue South, offer every status label in the world plus a few local symbols. Shoppers can also work credit cards at the Coastland Mall on US 41; however, the most productive browsing is available at Tin City on US 41 and Naples Bay. In this raffish milieu, gifts can be purchased at the old oyster processing plant or any of the 40 shops specializing in objects with seaside motifs. On a stormy day, it's a bit noisy with raindrops rattling on the old tin roofs.

Wealthy northerners, who first came to Naples around 1880 for the fishing, built homes around the pier and in the area now called Old Naples. The lifestyle changed in 1926 when the railroad was extended from Tampa. Two years later, The Tamiami Trail, a road cut through the Everglades linking South Florida communities on the Atlantic with those on the Gulf of Mexico was completed.

With added accessibility, tourists carrying golf bags as well as fishing poles arrived. Today, the Chamber of Commerce claims Naples has more golf courses per capita than any other city in Florida. There are at least 15 meticulously maintained public and semi-private courses in Naples and an even greater number of luxurious private clubs serving upscale housing.

Houses in the Port Royal area are in the process of being completely renovated, with classic styles such as Italian and Spanish gaining in popularity with clients.

Tennis, kyaking on a small lake and hiking on nature trails bordering the Everglades is available in the public parks. Cultural facilities include the Collier County Museum, the Philharmonic Center for the Arts, the 40-year-old Sugden Community Theatre, the Von Liebig Art center and the Teddy Bear Museum, which probably draws even more collectors than the two big art festivals — The Naples Downtown Art Festival, which stretches all the way down Fifth Avenue on the weekend following Christmas, and the Naples National Art Festival scheduled for February in Cambier Park.

Palm Cottage, an historic landmark built in 1895 of local materials, is a typical Florida Cracker house that it houses the Collier County Historical Society. The Palm Cottage, a strong indigenous style in most Florida communities where agriculture was the first industry, failed to leave a permanent mark on Naples.

Port Royal, a wealthy beachside area along Gulfshore Drive, was developed in the 1960s by an unhappy marriage of Bermuda style and ranch house. Now, the area is being completely renovated and British Colonial or Charleston revival are the favored style for multi-million dollar estates built on small quarter-acre lots.

An architect heavily involved in the facade lifting of Port Royal is Randy Stofft, who maintains offices in Delray Beach as well as Naples. "Our clients prefer traditional styles. We create homes that look better and earn even greater admiration as they age. We don't do trendy things, but we do add tropical touches to classic concepts," he reports.

Stofft believes in adapting classic styles, particularly Italian and Spanish, because even in antiquity, these basic forms were developed to shelter inhabitants from sun and sea. Another European category is gaining popularity, "We are beginning to see French influences in suggestions made by our clients," he noted.

Stofft and his staff of 15 have gained a lot of attention for a house created on Lantern Lane. In this instance, the ornamental touch of scalloped gables was added to a simple cottage style, a throwback to Newport.

"Teardowns account for more than 90 percent of the work we do in Port Royal," he said. "There are no vacant sites available on the beach. Houses that had to be demolished weren't landmarked because they were built in the 1960's."

Although Port Royal is not a gated or golf course community, it remains the most exclusive neighborhood in Naples. "Residents don't have golf courses at the back door, but they don't mind driving a short distance inland to private clubs where they hold memberships."

Naples is on the Gulf, but it's also on the mainland of the Florida peninsula. This is a limiting factor for waterfront property. There are no barrier islands off the coast of Collier County, so it's impossible to build causeways and develop sand spits into riverfront and ocean side property, a routine practice of turn of the century speculators who developed Miami Beach and Palm Beach. Most Naples residents believe Mother Nature favored them with that difference. ■

–*Agnes Ash*

COUNTRY CLUB COMMUNITIES:
A GULF-LOVER'S HEAVEN

Contrary to statistics reported in the census, golf is Florida's second language — it's spoken at the deli counter in the supermarket and during intermission at the opera. Golf courses have watering priority over car washes when there's a drought, and even those who don't play the game wear the shirts.

Florida owes its clean air and tolerable population density to golf. If it weren't for vast acreage devoted to fairways, the expensive land along both coasts would have been paved over long ago. Orange groves, truck farms and cattle grazing land are disappearing fast, but golf courses are multiplying, keeping Florida green for generations to come.

Naples has on its tax rolls the most expensive and ecology friendly golf club communities in the country. Communal facilities — lushly landscaped streets and greenswards, tennis courts and monarchical club houses — are standard facilities. Some communities also offer nature preserves, croquet courts and equestrienne trails.

These communities within a community are governed by codes often more strict than those of local government, translating to no

The interior of this Naples home reflects the classical architectural detailing currently in vogue in the design of upscale homes. Some of this detailing is evident in the use of heavy barrel roofs, archways and columns.

parking of recreational vehicles and no aluminum siding.

Through the past half century, Naples has been fortunate in the stability of its golf course communities. In cycles of economic slowdown, other Florida developments have failed to maintain or complete communal facilities. Naples; however, has established a reputation for being a safe haven for real estate investment, thanks to strongly capitalized land developers who could finance amenities until projects built out.

Membership initiation fees at established, exclusive clubs run as high as $100,000, an indication of the social and intrinsic value of residences in the community. Among the leading developments are Bay Colony, Quail West, Grey Oaks, Pelican Bay, Meda Terra, Twin Eagles, The Estuary and Bonita Bay.

Steve Watt, President of Gulfshore Homes, a quality construction company based in Bonita Springs, is building 6,000 to 10,000 square foot homes in these communities. He notes that Mediterranean styles are exceptionally popular. "This is a conservative community, so classic architecture is the first choice. The historic precedent is probably Addison Mizner, the self-taught architect who dictated the prevailing style of Palm Beach and Boca Raton."

Watt says his clients prefer beige to the vibrant pink walls that defined Mizner's work at the turn of the century. That color, according to Watt, is only for the boldest advocates of Mizner architecture. "Mizner touches are recognizable in barrel tile roofs, heavy columns, arches and cast stone, or wrought iron details," he says.

Watt admits that it's becoming more and more difficult to find skilled craftsmen to replicate the classic architectural detailing used in upscale construction. "In the past 10 years, we built 1,000 homes in Naples and Boca Raton. This enables us to keep quality workers busy, so they stay with us."

Watt, says the demographics of the area are changing rapidly, bringing much younger people to Naples. "Most of our clients are Midwesterners. They're making their fortune early in life, and building Florida vacation homes to use as primary residences when they retire, because five years down the road, housing in this area will be dramatically more expensive."

The size of the typical Collier County golf club community is about 1,000 acres according to Watt. Size varies, but most properties are at least one acre, and in some communities, there are restrictions on the size of the house that can be built on a lot.

Jim Boughton, principal of Boughton Architects Inc., has been commissioned to design four houses in the luxurious sub division of Little Harbour. "There are only 32 lots in Little Harbour, so our acceptance rate is running high," he says with a laugh. ■

–Agnes Ash

Finally...
South Florida's Own
Home & Design
Sourcebook

Call Toll Free at 888-458-1750

The South Florida Home Book, www.floridahomebook.com, is your final destination when searching for home improvement services. This comprehensive, hands-on-guide to building, remodeling, decorating, furnishing, and landscaping a home, is required reading for the serious and discriminating homeowner. With over 700 full-color, beautiful pages, this hard cover volume is the most complete and well-organized reference to the home industry. The Home Book covers all aspects of the process, including listings of hundreds of industry professionals, accompanied by informative and valuable editorial discussing the most recent trends. Ordering your copy of ***The South Florida Home Book,*** now, can ensure that you have the blueprints to your dream home, in your hand, today.

Order your copy today!

O R D E R   F O R M

THE SOUTH FLORIDA HOME BOOK

☐ YES, please send me _____ copies of the SOUTH FLORIDA HOME BOOK at $39.95 per book, plus $3 postage & handling per book.

Total amount sent: $_____   Please charge my: ☐ VISA   ☐ MasterCard   ☐ American Express

Card # _____ Exp. Date_____

Signature _____

Name _____ Phone ( ) _____

Address _____

City _____ State _____ Zip Code _____

Send order to: Attn: Book Sales—Marketing Dept., The Ashley Group, 1350 E. Touhy Ave., Suite 1E, Des Plaines, Illinois 60018
Or Call Toll Free at: 1-888-458-1750   Or E-mail ashleybooksales@cahners.com

All orders must be accompanied by check, money order or credit card # for full amount.

Hot Districts

Where the Unexpected Resides

I magine meeting a leading furniture designer who listens to your dreams and instinctively understands just what you want, or entering an antique shop and finding an elegant one-of-a-kind piece that is the perfect focal point for your foyer. Whether you're building a new residence or redecorating a single room, the search for furnishings and decorative art objects that speak to your spirit can be a joyous experience and one filled with discovery.

Every town boasts elegant shops and "appointment only" showrooms that are "hot" — places only the insiders know. Sometimes located on a popular shopping street, often tucked away in an outlying area, they are beloved shopping venues that leading interior decorators and architects frequent…and treasure.

Whether you're looking for a furniture or glass craftsman to bring your vision to life, custom moldings for a new residence or an exquisite, imported treasure to lend focus to a well-appointed room, these "hot" shopping venues can spark your creativity and shorten your search immeasurably. The problem is knowing just where they are.

We created this special section to help you locate these unique and popular shopping meccas. To make it easier, they have been divided into local areas that include the address and telephone number of each store, even an easy-to-follow map.

In a book designed to inspire you and get your creative juices flowing, this is the place where you can start to make it all become real. Whether quaint or cutting-edge, elegant or funky, in these pages you'll find shops that are the leading lights in today's galaxy of elegance, art and interior design. Peruse this special section and enjoy. Then go out and discover something wonderful!

Bird Road Art District

Decorating Finds in a Hidden Area

Travel west from Coral Gables and you'll discover this unique decorating venue neatly tucked away in an unassuming location. Once a quiet industrial park with row upon row of warehouses, today the Bird Road Art District has taken off. Recently revitalized, this area offers a rich array of antique shops, imported natural stone emporiums, furniture sources and custom glass designers. Come and discuss your decorating needs with these talented people. But be certain to call ahead of time. Although all of these shop owners and artisans will be happy to consult with you, many of them require an appointment.

Ⓐ Bonnin Ashley Antiques
4707 Southwest 72nd Ave.
305-667-0969
Mon.-Fri. 9:30 a.m.-5:30 p.m.;
Sat. 10 a.m.-5:30 p.m.
Warehouse by appointment.
Offering an exceptional selection of fine European and American furniture and accessories for more than 15 years. Visit their 10,000 square foot showroom.

Architectural Glass Arts, Inc.

Ⓑ Piedras International
1155 NW 76 Ave.
305-666-8555
Piedras International in Miami is a direct importer of fine natural stone, including French limestone, Jerusalem Stone and Marble found in some of the most exquisite quarries in France, Portugal, Spain, Greece and Italy. Architects and professional designers appreciate the Piedras International selection of hundreds of materials and styles on display in their showroom.

Ⓒ Architectural Glass Arts, Inc.
7414 S. W. 48 St.
305-284-8621
Consultations by appointment to luxury homeowners to aid in the design and development of the ultimate luxury bath. The truly frameless shower enclosures are custom made to exacting dimensions installed by experienced artisans. Do you know what 'truly frameless' means? Call us for an appointment to find out.

Ⓓ Art Teak Furniture
4691 S. W. 72nd Avenue #102
305-667-9291
Mon.-Sat. 10:30 a.m.-6 p.m.;
Sun. 11 a.m.-6 p.m.
www.artteak.com
Art Teak Furniture is the industry's source for exquisite, hand-made teak furniture and accessories. The aesthetic charm and ornate elegance of Indonesian teak is sure to captivate even the most discerning clientele.

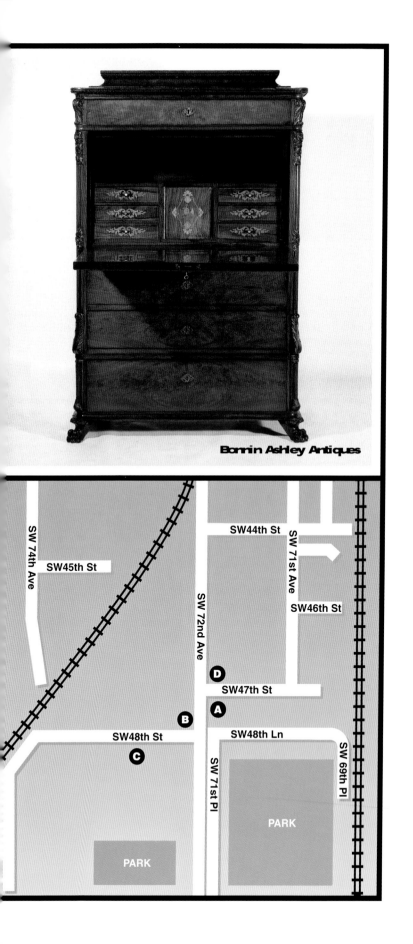

Bonnin Ashley Antiques

SW 74th Ave

SW 45th St

SW 44th St

SW 71st Ave

SW 46th St

SW 72nd Ave

D

SW 47th St

A

B

SW 48th St

SW 48th Ln

C

SW 71st Pl

SW 69th Pl

PARK

PARK

HOT DISTRICTS

Coral Gables

Spanish Charm and World Class Shopping

Inspired by the magnificent architectural style of the Mediterranean, Coral Gables is steeped in a rich, cultural heritage. Quaint and charming, this lovely town is the oldest area in Miami, and from day to night it explodes with unique shops to explore and enjoy. In its vibrant shopping area, you'll discover fine art, fabulous furnishings, original Art Nouveau, Art Deco and Venetian objets d'art, Swarovski crystal chandeliers, even elegant decorative hardware and bath fixtures. When it's time for lunch, you won't have to go far for a fabulous meal because Coral Gables is also known as the Fine Dining Capital of South Florida and boasts over 120 world class restaurants

Ⓐ Arredo Italiano
4018 Aurora St.
305-445-7780
Mon.-Fri. 9 a.m.-5 p.m.
Arredo Italiano offers for the first time in the United States the highest quality interior doors and architectural glass. The glass panes collection designed by Italian designers are the newest method homeowners are incorporating in their design style throughout the home. Visit our showroom to see just how different our interior doors are.

Ⓑ Opus 2000
201 Bird Road
305-448-4819
Opus 2000 offers the finest in Italian furniture and accessories. We specialize in

unique traditional furniture that is manufactured in the Old World methods. Our lighting accessories range from chandeliers in Swarovski crystal to table lamps with cobalt and amber.

Ⓒ Fiorelli Antiques
323 Aragon Ave.
305-441-2203
Mon.-Thurs. 11 a.m.-7 p.m.
Fri. 11 a.m.-9 p.m.; Sat. 11 a.m.-7 p.m.
Located in the heart of Coral Gables, Fiorelli Antiques showcases the finest array of rare and authentic 'objets d' art' from the turn-of the-century. The gallery specializes in Art Nouveau, Art Deco and Venetian Glass. All of them are originals from the Twenties and Thirties, and are signed by Daum-Nancy,

Arredo Italiano

Camille Faure, L.C. Tiffany, Rene Lalique, D. Chiparus, E. Galle, Dominique and others.

D The Americas Collection
2440 Ponce De Leon Blvd.
305-446-5578
Mon.-Fri. 10:30 a.m.-5:30 p.m.;
Sat. 12-5 p.m.
Gallery nights, hosted 7-10 p.m., every first Friday of the month.
We are a full-service gallery offering painting, sculpture, graphics, antique, maps framing, transportation and installation of artworks. We have a wide range of international artist from established masters to emerging talents, provides fascinating choices for both seasoned private collectors and corporate clients.

E Décor House
4119 Ponce de Leon
Mon.-Sat. 9:30 a.m.-6:30 p.m.;
Sun. 12-4 p.m.
Décor House is the exclusive retailer for Baker Furniture in Miami and is featuring the distinctive Continental Collection. A versatile selection of dining room, bedroom, occasional and upholstered furniture offers traditional elegance that creates a timeless sense of style. We specialize in exporting furniture to Latin America and around the world.

Décor House

F Farrey's Lighting and Bath
4101 Ponce de Leon Blvd.
305-445-2244
Also at: 1850 NE 146 St.
North Miami
305-947-5451
www.farreys.com
Farrey's Lighting and Bath offers a broad selection of lighting, decorative hardware and plumbing. From chandeliers to wall sconces, door knobs to cabinet knobs, and from faucets to sinks, if you can't find it at Farrey's, chances are it hasn't been made. Expert consultants will guide you through the process of creating the "Home of your Dreams."

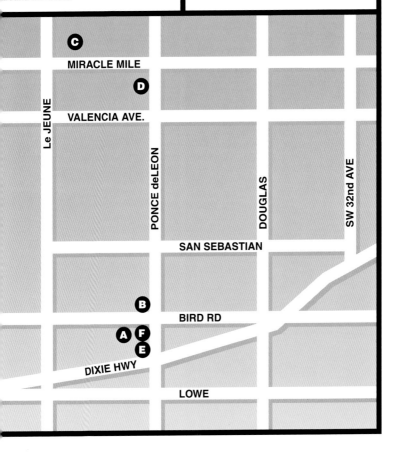

Miami Design District

Upscale Design in Downtown Miami

A four block, self-contained area that was originally a pineapple planta-tion, this 70-year-old mecca for decor and interior design called Decorator's Row is where you'll find the crème de la crème of Miami's most upscale decorating venues. The heart of this unique area is the inter-section of Northeast Second Avenue and Northeast 40th Street. Here you'll discover showrooms dedicated to fine quality antiques and exquisite accessories, state-of-the art wine care systems, elegant imported and domestic furniture and decorative art pieces. As well, you will find unique lighting and bath fixtures and high-end design services. In short, everything a well-appointed room should wear.

Ⓐ Leather Design Studio
101 NE 40th St.
305-572-0788
South Florida's premier showcase of fine leather furniture. Whether your style is con-temporary or traditional deco or Old World, we offer unique pieces built to the highest industry standards choose from hundreds of leather colors and textures. Many pieces also available in a selection of beautiful fab-rics.

Ⓑ Via Solferino
3920 NE 2nd Ave.
305-572-1182
Dilmos features Italian furniture with a highly unique concept for contemporary liv-ing. Its glamorous style originated in Milano and is rapidly spreading worldwide. The functional art pieces express a poetic value which are designed to enhance every living environment.

Ⓒ Evelyn S. Poole
3925 North Miami Ave.
305-573-7463
www.evelynpooleltd.com
Evelyn S. Poole, Ltd. Antique Gallery was the first, and still is, the premier source for very fine quality antiques in South Florida. The 5,000 square foot showroom specializes in statement pieces from large focal point furniture to small exquisite accessories from the 17th, 18th, 19th Century and Art Deco period. It has an excellent reputation amongst the interior design world and knowledgeable collectors. Many of the pieces are seen in articles featuring the houses of celebrities and the elite. An industry Foundation Member of the American Society of Interior Designers.

Ⓓ Chambrair, The Wine Care System
4100 N. E. 2nd Avenue
305-573-5120
Mon.-Fri. 10 a.m.-5 p.m.
Sat. by appointment.
www.chambrairusa.com
The Wine Care System caters exclusively to wine connoisseurs around the world. Engineered and crafted in Germany, the system uses state of the art components to recreate the conditions of a natural wine cellar found at the vineyards and chateaux of winegrowers throughout the world. Visit the Miami Design District showroom that features several climate controlled wine storage systems. Please call in advance to arrange for an exclusive demonstration.

Chambrair

E Sipure Design
135 NE 40th St.
305-576-2277
Mon.-Fri. 9:30 a.m.-5:30 p.m.
Sat. by appointment.
Sipure Design presents and distributes in exclusivity collections of furniture, lightings and accessories created by renowned European Contemporary designers. Owned and operated by an architect, the items, mostly imported from France, have been rigorously selected for the creativity and quality of their design and their high level end. Interior design services and assistance are available.

F Floral Designs
3841 NE 2nd Ave.
305-573-3232
Mon.-Fri. 9 a.m.-5 p.m.;
Sat. 10 a.m.-4 p.m.
Floral Designs is a custom manufacturer of high quality preserved and silk plants, trees and florals.

G Distinctive Interiors of Miami, Inc.
4141 N. E. 2nd Ave., Suite 102
305-571-5016
Mon.-Fri. 9 a.m.-5 p.m.
Distinctive Interiors of Miami offers one of a kind decorative art pieces as well as accessories from around the world. Even the most selective of clientele find our fur-

Showroom 84

nishings to be elegant and unique. Our expertise and experience provide you with a full range of design services. Visit our showroom in the Miami Design District.

H Showroom 84
3901 N. E. 2nd Ave.
305-573-5114
Mon.-Fri. 9 a.m.-5 p.m.
Sat. by appointment.
Showroom 84 is one of Miami Design District's largest and most popular showrooms to meet both your exterior and interior design needs. The Design District showroom offers two stories featuring a vast array of high quality domestic and imported furnishings. Another showroom is located at DCOTA.

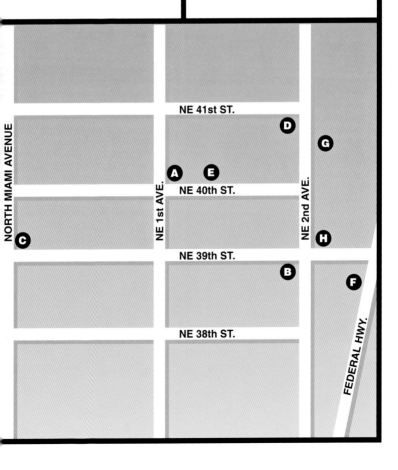

Naples

Old Florida Charm and Decorating Delights

If you're looking for a slice of charming, "Old Florida" you've come to the right place. In the old section of town, you'll stroll through tree-shaded neighborhoods with gracious, pastel-tinted homes. When it's time to shop, you'll discover treasures in several different shopping areas and, because Naples has become an ascending star in the galaxy of international travel, you'll join visitors from all over the world. Begin your shopping day with a delectable breakfast or lunch in the Village at one of the charming outdoor restaurants on 5th Avenue South, and then stroll over to 3rd Street where you'll discover a delightful array of boutiques. A mere five miles away are the Tamiami Trail and the Trade Center Way shopping areas, where you'll find handcrafted furniture and imported accessories, custom moldings and stonework, fireplace surrounds and custom faux finishing, as well as everything you need for a state-of-the art home entertainment area.

Ⓐ House of High Fidelity
5187 N. Tamiami Trail
941-262-0100
Mon.-Sat. 10 a.m.-5 p.m.
The House of High Fidelity has been bringing the best in home audio and video to the area for over 43 years. We offer AMX remote systems, audio visual equipment, televisions and plasma flat monitors, overhead projectors, and an extensive selection of speakers and in-wall speakers from Snell, Innovative Audio, Tannoy, Energy, Gallo, Sonance and VeloDyne.

Ⓑ Sweet Art & Design, Inc.
1813 J&C Blvd.
941-597-2110
We offer museum quality faux finishing, murals, trompe l'oeil and Venetian plaster. Come visit our studio–the ideas are endless.

Ⓒ Agostino's Design Group
3078 North Tamiami Trail
941-403-9108
Also at:
26811 South Bay Drive, Suite 132
Bonita Springs
941-992-3300
Truly a one-of-a-kind interior design firm, Agostino's Design Group is a family-owned and operated interior design studio that specializes in an international mix of custom hand-crafted furniture and antique accessories imported from Europe. With locations in Bonita Springs and Naples, their team of dedicated design professionals offer complete interior design service for the home. With inspirations collected from around the world, Agostino's Design Group pride themselves in bringing their clients exclusive furnishings to create customized interiors.

Agostino's Design Group

D Renaissance Plaster USA, LLC
6166 Taylor Rd., #102
941-591-8002
Mon.-Fri. 8:30 a.m.-5 p.m.
Sat. by appointment
We import high-quality plaster mouldings and architectural trim. Crown Moldings, Panel Trim, Niches, Corbels, Fireplace surrounds, columns, pilasters and ceiling medallions are available. We offer bespoke mouldings in period or contemporary styles as well as our standard products and complete refurbishment service from initial survey to final installations.

Renaissance Plaster

E Designer Audio
2011 Trade Center Way
941-514-4904
Mon.-Fri. by appointment
Offering custom audio/video, automated lighting, home automation, telephone system and home theatres. We are recognized as being in the "Top Ten Best of the Best" nationwide for home automation. Visit our state of the art showroom.

F Gulf Coast Marble & Granite, Inc.
6267 Lee Ann Ln.
941-566-7402
Mon.-Fri. 8 a.m.-6 p.m.
Sat. 9 a.m.-1 p.m.
With state-of-the-art technique in dimensional stonework, we specialize in countertop fabrication, tables, fireplaces, floor installation and cut to size marble, granite, limestone, travertine and natural stone for new residential and commercial construction and renovation projects. Quality-oriented craftsmanship.

G The Closet Company
3605 North Tamiami Trail
941-434-6655
Mon.-Fri. 9 a.m.-5 p.m.
Sat. by appointment
Southwest Florida's oldest locally-owned storage specialist with systems custom built to your specifications. Whether redesigning the closet space in the bedrooms or the storage space in the garage, we can simplify your life. Visit our showroom located in the heart of Naples' Tamiami Trial.

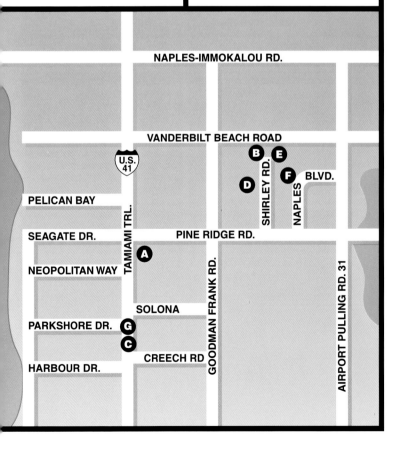

Palm Beach
Worth Avenue

Treasure Hunting in Palm Beach's Most Elegant Area

One of the world's most exclusive shopping streets, the Worth Avenue area in Palm Beach is synonymous with elegance. In this shopping mecca, art meets fashion, fashion meets interior design, and Florida's high society enjoys it all. Here, an amazing display of international and exclusive collections awaits. Stroll along the pleasant esplanade and receive star treatment as you explore this sophisticated destination that boasts a stunning array of luxurious shops and restaurants. Worth Avenue derives a considerable amount of its elegant ambience from the landscaped sidewalks and Mediterranean-style architecture designed by Addison Mizner over 70 years ago. How can you resist?

A A'Vare Design Group
337 E. Indiantown Rd., Suite 6
561-741-4010
A'Vare specializes in high-end residential and commercial projects throughout the US and the Caribbean Islands. Our dynamic blend of architecture and interior design, as well as construction management makes us truly full-service. We carry traditional and eclectic furniture, custom upholstery, decorative window treatments, area rugs, tapestries and creative accessories.

B Peacock Cabinetry
234 South County Road
561-833-3232
This elegant Palm Beach showroom displays only a sampling of what is possible with Christopher Peacock Bespoke English Cabinetry. Inspired by the rich treasury of Britain's furniture heritage, but built in the United States, Peacock cabinetry offers the best in handmade fitted furniture for the home with the highest level of personal service. Peacock's distinguished designers,

master craftsman and decorative artists, create rooms worthy of the finest homes built today.

C LaMaison Fleurie, Inc.
135 North County Rd. #25
561-833-1083
Mon.-Fri. 9 a.m.-5:30 p.m.
Located in upscale Palm Beach, LaMaison Fleurie specializes in residential homes.

D Florence Gallery
309 Worth Ave.
561-833-6660
Mon.-Wed. 10-6
Sat. 10 a.m.-10 p.m.; Sun. 12-5 p.m.
Florence Gallery offers hand-painted, oil recreations of the masters and popular artists. These museum quality recreations are painted by seven European master artists, each having studied the style, materials and techniques. Each painting is mounted in a custom frame chosen from our large inventory, or commission the painting you want in a size you need. You get the look you want and fabulous quality at a price you'll love.

E Stefen Jā Stüdēos
10 Governor's Ct.
561-775-0066
www.stefenjastudeos.com
South Florida is the perfect venue for custom aquatic theme designs by Stefen Jā Stüdēos. Unique coral reef sculptures bring to human environment the look and feel of the under sea world. Palm Beach Gardens is the newest hot spot for the ultimate in sub-tropic décor.

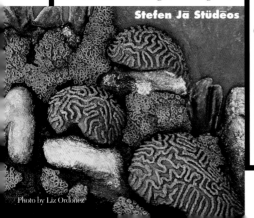

Stefen Jā Stüdēos

Photo by Liz Ordoñez

ⓕ Arte Ceramica
256 Worth Ave.
561-820-0032

Located in the Gucci Courtyard on Worth Avenue, Arte Ceramica is a direct importer of quality handmade, hand-painted Spanish ceramics and the finest custom wall-tile murals from select studios throughout Spain. Centuries old methods are used to shape the clay. Painted designs range from bright classic florals and 10th Century Moorish inspirations to intricate Renaissance scrolls. The tile murals display an array of subjects on rustic handmade tiles or more finely rendered reproductions of master painters. Custom projects are a specialty.

ⓖ Zeluck, Inc. Architectural Windows & Doors
202 Phipps Plaza
561-833-0092
By appointment.

Here is the solution for your unique window and door requirements. Made from Honduras Mahogany, Zeluck, Inc. offers an unrivaled selection and unequaled freedom for all types of architecture. In addition, most designs are both Dade County and Secci impact approved, thereby eliminating shutters. Visit the showroom to experience first-hand the precision, quality and enduring beauty of these products.

Photo by Sargent

A'Vare Design Group

ⓗ Avakian's Oriental Rugs
11940 US Highway One, Suite 108
561-626-6455
Mon.-Fri. 10 a.m.-5:30 p.m.;
Sat. 10 a.m.-6 p.m.

Avakian's Oriental Rugs displays a variety of rugs from around the world. Lavish rugs from as far away as India, Persia and China. Come visit our showroom located in Carl's Plaza in North Palm Beach.

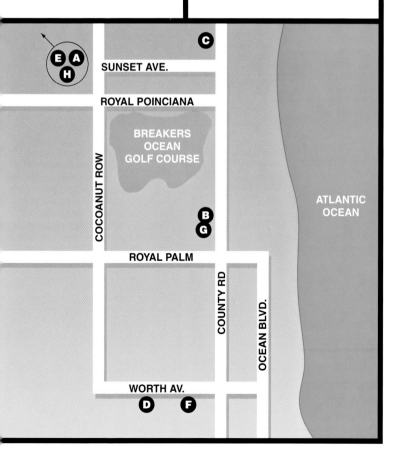

West Palm Beach

A Mile of Delightful Discoveries

West Palm Beach boasts several distinct shopping venues. The most unique is Antique Row, an unassuming area with a surprising array of shops and plenty of on-street parking. Here you'll discover more than 45 shops filled with treasures ranging from antique furniture, American and European Art Deco, and collectibles to oriental rugs, tribal tapestries and vintage linens. Browsing through these unique shops is such a delightful experience that you'll want to stay all day. And you can. When it's time for lunch, you'll find that Antique Row also boasts several charming al fresco restaurants.

❶ South Dixie Antique Row Association
West Palm Beach
Mon.-Sat. 10:30 a.m.-5 p.m.
www.westpalmbeachantiques.com
Just across the bridge from Palm Beach is a one-mile area known as Antique Row. West Palm Beach's Antique Row has over forty-five shops that convey the grandeur of Florida's past. For a Walker's Map, fax your name and address to (561) 588-3119 or visit our website.

Ⓐ ResourceASIA
500 Palm Street, Suite 24
561-659-6597
Tues.-Sat. 10 a.m.-5 p.m.
Specializing in teak furnishings for indoors and out, ResourceASIA provides harmonious elements for expressive and sensual environments. Styles range from Eastern simplicity to opulent carvings, all drawing their richness from the innate beauty of natural materials. From Bali and Java are antique and reproduction beds, tables, mirrors or reclining couches. For outdoors, you will find sleek teak and stainless steel table settings and lounges, or more traditional teak designs. Experience the blending of nature, art and function at ResourceASIA.

Ⓑ The Elephant's Foot Antiques
3800 S. Dixie Hwy.
561-832-0170
Mon.-Sun. 10:30 a.m.-5 p.m.
A major source for antique and decorative home furnishings since 1963, the large showroom displays an eclectic mix of one-of-a-kind antique furniture pieces from England and the continent. Decorative, painted and printed furniture is an integral part of their inventory. To further compliment the furniture the showroom is filled with a variety of antique and decorative accessories, including porcelains, silver, lamps, mirrors, painting and more. An ever-changing collection of chandeliers, both small and large, graces the showroom.

Ⓒ Christa's South Antiques & Seashells
3737 S. Dixie Hwy.
561-655-4650
Mon.-Fri. 10 a.m.-5 p.m.;
Sat. 11 a.m.-5 p.m.
Offering 17th, 18th and 19th Century antiques and decorations as well as custom framing. We also specialize in creating accessories and furnishings from seashells. We are located on Antique Row in West Palm Beach where there are more than 50 shops to browse.

Photo by Sig Bokalders

The Elephant's Foot Antiques

Dear Home Book Reader —

We hope that you have enjoyed our *Home Book*, and found it very resourceful for your dream home.

The following is a simple survey that we ask you fill out to receive your FREE COPY of **Distinguished Home Plans**. After filling out the survey, detach at the perforation and mail back to The Ashley Group.

We thank you for taking the time to fill out this survey; your FREE copy of **Distinguished Home Plans** is on its way!

Sincerely,
Maria Bronzovich, The Ashley Group

Receive your free copy today!

Please fill out and mail back today!

ashleybooksales@cahners.com

D Modern Venetian Blind
417 Bunker Rd.
561-585-2561
We are a family owned and operated man-ufacturer of interior window treatment. We have been serving the Palm Beaches since 1946. We fabricate woven wood roman shades, traditional wood venetian blinds, which can be custom stained or painted. Fabric laminated roller shades vertical blinds mini-blinds and more. All of our products can be motorized.

E Arc Stone III
3114 Tuxedo Ave.
561-478-8805
They have the largest selection of marble granite, tranatine, slate and limestone in Florida. Slabs tiles can be cut to size.

F Environmental Technology Control
2921 Australian Ave.
561-881-8118
Mon.-Fri. by appointment.
ETC provides sophisticated one-button operation of multiple features that trans-lates into easy to use electronic systems for homeowners. Pressing the 'Away Mode' on the keypad could activate several separate operations. The security system arms all windows, doors, and motion detectors, the thermostat adjusts the temperature and at night, interior lights turn on and off ran-domly to create the impression that some-

Photo by John Prinster

**John Prinster
Art Deco Moderne**

one is home. 'Vacation and Night Mode' are two popular design requests. Whatever your lifestyle, we'll design a system exclu-sively for you.

G John Prinster Art Deco Moderne
3735 S. Dixie Hwy.
561-835-1512
We are a specialty store handling fine furni-ture, lighting, sculpture, ceramics, mirrors and accessories all created by the leading designers and artisan of the 1920s, 1930s, and 1940s.

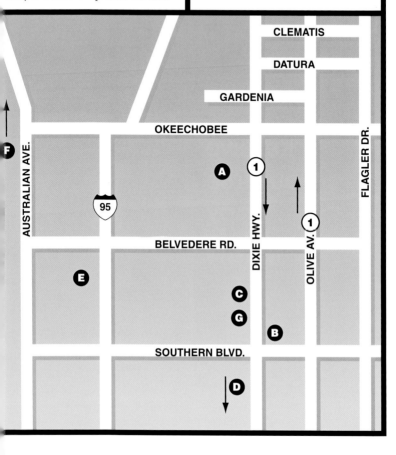

Finally...
South Florida's Own
Home & Design
Sourcebook

Call Toll Free at 888-458-1750

The South Florida Home Book, www.floridahomebook.com, is your final destination when searching for home improvement services. This comprehensive, hands-on-guide to building, remodeling, decorating, furnishing, and landscaping a home, is required reading for the serious and discriminating homeowner. With over 700 full-color, beautiful pages, this hard cover volume is the most complete and well-organized reference to the home industry. The Home Book covers all aspects of the process, including listings of hundreds of industry professionals, accompanied by informative and valuable editorial discussing the most recent trends. Ordering your copy of **The South Florida Home Book,** now, can ensure that you have the blueprints to your dream home, in your hand, today.

Order your copy today!

O R D E R   F O R M

THE SOUTH FLORIDA HOME BOOK

☐ YES, please send me _____ copies of the SOUTH FLORIDA HOME BOOK at $39.95 per book, plus $3 postage & handling per book.

Total amount sent: $_____   Please charge my: ☐ VISA   ☐ MasterCard   ☐ American Express

Card # _____   Exp. Date _____

Signature _____

Name _____   Phone ( ) _____

Address _____

City _____ State _____ Zip Code _____

Send order to: Attn: Book Sales—Marketing Dept., The Ashley Group, 1350 E. Touhy Ave., Suite 1E, Des Plaines, Illinois 60018
Or Call Toll Free at: 1-888-458-1750   Or E-mail ashleybooksales@cahners.com

All orders must be accompanied by check, money order or credit card # for full amount.

You can call any professional in this book TOLL FREE!

Need to contact a professional from the *South Florida Home Book*...use the Toll Free Number – Just dial **800-492-2708** and just enter the Extension number in their listing.

Sample Listing

INTERNATIONAL AUDIO VISUAL, INC ....**(954) 630-9797**
3215 NW 10th TCE #206, Fort Lauderdale   Fax: (954) 630-9775
See Ad on Page: 712, 713   800 Extension: 1139
Principal/Owner: Wade Gilbert
Website: www.iavi.com email: info@iavi.com
Additional Information: For the latest in home theater products and installation.

SOUTH FLORIDA
HOME
BOOK

800-492-2708

Photo courtesy of:
Quincy Johnson Architec

ARCHITECTS

sargent architectural photography

ARCHITECTURE AND INTERIORS

"To me, a building— *if it is* *beautiful* —is the love of one man;

he's made it out of his love for

space and materials. "

Martha Graham

photo courtesy of:
SGA Architects

The First Step

An architect is the first step in realizing your vision for your new or remodeled home. These professionals are not only skilled in the technical areas of space planning, engineering and drafting, but also happen to be experts in materials, finishes, energy efficiency, even landscaping. An architect takes the time to find out how you live, what your needs are, and how you'd like to see your dreams come into fruition, all the while keeping your budget in mind. These creative professionals can assemble seemingly disparate elements into a design that incorporates what you need with what you want, with grace, beauty and efficiency. We have the privilege of featuring the finest of these creative, technically proficient problem solvers to help you bring our ultimate home to life.

WHAT'S YOUR LIFESTYLE?

- Who lives in the house now?
- Who will live there in the future?
- Who visits and for how long?
- Do you like traditional, contemporary or eclectic design?
- Why are you moving or remodeling?
- What aspects of your current home need to be improved upon?
- Do you like functional, minimalist design, or embellishments and lots of style?
- Do you entertain formally or informally?
- How much time will you spend in the master bedroom? Is it spent reading, watching TV, working or exercising?
- What are the primary functions of the kitchen?
- Do you need a home office?
- Do you like lots of open space or little nooks and crannies?
- What kind of storage do you need?

BRINGING IDEAS TO LIFE

Whether you're building your dream home in the city, a second vacation home, or remodeling your home in the suburbs, it takes a team to design and build a high quality residential project. A team of an architect, builder, interior designer, kitchen and bath designer, and landscape architect/designer, should be assembled very early in the process. When these five professionals have the opportunity to collaborate before ground is broken, you'll reap the rewards for years to come. Their blend of experience and ideas can give you insights into the fabulous possibilities of your home and site you never considered. Their association will surely save you time, money and eventually frustration.

THE ARCHITECT - MAKING THE DREAM REAL

Licensed architects provide three basic, easily defined tasks. First, they design, taking into account budget, site, owner's needs, and existing house style. Second, they produce the necessary technical drawings and specifications to accomplish the desires of their clients, and explain to a contractor in adequate detail what work needs to be done. Lastly, architects participate in the construction process. This straightforward mission requires more than education.

It requires listening. The best architects have gained their status by giving their clients exactly what they want - even when those clients have difficulty articulating what that is. How? By creatively interpreting word pictures into real pictures. By eliciting the spirit of the project and following that spirit responsibly as they develop an unparalleled design.

It requires experience. Significant architects, such as those included in your Home Book, maintain a reputation for superiority because their buildings are stunningly conceived, properly designed and technically sound. If a unique, steeply pitched roof was custom-designed for you by a licensed architect with an established reputation, you can be confident that it is buildable.

Suggestions by an experienced architect can add value and interest to your new home or remodeling project. Because of their exposure to current, thoughtful design, they'll suggest you wire your home for the technology of the future, frame up an attic for future use as a second floor, or build your countertops at varying levels to accommodate people of different heights.

This area is blessed with many talented architects. It's not uncommon for any number of them to be working on a luxury vacation retreat in another country or a unique second home in another state. Their vision and devotion to design set a standard of excellence for dynamic design and uncompromising quality.

WORKING WITH AN ARCHITECT

The best relationships are characterized by close collaborative communication. The architect is the person you're relying on to take your ideas, elevate them to the highest level, and bring them to life in a custom design that's never been built before. So take your time in selecting the architect. It's not unusual for clients to spend two or three months interviewing prospective architects.

In preparation for the interview process, spend time fine-tuning your ideas. Put together an Idea Notebook (See 'Compile an Idea Notebook'). Make a wish list that includes every absolute requirement and every wild fantasy you've ever wanted in a home. Visit builder's models to discover what 3,000 square feet feels like in comparison to 6,000 square feet, how volume ceilings feel, or what loft living feels like. Look at established and new neighborhoods to get ideas about the relationship between landscaping and homes, and what level of landscaping you want.

GOOD COMMUNICATION SETS THE TONE

The first meeting is the time to communicate all of your desires for your new home or remodeling project, from the abstract to the concrete. You're creating something new, so be creative in imprinting your spirit and personality on the project. Be bold in expressing your ideas, even if they are not fully developed or seem unrealistic. Share your Idea Notebook and allow the architect to keep it as plans are being developed. Be prepared to talk about your lifestyle, because the architect will be trying to soak up as much information about you and your wishes as possible.

• Be frank about your budget. Although some clients are unrestricted by budgetary concerns, most must put some control on costs, and good architects expect and respect this. Great ideas can be achieved on a budget and the architect will tell you what can be achieved for your budget.

• However, sticking to your budget requires tremendous self-discipline. If there's a luxury you really want, (a second laundry room, a built-in aquarium) it's probably just as practical to build it into your design from the outset, instead of paying for it in a change order once building has begun.

COMPILE AN IDEA NOTEBOOK

It's hard to put an idea into words, but so easy to show with a picture. Fill a good-sized notebook with plain white paper, tuck a roll of clear tape and a pair of scissors into the front flap, and you've got an Idea Notebook. Fill it with pictures, snapshots of homes you like, sketches of your own, little bits of paper that show a color you love, notes to yourself on your priorities and wishes. Circle the parts of the pictures and make spontaneous notes. "Love the finish on the cabinets," "Great rug," "Don't want windows this big." Show this to your architect, and other team members. Not only will it help keep ideas in the front of your mind, but will spark the creativity and increase understanding within the entire team.

137

BUILT TO LAST

Custom home clients in the Chicago area are abandoning the quest for the big house in favor of designing a home of high quality, integrity and harmonious balance. When the emphasis is on using top quality materials and custom design to create a comfortable home, the result is truly built to last.

TOO BIG, TOO SMALL, JUST RIGHT?

If you're designing rooms with dimensions different from what you're used to, get out the tape measure. If you're down-sizing, can you fit the furniture into this space? Is the new, larger size big enough – or too big? Ask your architect, builder, or interior designer if there's a similar project you can visit to get a good feel for size.

• Ask lots of questions. Architects of luxury homes in the area are committed to providing their clients with information up front about the design process, the building process and their fees. These architects respect the sophistication and intelligence of their clientele, but do not necessarily expect them to have a high level of design experience or architectural expertise. Educating you is on their agenda.

• What is the breadth of services? Although this information is in your contract, it's important to know the level of services a firm will provide. There is no set standard and you need to be sure if an architect will provide the kind of services you want – from basic "no-frills" through "full service."

• Find out who you will be working with. Will you be working with one person or a team? Who will execute your drawings?

• Ask for references. Speak to past and current clients who built projects similar to yours. Ask for references from contractors with whom the architect works.

• Does the architect carry liability insurance?

• Ask to see examples of the architect's work – finished homes, job sites, and architectural plans. Does the work look and feel like what you want?

• Find out how many projects the architect has in progress. Will you get the attention you deserve?

• Decide if you like the architect. For successful collaboration, there must be a good personal connection. As you both suggest, reject, and refine ideas, a shared sense of humor and good communication will be what makes the process workable and enjoyable. Ask yourself, "Do I trust this person to deliver our dream and take care of business in the process?" If the answer is anything less than a strong and sure, "yes!," keep looking.

UNDERSTANDING ARCHITECTS' FEES AND CONTRACTS

Fees and fee structures vary greatly among architects, and comparing them can be confusing, even for the experienced client. Architects, like licensed professionals in other fields, are prohibited from setting fees as a group and agreeing on rates. They arrive at their fees based on:

(A) an hourly rate
(B) lump sum total
(C) percentage of construction cost
(D) dollars per square foot
(E) size of the job
(F) a combination of the above

Sample Budgets, Costs & Fees

CONTRACTOR:

Demolition & Protection: $2,500
Wood flooring:...$2,500
Countertops: $7,000
Tile backsplash: $2,000
Lighting/Electrical: $6,000
Plumbing: $6,000

Subtotal: $26,000
Contractor overhead & profit (15%): $3,900
Contractor Total **$29,900**

OWNER:

Cabinetry, furnished & installed: $40,000
High end appliances:..$15,000
Painting:..$2,500
Owner Total **$57,500**

Contractor + Owner **$87,400**
Architect or Designer Fee (15%)...............**$13,110**
Total Project Cost......................................**$100,510**

Assumes very good quality materials, contractors, and subcontractors. Construction cost estimated does not include structural work, windows, drywall or general carpentry. Range of fees is approximate.

A HIGH-QUALITY NEW HOME CONSTRUCTION SAMPLE

Size: ....4,500 square feet
Construction cost: ....$200 per square foot
(does not include the site cost or major landscaping)
Project structure:....................................Upscale South Florida location;
moderately high to high level of detail and complexity

Includes:
    Four or five bedrooms
    Four bathrooms
    Great room
    Home office
    Large American-style kitchen
    Dining room
    Three or four car garage
    Finished basement

Architect's fee: ....Survey results ranged from a low of $30,000 to a high range of $90,000-$120,000, based upon the type and quality of services offered.
Note: Architect's fee is approximately 15% of the cost of a project.

139

WHY YOU SHOULD WORK WITH A TOP ARCHITECT

1. They are expert problem solvers. A talented architect can create solutions to your design problems, and solve the problems that stand in the way of achieving your dream.

2. They have creative ideas. You may see a two-story addition strictly in terms of its function – a great room with a master suite upstairs. An architect immediately applies a creative eye to the possibilities.

3. They provide a priceless product and service. A popular misconception about architects is that their fees make their services an extravagance. In reality, an architect's fee represents a small percentage of the overall building cost.

The final quoted fee will include a set of services that may vary greatly from architect to architect. From a "no frills" to a "full service" bid, services are vastly different. For example, a no frills agreement budgets the architect's fee at two to seven percent of the construction cost; a full service contract budgets the architect's fee at 12 to 18 percent. Some firms include contractor's selection, bid procurement, field inspections, interior cabinetry, plumbing and lighting design, and punch list. Others don't.

One concrete basis for comparison is the architectural drawings. There can be a vast difference in the number of pages of drawings, the layers of drawings and the detail level of the specifications. Some include extra sketchbooks with drawings of all the construction details and in-depth written specs which call out every doorknob and fixture. Some offer impressive three-dimensional scale models to help you better visualize the end result, and computerized virtual walk throughs.

The benefit of a more detailed set of drawings is a more accurate, cost-effective construction bid. The more details noted in the drawings and text, the fewer contingencies a contractor will have to speculate on. The drawings are the sum total of what your contract with a builder is based upon. If a detail isn't included in the drawings, then it's not part of the project and you'll be billed extra for it.

Services should be clearly outlined in your contract. Many local architects use a standard American Institute of Architects (AIA) contract, in a long or short form. Some use a letter of agreement.

Have your attorney read the contract. Be clear that the level of service you desire is what the architect is prepared to deliver.

THE DESIGN PHASE

The architect will be in communication with you as your project progresses through the phases of schematic design, design development, preparation of construction documents, bidding and negotiating with a contractor, and contract administration (monitoring the construction). If any of these services will not be supplied, you should find out at your initial meeting.

The creativity belongs in the first phases. This is when you move walls, add windows, change your mind about the two-person whirlpool tub in favor of a shower surround, and see how far your budget will take you.

The time involved in the design process varies depending on the size of the project, your individual availability, and coordinating schedules.

A good architect will encourage you to take as much time as you want in the first phases. It's not always easy to temper the euphoria that comes with starting to build a dream home but the longer you live with the drawings, the happier you'll be. Spread the plans on a table and take an extra week or month to look at them whenever you walk by.

Think practically. Consider what you don't like about your current home. If noise from the dishwasher bothers you at night, tell your architect you want a quiet bedroom, and a quiet dishwasher. Think about the nature of your future needs. Architects note that their clients are beginning to ask for "barrier-free" and ergonomic design for more comfortable living as they age, or as their parents move in with them, and first floor master bedroom suites.

BUILDING BEGINS: BIDDING AND NEGOTIATION

If your contract includes it, your architect will bid your project to contractors he or she considers appropriate for your project, and any contractor you wish to consider. You may want to include a contractor to provide a "control" bid. If you wish to hire a specific contractor, you needn't go through the bidding process, unless you're simply curious about the range of responses you may receive. After the architect has analyzed the bids and the field is narrowed, you will want to meet the contractors to see if you're compatible, if you're able to communicate clearly, and if you sense a genuine interest in your project. These meetings can take place as a contractor walks through a home to be remodeled, or on a tour of a previously built project if you're building a new home.

If your plans come in over budget, the architect is responsible for bringing the costs down, except, of course, if the excess is caused by some item the architect had previously cautioned you would be prohibitive.

Not all people select an architect first. It's not uncommon for the builder to help in the selection of an architect, or for a builder to offer "design/build" services with architects on staff, just as an architectural firm may have interior designers on staff. ∎

AMERICAN ASSOCIATION OF ARCHITECTS

**AIA/Miami
3399 Ponce de Leon Blvd., Suite 104
Coral Gables, FL 33134
(305) 448-7488
www. aiamiami.org**

AIA/Miami is a professional association of licensed architects, with a strong commitment to educating and serving the general public. They sponsor free seminars called, "Working With an Architect" which feature a local architect speaking on home design and building. The Miami chapter also offers access to local architects' portfolios and provides a wealth of information in their Architect/Client Resource Center.

141

Architects

A'VARE DESIGN GROUP ....**(561) 741-4010**
337 E. Indiantown Rd., Suite 6, Jupiter   Fax: (561) 741-4011
See Ad on Page: 144, 314   *800 Extension:* 1002
Principal/Owner: Lorraine Alwaise
Website: www.avare.com
Additional Information: Award - winning design group. Making your vision a
reality!

AMES DESIGN INTERNATIONAL ....**(561) 274-6444**
203 Dixie Blvd., Delray Beach   Fax: (561) 274-6449
See Ad on Page: 176, 177   *800 Extension:* 1014
Principal/Owner: Shane Ames email: amesdesign@bellsouth.net
Additional Information: 20 years creating elegant and unique expressions of
architecture globally for the discerning domestic and international clientele.

B. DESIGN GROUP CORPORATION ....**(941) 592-0221**
2051 Trade Center Way, Naples   Fax: (941) 592-0077
See Ad on Page: 182   *800 Extension:* 1030
Principal/Owner: Anthony Boyatt

BORROTO ARCHITECTS PA ....**(305) 361-6181**
250 Crandon Blvd, Suite 49, Key Biscayne   Fax: (305) 365-9782
See Ad on Page: 173   *800 Extension:* 1040
Principal/Owner: Wilfredo Borroto
Website: www.borrotoarchitects.com email: borroto@msn.com
Additional Information: Award winning custom luxury residences, residential
developments, office buildings, hotels, yacht clubs, shopping centers and land
planning. Established in 1965.

BOUGHTON ARCHITECTS, INC...**(941) 596-7800**
6645 Willow Park Drive, Naples   Fax: (941) 596-7825
See Ad on Page: 147   *800 Extension:* 1042
Principal/Owner: James Boughton
Website: www.boughtonarchitects.com email: info@boughtonarchitects.com
Additional Information: Boughton Architects, Inc. is known for project design
innovation, detailed project documentation and active site administration services.

BRIDGES, MARCH AND CARMO ....**(561) 832-1533**
18 Via Mizner, 2nd Floor, Palm Beach   Fax: (561) 832-1520
See Ad on Page: 183   *800 Extension:* 1044

DAILEY & PARTNERS ARCHITECTS, P.A. ....**(561) 640-5281**
2 Harvard Circle, Suite 300, West Palm Beach   Fax: (561) 640-5283
See Ad on Page: 179   *800 Extension:* 1065
Principal/Owner: Edson Dailey / Roger Janssen / Jeremy Walter
email: dparchpa@aol.com

DYEHOUSE GESHAY & COMERIATO ARCHITECT ....**(941) 434-5455**
999 Fifth Ave Parkway, Naples   Fax: (941) 434-5736
See Ad on Page: 156, 157   *800 Extension:* 1075
Principal/Owner: John K. Dyehouse III
Website: dgcarc.com email: dgc@dgcarc.com
Additional Information: Dyehouse Geshay & Comeriato is a design/service ori-
ented architectural firm, fulfilling our clients dreams and aspirations.

HUMPHREY ROSAL ARCHITECT ....**(941) 598-3100**
801 Laurel Oak Drive, Naples   Fax: (940) 598-4266
See Ad on Page: 184   *800 Extension:* 1128

TERRY L. IRWIN ARCHITECTS ....**(407) 876-5353**
513 Main Street, Suite 100, Windemere   Fax: (407) 846-2138
See Ad on Page: 180   *800 Extension:* 1261
Principal/Owner: Terry L. Irwin
Website: irwinarchitects.com email: tliarchs@aol.com

continued on page **152**

MITCHELL O'NEIL, A.I.A.
A R C H I T E C T

947 NORTH ALT. A1A, SUITE C
JUPITER, FLORIDA 33477
561-746-1113   REG NO. 10338

WESSEL ASSOCIATES AIA

900 South US Highway One Suite 104
Jupiter, Florida 33477
561.747.4950
Fax 561.747.4184

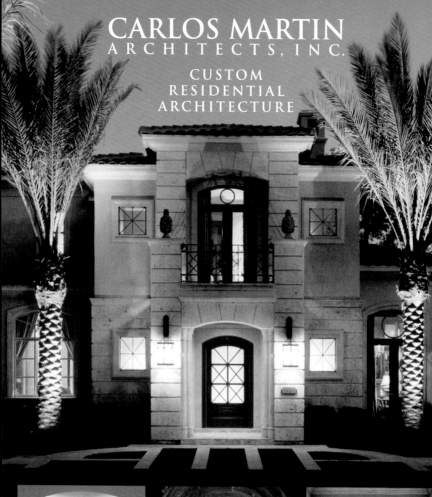

BAI

Boughton Architects, Inc.
6645 Willow Park Drive, Suite 200
Naples, Florida 34109
941.596.7800
fax 941.596.7825
FL DPR AA00002266
e-mail: info@boughtonarchitects.com

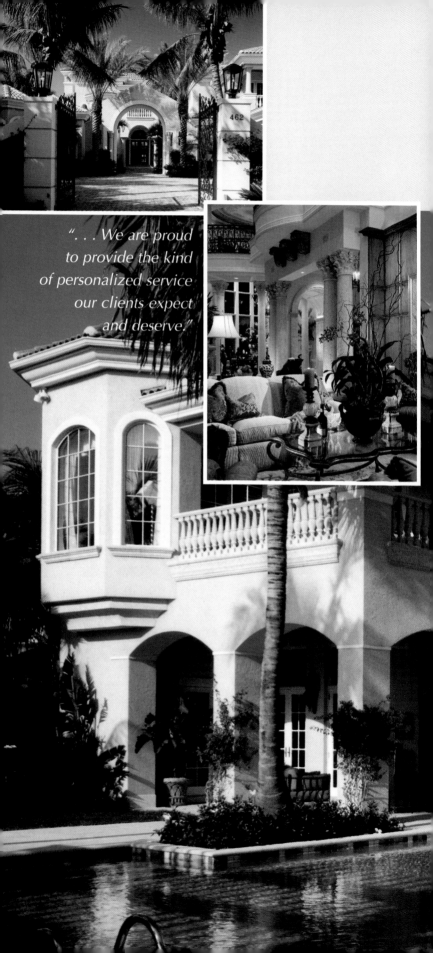

". . . We are proud to provide the kind of personalized service our clients expect and deserve."

SGA
ARCHITECTS
INCORPORATED

251A ROYAL PALM WAY, SUITE 600 PALM BEACH, FLORIDA 33480
561.832.1883   F. 561.832.1433

ARCHITECTURE AND PLANNING

Architecture

Interiors

continued from page **142**

QUINCY JOHNSON ARCHITECTS ....**(561) 997-9997**
949 Clint Moore Road, Boca Raton
See Ad on Page: 150, 151
Fax: (561) 997-1610
800 Extension: 1214
Principal/Owner: Quincy Johnson
Website: www.quincyjohnson.com email: info@quincyjohnson.com
Additional Information: We have a system which can guarantee on-time and under-budget design of your home.

CARLOS MARTIN ARCHITECTS, INC. ....**(954) 340-2650**
5100 W. Copans Road, Suite 700, Pompano Beach
See Ad on Page: 146
Fax: (954) 340-2649
800 Extension: 1046
Principal/Owner: Carlos A. Martin
Website: www.carlosmartinarchitects.com email: cam4arch@aol.com
Additional Information: Specializes in custom residential architecture inspired by the romantic revival periods of the 1920's and 30's.

MARK MCCREE, ARCHITECT ....**(561) 615-0636**
4753 Belvedere Road, West Palm Beach
See Ad on Page: 181
Fax: (561) 615-4549
800 Extension: 1176
Principal/Owner: Mark McCree
Additional Information: Award winning designs specializing in Mizner & old Florida vernacular.

KENNETH MILLER ARCHITECTS, P.A. ....**(561) 575-1442**
900 S. US Highway One, Suite 201, Jupiter
See Ad on Page: 132, 133, 153
Fax: (561) 575-1882
800 Extension: 1150
Principal/Owner: Kenneth R. Miller, A.I.A.
Website: kenmillerarchitects.com email: kmapa@bellsouth.net

NASRALLAH FINE ARCHITECTURAL DESIGN ....**(407) 647-0938**
507 N. New York Ave, Suite 300, Winter Park
See Ad on Page: 174, 175
Fax: (407) 647-2499
800 Extension: 1191
Principal/Owner: Mark Nasrallah
Website: www.nasrallah-aia.com email: markn@nasrallah-aia.com
Additional Information: Nasrallah specializes in luxury custom homes. Blending traditionalism with contemporary themes, award-winning with multi-disciplined firm creates diverse designs, which embody luxury, sophistication and comfort.

MITCHELL O'NEIL, A.I.A., ARCHITECT ....**(561) 746-1113**
947 N. Alternate A1A, Suite C, Jupiter
See Ad on Page: 143
Fax: (561) 746-1113
800 Extension: 1184
Principal/Owner: Mithchell O'Neil
email: oneilarchitect@juno.com

CHARLES HARRISON PAWLEY ARCHITECT ....**(305) 663-1600**
4515 Ponce De Leon Blvd., Coral Gables
See Ad on Page: 159 - 161
Fax: (305) 663-2777
800 Extension: 1054
Principal/Owner: Charles Pawley
Additional Information: Award - winning architecture incorporating optimal design solutions with the clients preferred style. New construction, remodeling and interior design.

PORTUONDO PEROTTI ARCHITECTS, INC. ....**(305) 442-1262**
4102 Laguna Street, Coral Gables
See Ad on Page: 172
Fax: (305) 442-1511
800 Extension: 1211
Principal/Owner: Rafael Portuondo

SGA ARCHITECTS ....**(561) 832-1883**
251 A Royal Palm Way, Sute 600, Palm Beach
See Ad on Page: 148, 149
Fax: (561) 832-1466
800 Extension: 1235

continued on page **178**

photography by architect

KENNETH MILLER ARCHITECTS, P.A.

RANDALL
STOFFT
ARCHITECTS

42 N. SWINTON AVENUE - DELRAY BEACH, FLORIDA 33444
561-243-0799 - FAX 561-243-0299 - NAPLES 941-262-7677

RANDALL
STOFFT
ARCHITECTS

42 N. SWINTON AVENUE - DELRAY BEACH, FLORIDA 33444
561-243-0799 - FAX 561-243-0299 - NAPLES 941-262-7677

DYEHOUSE
GESHAY &
COMERIATO

A R C H I T E C T

999   FIFTH   AVENUE   PARKWAY
NAPLES, FLORIDA   34102
941-434-5455 FAX: 941-434-5736 AA C001599
E-Mail: DGC@DGCARC.COM
WEB: WWW.DGCARC.COM

L. M. SILKWORTH, ARCHITECT, P.A.
1401 HIGHWAY A-1-A, SUITE 205
VERO BEACH, FLORIDA 32963

VOICE 1-561-234-4004
FAX 1-561-234-3111
e-mail: lmspa@atlantic.net

CHARLES H. PAWLEY
A R C H I T E C T   P A
FELLOW • American Institute of Architects

Since 1970, Charles Harrison Pawley, FAIA, has won over 30 American Institute of Architects awards, including the National AIA Award for Design and the Florida 25 Year Test of Time Award as well as two lifetime achievement awards, the Award of Honor for Design and The Gold Medal, both awarded in the same year - an unprecedented accomplishment.

4515 PONCE DE LEON BLVD • CORAL GABLES, FL 33146
TEL. 305.663-1600 • AR 4372 • FAX 305.663-2777

I. PAWLEY

CT PA
stitute of Architects

CORAL GABLES, FL 33146
72 • FAX 305.663-2777

162

Archi

A Return to Old World Charm

With design so firmly grounded in emotions, it's back to the future for some architects. Many people are nostalgic for the way things "used to be" and want their new homes to provide tranquility and security.

To meet their clients' lifestyle requirements, several South Florida architects have turned to classical architecture. They are integrating aspects of centuries-ago Spanish, French, English and Italian architecture into today's residential designs.

Nostalgia for the way things "used to be" has sparked a desire for a return to more traditional designs. This grand, new Spanish Colonial residence conveys the history and timeless elegance of this period through a close attention to detail.

Photo by Laurence Taylor

itects

Palm Beach architect Spencer Goliger, SGA Architects, sees some clients favoring Manor and Georgian architecture from England's 17th and 18th centuries. "They want a sense of living in a castle—to feel secure and grand," he said. "Spaces are much bigger and more specific for separate functions."

"They want large drawing rooms, 500-square-foot kitchens, six- or eight-car garages, huge wine cellars, and meditation and steam rooms. They also want a club room with a media center, fireplace and a smaller library area for computers," he said.

164

Archi

To make the homes look older and more European, Goliger often uses flat tiles for the roof. For the flooring, he uses real antique terracotta, limestone or Jerusalem stone.

Mark Nasrallah, Nasrallah Fine Architectural Designs, is also seeing a return to more traditional designs. "It's the single most important trend I've noticed," said the Winter Park architect. His firm has designed a number of period homes, recently completing two Spanish Colonial residences in Orlando and Bolivia—using concepts from the 15th century.

A combination of classical and Mediterranean architecture is evident in the columns and archways that line the pool area, and the exotic stone terrace adds to the sense that a person could very well have been transported to a villa in the south of Italy.

Photo courtesy of SGA Architects
Photo by Laurence Taylor

itects

To convey the history and timeless elegance of this period, Nasrallah focuses on attention to detail.

"For trim, the clients want sconces, rope details, and corbels and arches for certain areas," he said. "Roofing materials such as cap and pan barrel tile and a simulated slate roof are used. For flooring, we utilize Cantera stone on the interior and exterior."

The intricate ironwork on this residence reflects the current focus on detailing—both inside and outside. As an expression of the current desire for architectural styles from the past, this English Georgian home makes an elegant statement.

Photo courtesy of SGA Architects

Archi

Boca Raton architect Quincy Johnson, Quincy Johnson Architects, has noticed clients returning from Europe with a greater appreciation and desire for exterior elements, including pools with fountains, waterscapes, and landscaping for privacy.

itects

The dramatic entryway to this house is enhanced with the use of beautifully detailed materials. Every aspect of this presentation has been carefully considered, from the cap and pan barrel tile on the roof, to the imposing wooden doors.

168

Photo courtesy of Nasrallah Fine Architectural Designs

Archi

The use of concepts from the 15th century gives this Spanish Colonial residence a distinctive and romantic presentation. The combination of pan barrel and flat tile on the roof and thoughtful exterior detailing create a sense of security and grandeur.

Making an Entrance

In some case, these architects said they are asked to create dramatic entryways. Clients want distinctive, romantic foyers enhanced with beautifully detailed materials.

And if eyes are the windows to the soul, the entryway is a reflection of the interior.

"The entrance is the most important experience in the entire home," said Johnson. "It's the perfect place to create a grand staircase that's 360 degrees and 20 feet in diameter. It's also perfect for niches for artwork and a long diagonal view, perhaps one that focuses on a swimming pool with a disappearing edge."

Foyers also are imposing in size, according to Nasrallah. "Some are two stories high and have about 1,000 to 1,500 square feet of space for the foyer and the grand stairway," he said.

And, there is a focus on detailing in this area, said Nasrallah.

itects

"These homes have modern
like they could have been
he said. "They retain their

170

The elegant combination of classical and Mediterranean architectural influences in this residence covey a sense of timeless elegance. Every detail has been carefully considered, from the variegated terra cotta tiles on the roof to the manner in which the arched entryway is reflected in the window design.

Photo courtesy of Qunicy Johnson Architects

Archi

conveniences, but look
built 300 years ago,"
value."

—*Mark Nasrallah*

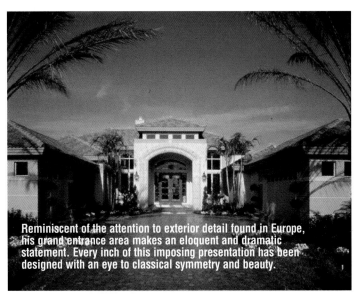

Reminiscent of the attention to exterior detail found in Europe, this grand entrance area makes an eloquent and dramatic statement. Every inch of this imposing presentation has been designed with an eye to classical symmetry and beauty.

Photo courtesy of Qunicy Johnson Architects

"Banisters might have a wrought design. The walls and columns are cut limestone, the stairs are of limestone, groin vaults and arches are plaster trimmed in limestone, and surround arches are of real plaster, not drywall."

Though many clients want to make a statement at the entranceway to their homes, Goliger said some of his clients want drama elsewhere in the home—a foyer in front of their powder room.

"This is so guests won't have to walk straight into the powder room," said Goliger. "Years ago, you might see a foyer before a bath area with a telephone in it. It may have been about 6 feet by 6 feet. Now some clients ask for foyers that measure up to 10 feet by 10 feet, where they might place a comfortable lounge and a desk."

Nasrallah, though, believes that money—another powerful influence—is the reason many people are turning to classical architecture. ■

—Lois Prunner

itects

PORTUONDO PEROTTI
A R C H I T E C T S

CUSTOM RESIDENTIAL DESIGN
4102 LAGUNA ST. • CORAL GABLES, FL 33146
TEL 305-442-1262 • FAX 305-442-1511
URBAN DESIGN • ARCHITECTURE • INTERIOR DESIGN

BORROTO
ARCHITECTS

260 Crandon Boulevard, Suite 49
Key Biscayne, Florida 33149
305.361.6181 Fax: 305.365.9782
Website: www.borrotoarchtects.com
e-mail: borroto@msn.com

Principal/Owner: Wilfredo Borroto, AIA
Junior Partner: Otto Z. Borroto

Description: Award winning international
architects and planners since 1965.
Residences, office and apartment
buildings, shopping centers, hotels and
yacht clubs, land planning.

Equally at ease creating the dream residence of an eccentric art collector
as planning a futuristic high rise

Photos: Everett & Soulé

NOW AVAILABLE! A portfolio that features a selection of masterfully designed, view-oriented homes ranging from 3,000–40,000 square feet for $45 US dollars (plus shipping and handling). MasterCard and Visa accepted.

© Everett & Soulé

NASRALLAH
FINE ARCHITECTURAL DESIGN

Mark P. Nasrallah, AIA
Telephone (407) 647-0938
Fax (407) 647-2499
www. nasrallah-aia.com

Ames Design International

Architecture & Design

203 Dixie Boulevard, Delray Beach, Florida 33111

Ph: 561-271-6111   AAC001720   Fax: 561-271-6119

E-mail: Ames.Int@BellSouth.net

Architects

continued from page **152**

L. M. SILKWORTH ARCHITECT P.A. ....**(561) 234-4004**
1401 Highway A-1-A, Suite 205, Vero Beach   Fax: (561) 234-3111
See Ad on Page: 158   *800 Extension:* 1157
Principal/Owner: L. M. Silkworth, AIA
email: lmspa@atlantic.net

SMITH & MOORE ARCHITECTS INC. ....**(561) 835-1888**
1500 S. Olive Avenue, West Palm Beach   Fax: (561) 832-7015
See Ad on Page: 185   *800 Extension:* 1238
Principal/Owner: John Moore

SMITH ARCHITECTURAL GROUP INC. ....**(561) 832-0202**
205 Phipps Plaza #B, Palm Beach   Fax: (561) 832-3443
See Ad on Page: 186   *800 Extension:* 1239
Principal/Owner: Jeffery W. Smith

RANDALL STOFFT ARCHITECTS, P.A. ....**(561) 243-0799**
42 N. Swinton Avenue, Delray Beach   Fax: (561) 243-0299
See Ad on Page: 154, 155   *800 Extension:* 1219
Principal/Owner: Randall Stofft
email: stofft@bellsouth.net
Additional Information: Randall Stofft Architects has offices located in Delray
Beach and Naples, Florida.

WESSEL ASSOCIATES AIA ....**(561) 747-4950**
900 South US Highway One, Suite 104, Jupiter   Fax: (561) 747-4184
See Ad on Page: 145   *800 Extension:* 1272
Principal/Owner: Mitchell Miller
Website: www.wesselaia.com email: alw@flinet.com

Photo: R.P. Janssen

Photo: C.J. Walker

Photo: R.P. Janssen

Dailey & Partners Architects, P.A.

2 Harvard Circle, Suite 300
West Palm Beach, Florida 33409
Tel: 561-640-5281 Fax: 561-640-5283

Terry L. Irwin Architects, P.A.

513 Main Street
Suite 100
Windermere, FL 34786

T: (407) 876-5353
F: (407) 876-2138

www.irwinarchitects.com

Lauren C. VanArman

MARK
McCree
ARCHITECT

4753 Belvedere Rd.   West Palm Beach, FL 33415   Tel: 561-615-0636 Fax: 561-615-4549
AERO CLUB, WELLINGTON-JONATHAN'S LANDING, JUPITER-LOXAHATCHEE RIVER, TEQUESTA-JUPITER ISLAND, HOBE SOUND

AR-0014248

"B" DESIGN CORP
Architects, Designers, & Planners

2051 Trade Center Way
Naples, Florida 34109
(941) 592-0221

ARCHITECT NO. 011330
DBPR NO. AA0003308
N C A R B
THE NATIONAL COUNCIL OF
ARCHITECTURAL REGISTRATION BOARDS
NO. 010800.

A I
B D.

Award
Winning

Custom
Homes

Bridges, Marsh & Carmo, Inc.

Chartered Architects

Eighteen Via Mizner
Palm Beach, FL 33480
561 832 1533
Fax: 561 832 1520
www.bmcarch@aol.com

Jennifer Deane

Ed Chappell

Jennifer Deane

SMITH AND MOORE ARCHITECTS, INC.

1500 South Olive Avenue
West Palm Beach, Florida 33401
Telephone: (561)835-1888   Fax: (561)832-7015
E-mail: smarch99@aol.com
Website: smithmoorearchitects.com

SMITH
ARCHITECTURAL
GROUP, INC.

PALM BEACH   NEW YORK

CUSTOM
HOME BUILDERS

&

REMODELERS

WORTH
BUILDERS
OF PALM BEACH, INC.
1137 CLARE AVENUE
WEST PALM BEACH, FL 33401
561-832-0500
CGC 011891
© SARGENT

"*The* *beautiful* rests on the FOUNDATION of the *necessary.* "

Ralph Waldo Emerson

From the Ground Up

One of the key players in every home building and remodeling success story is the contractor. Architects envision possibilities, but contractors create new realities. While design/build teams of architects and contractors are becoming increasingly popular, the home in which you will be living will be the direct result of your contractor's efforts and expertise.

So much of your satisfaction in the final outcome depends upon the selection of the right contractor. It is essential to choose a company or individual with whom you have a good rapport, who has excellent references as well as experience with your type of project.

While the planning phase of a new home or remodeling project may be exciting, creating the finished product is hard work. Seek out a contractor whose attention to quality detail, willingness to listen to your concerns, and in-depth of knowledge of the trades assures you a smoother road on the way to your new home.

THE TEAR-DOWN TREND

Land for new residential construction is getting harder to find, and "tear-down" renovations are becoming more common. There are often mixed emotions in an existing neighborhood as old structures come down. If you are considering a "tear-down" property, be sure you work with a builder and architect who are sensitive to the character of the neighborhood, and will help you build a home that fits in.

HOME BUILDER SOURCES

Florida Home Builders Association (FHBA) 201 E. Park Ave. Tallahassee, FL 32301 (805) 224-4316 www.fhba.com

Tampa Bay Area Chapter NARI National Association of the Remodeling Industry (NARI) (727) 578-2207 www.nari.org

SETTING THE STANDARD FOR QUALITY

A strong commitment to providing top quality materials and craftsmanship is the most important contribution a builder can make to your professional team. Working in concert with your architect, interior designer, kitchen and bath designer and landscape architect/designer, a custom home builder will take the designs, and your dreams, and make them happen. Selecting a builder who shares your dedication to building only the best is one of the best ways you can build quality into your new home. This kind of quality is as tangible as it is intangible. You can see it in the materials used – not necessarily the most expensive, but always the best for the situation. More interestingly, you can feel it. There's an unmistakable sense of integrity in a well-built home, of a dream fulfilled.

MAKE "QUALITY-DRIVEN" DECISIONS

Instead of instructing a builder to "build me a big house," or a "big kitchen" today's custom home buyer is more likely to say, "Build me the best house or kitchen my budget will allow." The emphasis has shifted from quantity ("I want it all") to quality ("I want the best"), and from taking the lowest bid to fairly compensating the builder who submits the best package of products and services. Smart, value-oriented customers realize that dollars spent today will soon be forgotten, whereas the level of quality those dollars bought will be appreciated for years.

As a custom home client, you must determine what's most important to you and what investment you'll make to achieve it. Good builders will help you set priorities and meet your goals. They've been through the process and know to be exacting, setting their expectations as high as their high-end clients do.

IS IT A(ARCHITECT) BEFORE B(BUILDER) OR B BEFORE A?

Answering this question can seem like the "chicken or the egg" riddle: Do you hire the builder first, the architect first, or choose a design/build firm, where both functions are under the same roof?

If you work first with an architect, his or her firm will recommend builders they know have a track record in building homes of the same caliber as yours. Most likely, your architect contract includes bidding and negotiation services with these builders, and you may expect help in analyzing bids and making your selection. Your architect contract also may include construction administration, where the architect makes site visits to observe construction, review the builder's applications for payment, and help make sure the home is built according to the plans.

Perhaps you've seen previous work or know satisfied clients of a custom home builder, and wish to work with him. In this scenario, the builder will recommend architects who are experienced in successfully designing homes and/or additions similar to what you want. The builder will support you and the architect will cost control information through realistic cost figures, before products are integrated into the house.

If you like the idea of working with one firm for both the architectural design and building, consider a design/build firm. Design/build firms offer an arrangement that can improve time management and efficient communication, simply by virtue of having both professional functions under the same roof. There is also added flexibility as the project develops. If you decide you want to add a feature, the design/build firm handles the design process and communicates the changes internally to the builder. When you interview a design/builder firm, it's important to ascertain that the firm has a strong architectural background, with experienced custom home architects on staff.

All scenarios work and no one way is always better than the other. Make your choice by finding professionals you trust and with whom you feel comfortable. Look for vision and integrity and let the creative process begin.

FINDING THE RIGHT BUILDER

The selection of a builder or remodeler is a major decision, and should be approached in a thoughtful, unhurried manner. Allow plenty of time to interview and research at least two candidates before making your choice. Hours invested at this point can save months of time later on.

At the initial interview, the most important information you'll get is not from brochures, portfolios, or a sales pitch, but from your own intuition. Ask yourself: Can we trust this person to execute plans for our dream home, likely the biggest expenditure of our lifetime? Is there a natural two-way communication, mutual respect, and creative energy? Does he have the vision to make our home unique and important? Is his sense of the project similar to ours? Will we have any fun together? Can we work together for at least a year?

If you answer "Yes!", you've found the most valuable asset – the right chemistry.

TEN GOOD QUESTIONS TO ASK A BUILDER'S PAST CLIENTS

1. Are you happy with your home?
2. Was the house built on schedule?
3. Did the builder respect the budget and give an honest appraisal of costs early on?
4. Did the builder bring creativity to your project?
5. Were you well informed so you properly understood each phase of the project?
6. Was the builder accessible and on-site?
7. Does the builder provide good service now that the project is complete?
8. How much help did you get from the builder in choosing the products in your home?
9. Is the house well built?
10. Would you hire the builder again?

193

IT TAKES HOW LONG?

Some typical construction time frames:

Total Kitchen Remodel:
From total demolition to installation of new cabinets, flooring, appliances, electrical, etc.
SIX – EIGHT WEEKS

A 1,400 Sq. Ft. Addition:
New first floor Great Room & powder room, extension of the existing kitchen; master suite upstairs.
FOUR – SIX MONTHS

Total Home Remodel:
An 1,800 sq. ft. Colonial expanded to 4,000 sq. ft. All spaces redefined, added third floor, three new baths, new high-end kitchen, deck.
SIX – NINE MONTHS

These estimates depend on factors such as the size of the crew working on your project, the timeliness of decisions and delivery of materials.

TAKE TIME TO CHECK REFERENCES

The most distinguished builders in the area expect, even want, you to check their references. More luxury home clients are taking the time to do this research as the move toward quality workmanship continues to grow.

Talk to clients. Get a list of clients spanning the last three to five years, some of whom are owners of projects similar to yours. Call them and go visit their homes or building sites. Satisfied customers are only too happy to show you around and praise the builder who did the work. If you can, speak with a past client not on the builder's referral list. Finding one unhappy customer is not cause for concern, but if you unearth a number of them, cross that builder off your list.

Visit a construction site. Clients who get the best results appreciate the importance of the sub-contractors. Their commitment to quality is at the heart of the job. Do the sub-contractors appear to be professional? Are they taking their time in doing their work? Is the site clean and neat?

Contact subcontractors with whom the builder has worked. If they vouch for the builder's integrity and ability you'll know the firm has earned a good professional reputation. Meeting subcontractors also provides a good measure for the quality of workmanship you'll receive.

Visit the contractor's office. Is it well-staffed and organized? Do they offer the technology for virtual walk-throughs? Do you feel welcome there?

Find out how long the builder has been in business. Experienced custom builders have strong relationships with top quality sub-contractors and architects, a comprehensive knowledge of products and materials, and know how to provide the best service before, during and after construction.

Ask how many homes are currently being built and how your project will be serviced. Some builders work on several homes at once; some limit their total to ten or twelve a year.

LAYING A FOUNDATION FOR SUCCESS

Two documents, the contract and the timeline, define your building experience. The contract lays down the requirements of the relationship and the timeline delineates the order in which the work is done. While the contract is negotiated once at the beginning of the relationship, the timeline continues to be updated and revised as the project develops.

THE CONTRACT

The American Institute of Architects (AIA) provides a standard neutral contract which is widely used in the area, but some firms write their own contracts. As with any contract, get legal advice, read carefully, and assume nothing. If landscaping is not mentioned, then landscaping will not be provided. Pay careful attention to:

• Payment schedules. When and how does the builder get paid? How much is the deposit (depends on the total cost of the project but $10,000 to $25,000 is not uncommon) and will it be applied against the first phase of the work? Do you have the right to withhold any payment until your punch list is completed? Will you write checks to the builder (if so, insist on sworn waivers) or only to the title company? Remodeling contracts typically use a payment schedule broken into thirds – one-third up front, one-third half-way through the project, and one-third at completion. You may withhold a negotiated percentage of the contract price until you're satisfied that the terms of the contract have been met and the work has been inspected. This should be stipulated in the contract. Ten percent is the average amount to be held back, but is negotiable based on the overall size of the project.

Builders and remodeling specialists who attract a quality-minded, high end custom home client, are contacted by institutions offering attractive construction or bridge and end loan packages. Ask your contractor for referrals if you want to do some comparative shopping.

• The total cost - breakdown of labor and materials expenses.

• Change order procedures. Change orders on the average add seven to ten percent to the cost of a custom home. Be clear on how these orders are charged and the impact they eventually will have on the timetable.

• The basic work description. This should be extremely detailed, including everything from installing phone jacks to the final cleaning of your home. A comprehensive list of specified materials should be given, if it hasn't already been provided by your architect.

• Allowances. Are they realistic? This is one place where discrepancies will be evident. Is Contractor A providing $75,000 for cabinets while Contractor B is providing $150,000?

• Warranty. A one-year warranty, effective the date you move in, is standard in this area.

TRUTH ABOUT CHANGE ORDERS

The building process demands an environment that allows for changes as plans move from paper to reality. Although you can control changes through careful planning in the preliminary stages of design and bidding, budget an extra seven to ten percent of the cost of the home to cover change orders. Changes are made by talking to the contractor, not someone working at the site. You will be issued a change order form, which you will sign and return to the contractor. Keep your copies of the forms together in one folder. Avoid last minute sticker shock by being diligent in keeping a current tab on your change order expenses.

195

SOURCES FOR HISTORIC PROPERTIES

Dade Heritage Trust, Inc. 190 SE 12th Terrace, Miami, FL 33131 (305) 358-9572 www. dadeheritagetrust .org Contact them for information about your home and be sure to ask about their Dade Heritage Days Festival calendar of events.

The National Trust for Historic Preservation 1785 Massachusetts Avenue, N.W. Washington, D.C. 20036 (202) 588-6000 Having a home listed on the National Register doesn't restrict homeowners from demolishing or making changes, (local restrictions do that) but offers possible financial assistance and tax credits for renovations, and limited protection against federal 'takings.' The organization sponsors programs, publishes newsletters and books, and advocates preservation.

Local foundations and historical societies are established in most of the South Florida area communities that have older homes.

THE TIMELINE

This changeable document will give you a good indication if and when things will go wrong. Go to the site often enough to keep track of the progress according to the timeline. Do what you need to do to keep the project on schedule. One of the main causes of delays and problems is late decision-making by the homeowner. If you wait until three weeks prior to cabinet installation to order your cabinets, you can count on holding up the entire process by at least a month. (You'll also limit your options to cabinets that can be delivered quickly.)

THE SECOND TIME'S A CHARM

Today's lifestyles demand a home that's flexible. As homeowners become increasingly sophisticated in their knowledge and awareness of the exciting possibilities that can be built into a home, they're designing custom additions and renovations that match their individual style. People who entertain formally, who like to have caterers and chefs come into their kitchens to prepare a special meal, build fabulous multi-zone kitchens with elegant dining areas. Those who operate a business build dedicated offices, with separate entrances and conference areas. Empty nesters add on or re-configure existing space for a luxury first floor master suite, and use the upper level as storage and guest rooms for visiting children and grandchildren.

Renovating a home offers the unique excitement of reinventing an old space to serve a new, enhanced purpose. It's an evolutionary process, charged with creative thinking and bold ideas. If you enjoy a stimulating environment of problem solving and decision making, and you're prepared to dedicate the needed time and resources, remodeling will result in a home which lives up to all of your expectations. You'll be living in the neighborhood you love, in a home that fits your needs.

Top caliber remodeling projects are achieved by remodeling specialists who create excellent plans which meet the needs of their client, the best quality workmanship and materials, and considerable client involvement.

They work on jobs as contained as updating a bathroom or adding storage, and as complex as renovating or enlarging a classic or historic home.

A successful addition or renovation is so elegantly seamed into the original structure, both inside and out, that the work is all but unnoticeable. An achievement of this magnitude requires an extensive amount of care in planning and execution.

THE LUXURY OF SUPERIOR SERVICE

Clients of top quality remodeling specialists expect a high level of individualized service, and when they fulfill their client responsibilities in the project, they aren't disappointed. Involved clients are granted a high degree of personal attention from the very beginning of the process.

As the planning and eventually the building project unfolds, a top remodeler will keep you up to date and on track with your decision-making.

This service and accessibility will save you time and money and add to your enjoyment of the project. You may speak to each other every day during the most intensive period of decision making.

UPDATING THE CLASSICS

Many homeowners at the end of the century are attracted to the historic architecture in these older neighborhoods. Their maturity and classicism are factors that persuade homeowners to make an investment in an old home and restore, renovate or preserve it, depending on what level of involvement interests them and the significance of the house. Renovations include additions and updating or replacing systems in the house. Restorations involve restoring the building to the specifications original to the house. Preservation efforts preserve what's there.

Like any remodeling project, it's an emotional and personal experience, only more so. Staying within the confines of a certain period or style is difficult and time consuming. That's why it's crucial to find an experienced architect and builder who share a reverence for tradition and craftsmanship to bring about a successful result. At your interview, determine if his or her portfolio shows competence in this specialty. It's vital to find a professional who understands historic projects and knows experienced and qualified contractors and/or subcontractors who will do the work for you. Ask if he or she knows experienced contractors who work in historic districts and have relationships with knowledgeable, experienced craftsmen. If you want exterior features, like period gardens or terraces, ask if it will be included in the overall plan. Make sure he or she has sources for you to find period furnishings, sconce shades or chimney pots.

There are many construction and design issues particular to old homes. The historic renovation and preservation experts featured in the following pages bring experience, creativity and responsibility to each project.

A LUXURY ADDITION ON AN HISTORIC HOME

Suburban Arts and Crafts-Prairie Home, circa 1915.
• All windows, trim, casings, and other details to match the original brick.
• Full, finished basement, with bar and workout area.
• First level family room, dining room and new kitchen.
• Upper level master suite and office. Stone terrace and garden.

Total Project Cost: $500,000, including architectural fees.

CLEAN UP TIME: Now or Later?

Your remodeling contract should be specific about clean-up. Will the site be cleaned up every day, or at the end of the project? Everyday clean-up may add to the price, but is well worth the extra expenditure.

CREATE A RECORD

You have a team of highly qualified professionals building your home, but the ultimate responsibility is on your shoulders. So keep track of the project. Organize a binder to keep all of your samples, chips, change orders, and documents together. Make copies for yourself of all communication with your suppliers and contractor. Take notes from conversations and send them to the contractor. This can help eliminate confusion before a problem occurs.

SETTING PRIORITIES

Choosing the "must-have" features and learning to live without others can be a highly-charged issue for the custom home client. Your builder will help you make these decisions, by giving you accurate quotes and emphasizing the features you need to build a quality home.

RESPECT YOUR ELDERS

Before you fall in love with an old house, get a professional opinion. Find out how much is salvageable before you make the investment. Can the wood be restored? Have the casings been painted too many times? Is the plaster wavy and buckled? Can the house support ductwork for central air conditioning or additional light sources?

Are you really compatible? The biggest mistake prospective historic home owners make is planning to change the nature of the house. If the house can't be made livable to your standards, while staying true to the architecture and style of the home and neighborhood, look for another property. People who live in historic neighborhoods expect new owners will do their part to keep the distinctive character of the area intact. Be sensitive to and aware of that expectation.

Notable remodelers are often contacted for their expert advice prior to a real estate purchase and Realtors® maintain relationships with qualified remodelers for this purpose. They also keep remodelers informed of special properties suitable for custom renovations as they become available.

PRIVACY? WHAT'S THAT?

Remodelers overwhelmingly agree their clients are happier if they move to a temporary residence during all, or the most intensive part, of the renovation. The sight of the roof and walls being torn out, the constant banging and buzzing of tools, and the invasion of privacy quickly take their toll on children and adults who are trying to carry on family life in a house full of dust. Homeowners who are well-rested from living in clean, well-lighted temporary quarters enjoy better relationships with each other, their remodeler and sub-contractors.

Not only will you save your sanity by vacating your home, you may also save a significant amount of money while shortening the time it takes to complete the job. A plumber, for instance, won't have to make two trips to your house – once to make it temporarily livable and again to do the majority of the required plumbing work. Contractors always protect the inside of a home from the elements during construction, but if you will be in the house, additional protection must be provided. By staying home, you may add as much as two percentage points to the cost of the remodeling project and weeks or months to the timeline.

Common hideaways are rental homes, suite-type hotels, the unoccupied home of a relative, or a long vacation trip.

CONTEXTUALISM

Popular styles and trends take a back seat to establishing harmony with the neighborhood and within a house itself.

Property owners want their newly built home to fit in with the other houses in their neighborhood – to respect and complement any established architecture. Homeowners who remodel or add on, who forego moving because they love their homes and neighborhoods, are ardent supporters of contextual design, which works within the aesthetic of the original home. They insist on an addition that blends in with the existing structure, stays in context with other rooms and doesn't intrude on the look or feel of the neighborhood. The result: a home of perfect proportion that is appealing to the eye, fits the land, and doesn't overpower the neighborhood.

A WORD ABOUT FINANCING OF REMODELING PROJECTS

Payment schedules in remodeling contracts typically require a deposit or a first payment at the start of the project with subsequent payments due monthly or in conjunction with the progress of the work.

It is within your rights to withhold a negotiated percentage of the contract price until you're satisfied that the terms of the contract have been met and the work has been inspected. This should be stipulated in the written contract. Ten percent is the average amount to be held back, but is negotiated based on the overall size of the project.

Remodeling specialists who attract a quality-minded clientele are kept abreast of the most attractive remodeling loans on the market by lenders who specialize in these products. Ask your remodeler for referrals to these financial institutions. ■

THAT'S ENTERTAINING

The need for more efficient, flexible and expanded space for entertaining is one of the main reasons Chicago area homeowners decide to remodel their homes. As home becomes more central to our lifestyle, comfortable entertaining becomes a priority, especially in the new, multi-functional kitchen.

199

ALCOR, INC...**(561) 375-8854**
9637 Plumeria Way, Boynton Beach
See Ad on Page: 205
email: alcor_inc@msn.com

Fax: (561) 966-2953
800 Extension: 1010

ALONSO & ASSOCIATES...**(561) 837-9820**
361 S County Road, Palm Beach
See Ad on Page: 240, 241
Principal/Owner: Rene Alonso
email: alonsoassoc@aol.com
Additional Information: Our company has been in the custom home building
business for 20 years in South Florida.

Fax: (561) 837-9830
800 Extension: 1012

BOMAR BUILDERS, INC. ....**(954) 428-2522**
550 Fairway Drive, Suite 104, Deerfield Beach
See Ad on Page: 201
Principal/Owner: Robert G. Mayer
Website: www.bomarbuilders.com email: bob@bomarbuilders.com
Additional Information: Bomar Builders, Inc. specializes in the construction of
personalized incomparable custom oceanfront, intracoastal, and country club
residences from the timeless classics to contemporary.

Fax: (954) 428-0024
800 Extension: 1037

BREAKSTONE HOMES ....**(305) 705-0001**
1200 Ponce de Leon Blvd., Coral Gables
See Ad on Page: 212 - 216

800 Extension: 1043

CELEBRATION HOMES, INC. ....**(561) 691-1828**
1911 US Highway 1, Suite 208, North Palm Beach
See Ad on Page: 246, 247
Principal/Owner: Richard J. Greco
Website: www.wemakeitfun.com email: rjgreco@evcom.net
Additional Information: We build a quality product, on time, under budget, with
personal service and we make it fun.

Fax: (561) 691-1830
800 Extension: 1049

CORNERSTONE DEVELOPERS INC. ....**(941) 594-7985**
1827 Trade Center Way, Suite 3, Naples
See Ad on Page: 254, 255

Fax: (941) 594-0078
800 Extension: 1062

TERRENCE CUDMORE BUILDER INC. ....**(561) 477-7375**
8075 Twin Lake Drive, Boca Raton
See Ad on Page: 218, 219

Fax: (561) 477-6274
800 Extension: 1260

continued on page **210**

"When you're talking about building a house,
you're talking about dreams."

Robert A.M. Stern

BOMAR BUILDERS
FINE ESTATE HOMES

Builders of personalized incomparable custom oceanfront, intracoastal, and country club residences from the timeless classics to comtemporary

Bomar Builders, Inc.
(954) 428-2522
550 Fairway Drive, Suite 104
Deerfield Beach, FL. 33441
www.BomarBuilders.com

Enterprise Contractors Inc.

2210 N. Federal Highway
Del Ray Beach, FL 33483
561-279-0311

STATE LICENSED GENERAL CONTRAC-
TOR

Alex Villegas
9637 PLUMERIA WAY
BOYNTON BEACH, FL 33426

OFFICE: 516-375-8854
FAX: 561-966-2953

Experience to meet

614 S. Federal Highway, Fort Lauderdale, FL 33301 **954/764-6550**

the highest standards...

Yours

The Team Approach

Homeowners enjoy a wealth of new design and technology options. This makes it possible to achieve every detail of their dream, but it requires a longer, more involved planning process. The choices are almost limitless — from exciting theme pools with rockscapes and waterfalls to sophisticated "one touch" computer systems that create elaborate sound and lighting effects.

In addition, many teams are tapping an entire world of building materials to create "authenticity" — a sense that a new home has existed for years. Using today's technologies, they can source the right products, including aged roof tiles, antique timbers and weathered iron railings.

In today's complex custom homebuilding environment, good old-fashioned teamwork is the key to successful design and construction. The most successful teams are created by the early selection of a design-builder or general contractor, an architectural design firm, engineering consultants, interior designers, and a whole slew of specialty consultants like landscape designers, lighting designers and electronics integration experts. Communication is vital, as team members may be located in different parts of the country, or across the globe.

Each team member brings talent, knowledge and experience in design, materials specifications, budget control, scheduling, coordination, and construction for the overall benefit of the homeowner. Through proper planning and coordination in the design phase, the homeowner has taken the first step toward creating a truly one-of-a-kind masterpiece.

W. Grey Marker, *Miller Construction Company*

WILLIAMS CONSTRUCTION

QUALITY CUSTOM HOMES
CONSTRUCTION MANAGEMENT
DESIGN/BUILD - SINCE 1986

continued from page **200**

ECCLESTONE ESTATE HOMES ....**(561) 627-1270**
357 Hiatt Drive, Suite A, Palm Beach Gardens   Fax: (561) 624-0258
See Ad on Page: 245   *800 Extension:* 1077
Principal/Owner: Llwyd Ecclestone III
Website: www.ecclestonehomes.com email: lecclestone@ecclestonehomes.com
Additional Information: Design/Build and construction management of homes
from $1,000,000 and up.

ECI/ENTERPRISE CONTRACTORS INC. ....**(800) 293-9701**
2210 North Federal Hwy, Delray Beach   Fax: (561) 279-0311
See Ad on Page: 204   *800 Extension:* 1078
Principal/Owner: Ron & Brian Brito
email: eciwork@aol.com
Additional Information: Commercial and Residential. General Contracting. New
or renovation, including historical. Where your ideas come to life.

ELLEMAR ENTERPRISES ....**(561) 394-4004**
6885 SW 18 Street, Suite 7, Boca Raton   Fax: (561) 394-4572
See Ad on Page: 230, 231   *800 Extension:* 1081
Principal/Owner: Mark D. Rothenberg
Website: www.ellemar.com email: info@ellemar.com
Additional Information: Luxury custom home builder. "Nothing overlooked,
nothing left to chance, perfection pure & simple."

WILLIAM ENNIS COMPANY ....**(561) 747-4195**
938 N. Old Dixie Highway, Jupiter   Fax: (561) 747-6240
See Ad on Page: 211   *800 Extension:* 1273
Principal/Owner: Bill Ennis
Website: www.ennisco.com email: wec@ennisco.com
Additional Information: Twenty years building fine custom homes, all having the
distinguished trademark of quality and impeccable craftsmanship.

EURO HOME ....**(561) 655-5533**
PO Box 2558, Palm Beach   Fax: (561) 832-5417
See Ad on Page: 234, 235   *800 Extension:* 1086

GENERAL CONTRACTOR SEVICES INC. ....**(561) 471-7303**
1401 Forsythe Road, West Palm Beach   Fax: (561) 471-7305
See Ad on Page: 252, 253   *800 Extension:* 1107
Principal/Owner: Philip Modenos
email: philipgcs@aol.com
Additional Information: Award winning builder - combining toatal customer
service with the finest quality and craftsmanship.

GULFSHORE HOMES ....**(941) 947-2929**
23815 Addison Place Court, Bonita Springs   Fax: (941) 947-3555
See Ad on Page: 232, 233   *800 Extension:* 1116
Principal/Owner: Steven M. Watt, President

HEDRICK BROTHERS CONSTRUCTION CO., INC....................**(561) 844-6608**
1100 Technology Place, Suite 122, West Palm Beach   Fax: (561) 844-9645
See Ad on Page: 217   *800 Extension:* 1121
Principal/Owner: Dale Hedrick

continued on page **238**

*Mastering the art
of custom homebuilding*

WILLIAM ENNIS
COMPANY

938 N. Old Dixie Hwy., Jupiter, FL 33458
Tel: (561) 747-4195 • Fax: (561) 747-6240
www.ennisco.com

The Breakstone Custom Homebuilding Center makes the limited unlimited. The impossible possible. And the unbelievable believable.

Enjoy the stress-free pleasure of creating your own Breakstone Original.

Gathered together under one roof in our huge, new 15,000 sq. ft. permanent facility are award-winning in-house architects, interior designers and builders, along with a

Way You Build A Custom Home.

mind-boggling array of models, floorplans

and samples. Everything you need to

create the home of your dreams, all

packaged at one easy-to-understand,

all-inclusive, guaranteed price.

Build on your lot.

Our lot.

Or one we find together.

freedom

Breakstone
CUSTOM LUXURY HOMEBUILDERS

Chateau Chambord,
Loire Valley, France

Own A Breakstone Original.

L Luxury homebuyers are discovering that creating their dream home is no longer just a dream. They're building Breakstone Originals at the Breakstone Custom Homebuilding Center in Coral Gables, Florida.

Our unique homebuilding facility is the first of its kind anywhere in America.

choices

Breakstone buyers may build on their lot, on one we own, or on one the buyer and we find together. Our spacious 15,000 sq. ft. permanent Center makes building your dream home simple and enjoyable. Every element comes together under award-winning, on-staff architects and internationally acclaimed interior designers. There are model kitchens, bathroom, living room, media room, kids room and more, as well as thousands of options and materials on display: fixtures, appliances, custom cabinets, fireplaces, home theaters, and countless other design elements.

Neuchwanstein Castle,
Bavaria, Germany

Come, be one of the first to see the future of luxury homebuilding.

Just as you are one of a kind, so every

Breakstone Home is an original, inspired by your

unique vision and lifestyle as you move from wish list

to blueprint to finished home. You

must experience it.

Breakstone

CUSTOM LUXURY HOMEBUILDERS

Broker inquiries more than welcome. Open 7 Days A Week • Hours: 10 AM-6 PM
• 305.705.0001 • 1200 Ponce de Leon Boulevard • Coral Gables

See The Breakstone Custom Homebuilding Center Firs

If you're contemplating a luxury home, you must see the Breakstone Custom Homebuilding Center. It will transform your idea of your choices. Every phase of the process is simplified, so you can visualize and create with total comfort and ease. Everything is under one roof in a permanent building, including architects, designers, models and sample materials.

Build on your site, on one we own, or we can find one together.

Enjoy award-winning Old World craftsmanship and top-of-the-line materials, all on display. Best of all, you'll know your budget and schedule will be met and that we are here for you now and in the future.

Breakstone

CUSTOM LUXURY HOMEBUILDERS

Palace Of Fine Arts,
San Francisco, California

Broker inquiries more than welcome. Open 7 Days A Week • Hours: 10 AM-6 PM
• 305.705.0001 • 1200 Ponce de Leon Boulevard • Coral Gables

HEDRICK BROTHERS
CONSTRUCTION CO., INC.

GENERAL CONTRACTOR
FL License No. CGC013137

Meeting the challenges of a challenging world.

1100 Technology Place, Suite 122
West Palm Beach, FL 33407-4693
Telephone: (561) 844-6608
Facsimile: (561) 844-5290
e-mail: bclemens@hedrickbrothers.com

TERENCE
CUDMORE
BUILDER INC.

8075 Twin Lake Drive • Boca Raton, FL 33496
(561)477-7375 • Fax (561)477-6274
Beeper (561)874-2004
Lic.#CG041975
e-mail: tcudmore@gate.net

SRD BUILDING CORP.
855 S. Federal Highway, Suite 111
Boca Raton, FL 33432
561.395.2150

*It's all about...***Exceeding Expectations**
Exceptional Quality
Personal Attention

FINE

222

HomeB

FINISHES

I t's the most exciting time for homeowners. Construction on their new home is nearing an end. The finishes they selected, from flooring to trimwork to paint, will be installed, added or completed. And, when the work is done, the homes will reflect their owners' creativity and individuality.

Many luxury homeowners use stone in places other than flooring. The natural grandeur of stone for cornices, window and door surrounds, or columns, as seen in this gracious dining room, creates an elegant mood and reflects the owner's creativity and individuality.

Photo courtesy of Lavelle Construction & Development Corp.

Photo courtesy of Terence Cudmore Builders
Photo by FLA Air Shots Inc.

As clients become more knowledgeable about building materials, they often choose sophisticated products and techniques to make a statement in their new homes. For a traditionally designed home, they might select a custom trim package to soften or accentuate the lines of certain areas. In a classically designed home, they might select faux painting to create a subtle mood or elegant stone to impart ruggedness.

Terry Cudmore, owner of Terence Cudmore Builder, Inc., in Boca Raton, said many of his clients like to use stone for their new homes because of its earthy, natural look. They also like using it in places other than flooring. One of his clients wants to create a very unusual exterior finish requiring the extensive use of Canterra stone.

 "We are using the stone in numerous areas for cornices, crown moldings, columns, window and door surrounds and window sills," he said.

HomeB

For home interiors, Cudmore said some of his clients are using shell stone on fireplaces and columns to convey a natural feeling. The kitchen area is also an excellent place to feature stone, particularly limestone.

"We use limestone for the large expanses of countertops because of the way it looks. Here again, clients want a natural look. They don't want to use a manmade product like Corian. The limestone is a very dense material, and once it's sealed, there is no maintenance."

But one of the most important decisions homeowners must make is selecting finishes for their unfinished walls—walls that seem as stark as an artist's blank canvas. Ron Palladino, owner of Lavelle Construction in Jupiter, said many of his clients are asking for paint.

"This replaces wallpaper in most main areas," he said. But they don't just want paint—they want paint applied creatively."

According to Palladino, this is easily accomplished.

"Our painters can do almost anything with paint," he said. "They do faux painting and can do any texture the clients come up with to create the mood they desire for that area."

Palladino said that with the faux painting, textures range from marble to leather-look finishes. Sometimes clients want a glaze applied over

The fine finishes on a home's exterior bring together the complete look of the home, marrying it with the landscaping and overall presentation luxury homeowners crave.

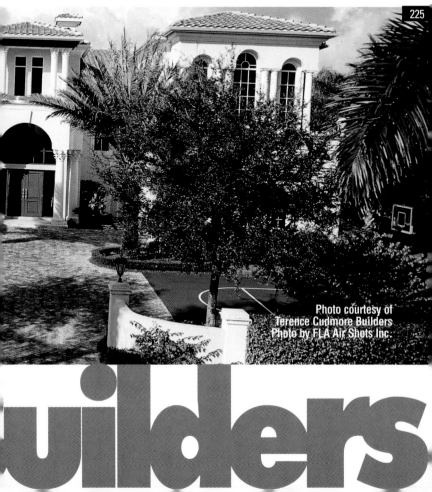

Photo courtesy of Terence Cudmore Builders
Photo by FLA Air Shots Inc.

uilders

In more and more homes, hand-applied faux painting is replacing wallpaper. With a choice of styles that range from marble, as shown, to leather or fabric, the hand-textured wall is compatible with both traditional and contemporary interior decoration.

226

Photo courtesy of
Lavelle Construction & Development Corp.

Embellishing an interior area or room with custom trim and fine trim detailing adds a touch of elegance and can make a luxury residence truly unique.

Photo courtesy of Lavelle Construction & Development Corp.

227

hand-textured walls in the main areas of the home, such as the living room, library and entryways. It creates a feeling of warmth and implies the look of fabric.

Exteriors are another desirable place for faux painting, according to Palladino.

"It's an excellent way of making new homes look older," he said.
"We use a glazing technique primarily in earth tones. For accents, we incorporate a splash of color in the trim work."

Whether the clients' homes are traditional or contemporary, Palladino said faux painting and other glazing or painting techniques are compatible with these designs.

Contractor John Winfield, president of Winfield Companies, builds luxury residences for clients in Naples. They, too, expect quality custom finishes. Winfield said that many of the homes he builds are traditional, and some clients request custom trim or molding packages to embellish these interior areas.

"These molding packages are made exclusively for each home," said Winfield. "Depending on the design and specifications, the package may include numerous trim detailing, such as baseboards, casings, corbels, arches, wainscoting and rope details."

228

Winfield recently completed extensive trim work on two homes. "And they used a great deal of it," he said. One home had 2,000 linear feet of crown molding and the other had 3,000 linear feet," said Winfield. "Clients want what is unique and what no one else has."

In addition to the trim packages, Winfield said he also uses wood in a variety of areas.

"When we do a staircase, we often use mahogany banisters," he said. "And clients often request that we use this wood for their doors."

But some clients like to use finishes in unexpected places. Palladino recalls one of the most unique jobs a client wanted.

"It involved the bathroom," he said. "They wanted their toilet faux painted like marble to match the floor. We did it for them." ■

—*Lois Prunner*

Having become more knowledgeable, clients are choosing sophisticated products and techniques to make a statement with their homes.

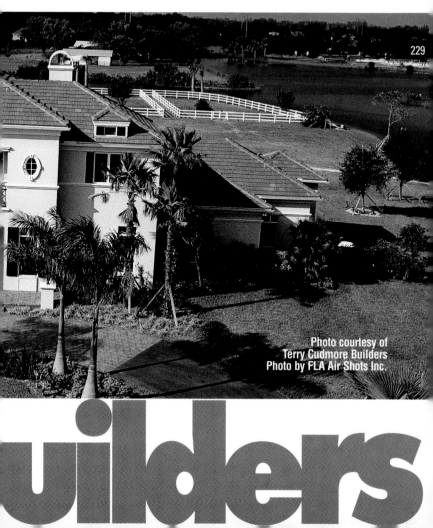

229

Photo courtesy of
Terry Cudmore Builders
Photo by FLA Air Shots Inc.

THE 2000 HOME & CONDO DREAM HOME WAS BUILT

IN QUAIL WEST GOLF COUNTRY CLUB,

NAPLES, FLORIDA. THIS $9,000,000 ESTATE HOME

SOLD PRIOR TO COMPLETION.

GH

FORM

FUNCTION

DESIGN

CREATIVITY

AESTHETICS

REGIONAL

AND NATIONAL

MULTI-AWARD

WINNER

GULFSHORE

HOMES

BUILDING IN

THESE FINE

COMMUNITIES:

BAY LAUREL

ESTATES,

THE ESTATES

AT BAY COLONY

GOLF CLUB,

GREY OAKS,

MEDITERRA,

PELICAN BAY

AND

QUAIL WEST

CONSIDER THE **POSSIBILITIES**.
TALK TO US.

FOR A PRIVATE CONSULTATION
CONTACT STEVEN M. WATT, PRESIDENT
GULFSHORE HOMES, 23815 ADDISON PLACE COURT
BONITA SPRINGS, FLORIDA 34134   941.947.2929

GH
Gulfshore Homes

SOUTHWEST FLORIDA'S
PREEMINENT
CUSTOM
ESTATE HOMEBUILDER

Euro Homes

249 PERUVIAN AVENUE

PALM BEACH

FLORIDA 33480

561.655.5533

PALM BEACH'S PREMIER BUILDER

CAN BECOME
A REALITY...

Custom Home Builders

continued from page **210**

JOHANSON HOMES, INC...**(561) 287-5733**
1501 Decker Avenue, Suite A101, Stuart   Fax: (561) 287-5718
See Ad on Page: 249   800 Extension: 1148
Principal/Owner: Charles Johanson
email: johansonhomes@aol.com
Additional Information: Celebrating 15 years building exclusive custom homes "In the tradition of old world craftsmanship".

LAVELLE CONSTRUCTION & DEVELOPMENT, CORP. ....**(561) 748-6844**
801 Maplewood Drive, Suite 3, Jupiter   Fax: (561) 748-6845
See Ad on Page: 236, 237   800 Extension: 1162
Principal/Owner: Ronald J. Palladino / Charles A. Lavelle
email: lavelleconstruct@aol.com
Additional Information: Luxury custom home builder and remodeling specialist.

MILLER CONSTRUCTION COMPANY ....**(954) 764-6550**
614 South Federal Highway, Ft. Lauderdale   Fax: (954) 964-5418
See Ad on Page: 206, 207   800 Extension: 1181

MIKE NOURSE CONSTRUCTION...**(941) 262-7228**
1076 Industrial Blvd., Naples   Fax: (941) 262-2275
See Ad on Page: 242, 243   800 Extension: 1180
Principal/Owner: Mike Nourse, Mike Nourse Jr. & Mark Nourse
Website: www.nourseconstruction.com email: info@nourseconstruction.com
Additional Information: A family owned business.

POLO HOMES OF PALM BEACH, INC. ....**(561) 833-7331**
205 Worth Ave., Suite 203, Palm Beach   Fax: (561) 835-6977
See Ad on Page: 202, 203   800 Extension: 1209
Principal/Owner: Misbah Ahbad
Website: polohomesofpalmbeach.com
Additional Information: We also do additions, remodeling and historic renovations.

R.J. HOMES ....**(561) 734-6663**
9185 Perth Road, Lake Worth   Fax: (561) 734-3901
See Ad on Page: 251   800 Extension: 1215
Principal/Owner: Rod Regan
Website: rjhomes.net email: rodjregan@aol.com
Additional Information: Family owned company providing design, color consulting, and interior design in house.

SRD BUILDING CORP ....**(561) 395-2150**
855 S. Federal Highway, Suite 111, Boca Raton   Fax: (561) 395-8434
See Ad on Page: 220, 221   800 Extension: 1247
Principal/Owner: Scott Dingle
Website: www.s-r-d.com

WILLIAMS CONSTRUCTION SERVICES INC...........................**(561) 791-8168**
5530 Duckweed Road, Lake Worth
See Ad on Page: 209   800 Extension: 1274
Principal/Owner: Richard C. Williams

238

continued on page **250**

© SARGENT

CUSTOM RESIDENTIAL BUILDING
and
RENOVATION SERVICES

WORTH BUILDERS
OF PALM BEACH, INC.

1137 CLARE AVE. WEST PALM BEACH, FL *33401*
561-832-0500

CGC 011891

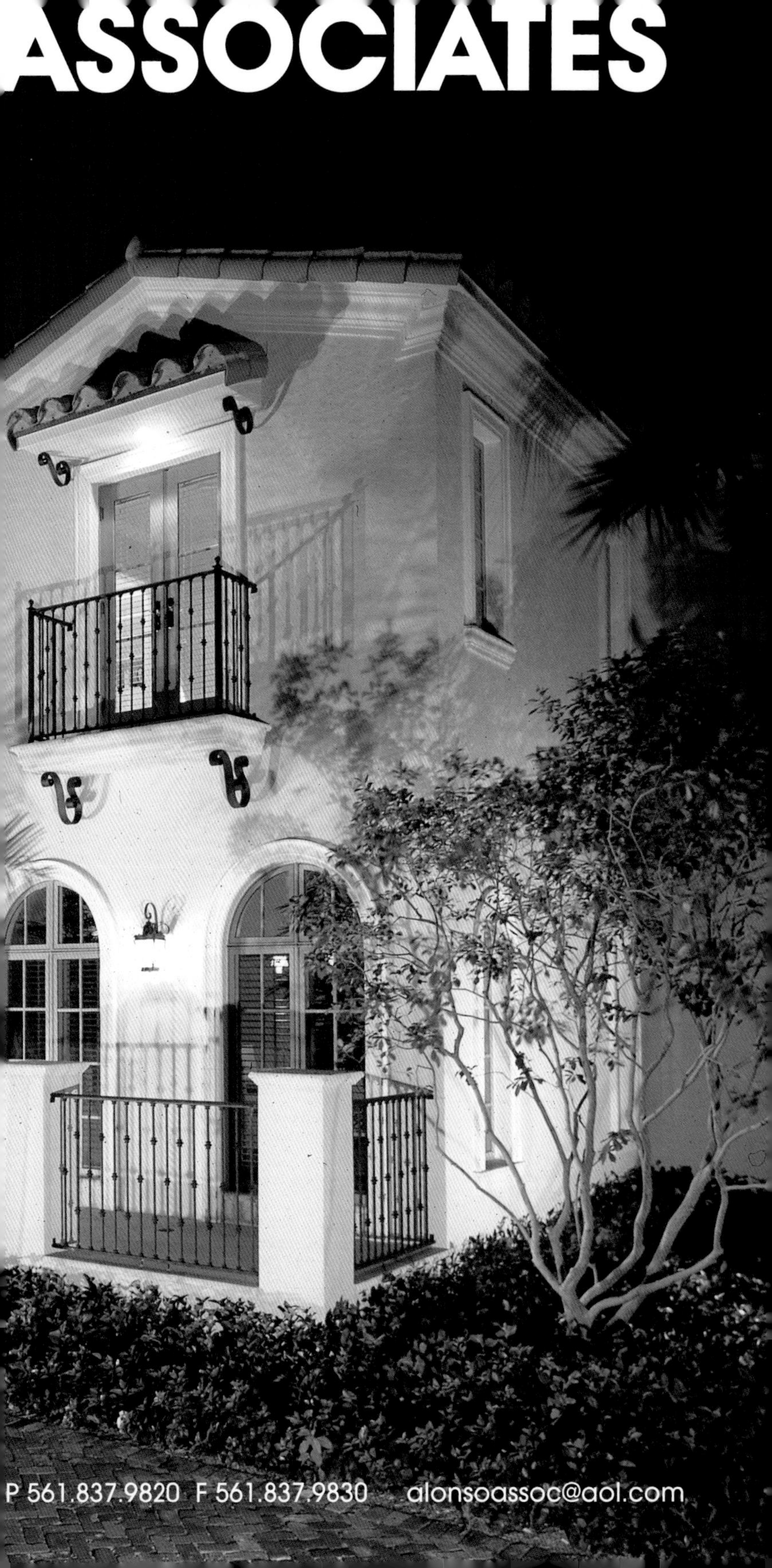
ASSOCIATES
P 561.837.9820 F 561.837.9830 alonsoassoc@aol.com

MIKE NOURSE CONSTRUCTION, INC.

1076 Industrial Boulevard
Naples, FL 34104
Phone 941-262-7228 • Fax 941-262-2275
www.nourseconstruction.com

Avoiding New Home Construction Detours

There's a vast disparity between the new custom estate home that you see in your mind's eye, and the task of transforming that image into reality. It could be compared to a winding road, with many possible detours along the way.

Obviously, getting off to the right start is important, and, on this particular journey, that means choosing your builder carefully. Always ask for references from other homeowners, and ask about the quality of service during and after construction. Tour model homes to determine which builder has demonstrated an ability to complete the job to your satisfaction. Once you've selected a builder, ask to meet the individual who will supervise your home's day-to-day construction.

If you've engaged an architect, involve your builder before drawings are executed. The practitioners of these two disciplines must work together to assure that the creative concepts you have in mind can actually be produced. Before pencil drawings are converted to computer-assisted plans, assemble a team of professionals who specialize in landscape architecture, interior design and kitchen design.

There's a purely practical reason to involve these specialists early in the process. Each one has specific knowledge — such as appropriate site elevations, finish materials availability and how well a dramatic kitchen form will actually function — which will keep construction on schedule, and help identify necessary modifications while revisions are still cost-effective. "Fixing" something later is always more expensive than building it right the first time.

One final recommendation: When friends and family members offer their opinions, thank them politely, but heed the professionals. With proper scheduling, meticulous supervision and clear communication, even occasional delays will be nothing more than minor bumps in the road.

Steven M. Watt, *Gulfshore Homes*

Architectural Excellence...
Discriminating Design

Celebration Homes Inc

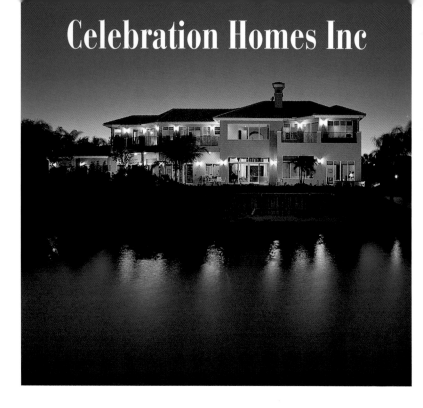

www.wemakeitfun.com

because a new home
is time for celebration

Custom Home Builders

continued from page **238**

WINFIELD COMPANIES ....**(941) 593-3100**
10001 Tamiami Trail N., Naples   Fax: (941) 593-3150
See Ad on Page: 248   *800 Extension:* 1275
Principal/Owner: John Winfield
email: jwinfield@winfieldcompanies

WORTH BUILDERS OF PALM BEACH, INC. ....**(561) 832-0500**
1137 Clara Avenue, West Palm Beach   Fax: (561) 832-3871
See Ad on Page: 188, 189, 239   *800 Extension:* 1276
Principal/Owner: Thomas Eastwood
Additional Information: Worth Builders services Palm Beach & Martin counties, building new custom residential homes and remodeling luxury residences.

"When you're talking about building a house, you're talking about dreams."

Robert A.M. Stern

General Contractor Services

Winner of a GCBA Gold Prism Award 2000

General Contractor Services

Lake Worth, Florida
License # CG C057454
Tel: (561) 471-7303 Fax: (561) 471-7305

Combining Total
Customer Service
With The Finest
Quality &
Craftsmanship

Petra of Naples, Ltd.

Cornerstone Group of Companies

Capstone Builders
of Southwest Florida, Ltd.

Photography: Oscar Thompson

Genesis Custom
Homes, Ltd.

Cornerstone Developers, Inc.
1827 Trade Center Way, Suite 3
Naples, FL 34109
(941) 594-7985
Fax: (941) 594-0078
jmj@cornerstonedevelopers.com

It Should be Fun

As you embark on the journey of designing and building your new home, keep in mind that this process should be an exciting and rewarding experience. It should be fun. It should be gratifying to see your dreams become a reality and to see your desires take the shape of a tailor-made home.

All too often, however, people get involved in designing and building a new home and they get "lost" in the process. They become overwhelmed by all of the decisions and choices needing to be made, and after a while, they can't see the forest for the trees. They stop having fun.

A good architect will try to keep it fun. He is there to help you throughout the process. His job is to organize your ideas and needs into a design expressing your individuality and your tastes. A good architect guides you through the decision-making process, and helps you to maintain a proper perspective on the whole project. A good architect makes it simple, he makes it rewarding and enjoyable. When you work with a qualified architect, he'll help your experience be as satisfying as the home you are building.

John K. Dyehouse, *Dyehouse Geshay & Comeriato Architects*

INTERIOR DESIGNERS

Perla Lichi Design

Lifestyles for the 21st Century

INTERIOR DESIGNERS

Perla Lichi Design, established in 1990, is dedicated to creating personal environments that are aesthetically pleasing as well as practical and functional. The goal is to please each client and leave them happy, nurturing environments where they will live in harmony and good health.

7127 North Pine Island Road
Tamarac, FL 33321
Tel: 954-726-0899 Fax: 954-720-5828
FL ID. No.1727 ◆ FL IB. No. 1037 ◆ FL IB. No. 1039
www.perlalichi.com

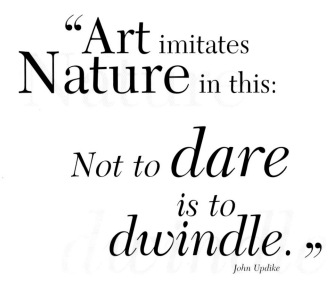

"Art imitates Nature in this:

Not to *dare* is to *dwindle*. "

John Updike

261

photo courtesy of:
Maria Freedman

Inner Beauty

It may be as simple as a fresh look at the familiar. Or it may be an involved process requiring major renovation. In either case, interior designers can bring your ideas to life by demystifying the daunting task of designing a home.

With their years of professional experience and the tools that they have at their fingertips, designers can orchestrate, layer by layer, design elements that together compose an inviting and harmonious décor. For this collaboration to be a success however, requires communication and trust. By listening to your dreams and by understanding your needs, designers can fashion workable rooms that are a visual delight, reflect your personality and speak to your spirit. The end result of a productive partnership should be a happy homeowner who can exclaim, "I've always known that this was a great house, but now it's home!"

Interior Design

FIVE THINGS YOU SHOULD KNOW

1. **Know what level of guidance you want:** A person to handle every detail, someone to collaborate with you, or simply an occasional consultation?

2. **Know what you're trying to achieve.** Start an Idea Notebook, filling it with pictures of rooms you like and don't like. This will help you define your style and stay true to your goal.

3. **Know your budget.** Prices of high end furnishings know no upper limit. Adopt a "master plan," to phase in design elements if your tastes are outpacing your pocketbook.

4. **Know what's going on.** Always ask; don't assume. Design is not a mystical process. Good designers can explain your project (and they'll want to).

5. **Know yourself.** Don't get blinded by beauty. Stay focused on what makes you feel "at home," and you'll be successful.

WHERE STRUCTURE MEETS INSPIRATION

A great interior designer, like a great architect or builder, sees space creatively, applying years of education and experience to deliver a distinguished residence at the highest level of quality in an organized, professional manner. Intensely visual, these talented individuals imprint a home with the spirit and personality of the family living there.

Creativity, that special talent to see the possibilities in a living room, library, or little reading nook, is the most important asset an interior designer will bring to a project. Particularly in upper-end interiors, where the expense of the antique accessories, sumptuous fabrics and imported furnishings is often a secondary concern, the creative vision driving the design choices and placement decisions is what makes a room extraordinary.

Just as an inventive spirit allows talented designers to apply their flair for putting things together in creative and welcoming ways, education and business experience are what get the wonderful concept off the computer or drawing paper and into reality.

A top quality interior designer who is licensed by the state is well educated in the field of interior design, usually holding a bachelor's or master's degree in the subject. This educational background coupled with practical experience is vital. You need not know where to get the best down-filled pillows, or when French fabric mills close each summer. You need not learn the difference between French Country and English Country, how to match patterns, or correctly balance a floor plan. Rely on a knowledgeable designer for that information.

A great interior designer also handles the "nuts and bolts" business end of the project. With skill and experience in placing and tracking orders, scheduling shipping, delivery, and installation, the designer can bring your project to its perfect conclusion.

AN INTERIOR DESIGNER IS A TEAM MEMBER

Choose an interior designer when you select your architect, builder, and landscape architect. A skilled designer can collaborate with the architect on matters such as window and door location, appropriate room size, and practical and accent lighting plans. In new construction and remodeling, try to make your floor plan and furniture choices simultaneously, to avoid common design problems, like traffic corridors running through a formal space, or awkward locations of electrical outlets.

CREATE THE BEST CLIENT-DESIGNER RELATIONSHIP

Talk to the best interior designers in the area and they'll tell you how exciting and gratifying it is for them when a client is involved in the process. This is happening more and more as homeowners turn their attention to hearth and home, and dedicate the time and resources to achieve a style they love.

To establish the most successful and pleasant relationship with an interior designer, make a personal commitment to be involved.

Start by defining your needs, in terms of service and the end result. Have an interior designer involved during the architectural drawing phase of a new or renovation project, and get the process started early. Be clear about how much help you want from a designer. Some homeowners have a strong sense of what they want and simply need a consultant-type relationship. Others want significant guidance from a professional who will oversee the entire process.

Set up a relationship that encourages an open exchange of ideas. In pursuit of personal style, you must be comfortable trusting a professional designer to interpret your thoughts and needs. You must be comfortable saying, "No, I don't like that," and receptive to hearing, "I don't think that's a good idea."

Be forthcoming about your budget. Not all interiors are guided by a budget, but the majority are. Your designer must know and respect your financial parameters and priorities. If a gorgeous dining room table is a top priority, objets d' art can be added later as you find them. Prices of exquisite furniture, custom carved cabinets, and other high end furnishings know no upper limit. Be realistic about what you will spend and what you expect to achieve. Do some research in furniture stores and specialty shops, starting with those showcased in this section. If your expectations temporarily exceed your budget, phase in the decor over a period of time.

Lastly, be inquisitive as the design unfolds. This is a creative effort on your behalf, so let yourself enjoy it, understand it and be stimulated by it.

START THINKING VISUALLY: STOP, LOOK AND CLIP

Before you start scheduling initial interviews with interior designers, start compiling an Idea Notebook – it's the best tool for developing an awareness of your personal style. Spend a weekend or two with a pair of scissors, a new Idea Notebook, and a stack of magazines, (or add a section to the Idea Notebook you made to inspire your architecture and building plans).

UNDERSTANDING "ECLECTIC"

Eclectic means "not following any one system, but selecting and using what seems best from all systems."

Its popularity in interior design stems from the unique look it creates. Mixing the best from different styles creates a dynamic that's totally different from an application of one chosen style. The overall effect is casual and comfortable, "dressed up" in a less formal way.

Eclectic can mean a mixing of styles within one room, like a rich Oriental rug paired with a denim sofa, or between rooms, like an 18th Century dining room leading into an Early American kitchen. The possibilities for accents and appointments are unlimited because there are no restrictions.

263

IMMERSE YOURSELF

The more exposure you have to good design, the easier it becomes to develop your own style.

• Haunt the bookstores that have large selections of shelter magazines, and stacks of books on decorating, design and architecture.

Prairie Avenue
Book Shop
418 South
Wabash Street
(312) 922-5184
www.pabook.com

• Attend show houses, especially the Designer Showcase homes presented twice annually by ASID, and visit model homes, apartments or lofts
• Visit the South Dixie Antique Row and take advantage of its vast array of antiques and collectibles.

Make this a record of your personal style. Include pictures of your favorite rooms, noting colors, fabrics, tile, carpet, fixtures, the way light filters through a curtain, anything that strikes your fancy. Circle the design elements in a room that you'd like to incorporate into your own home décor and make comments regarding those elements you don't care for. Think hard about what you love and loathe in your current residence. Start to look at the entire environment as a rich source of design ideas. Movies, billboards, architecture, clothing – all are fascinating sources for visual stimulation.

Then, when you hold that initial meeting, you too will have a book of ideas to share. Although a smart designer will be able to coax this information from you, it's tremendously more reliable to have visual representations than to depend on a verbal description. It also saves a tremendous amount of time.

THE INTERIOR DESIGN PROCESS: GETTING TO KNOW YOU

Give yourself time to interview at least two interior designers. Invite him or her to your home for a tour of your current residence and a look at items you wish to use in the new environment. If you're building or remodeling, an interior designer can be helpful with your overall plans when they're given the opportunity to get involved early in the building process.

During the initial meeting, count on your intuition to guide you toward the best designer for you. Decorating a home is an intimate and very personal experience, so a comfortable relationship with a high degree of trust is absolutely necessary for a good result. You may adore what a designer did for a friend, but if you can't easily express your ideas, or if you feel he or she isn't interested in your point of view, don't pursue the relationship. Unless you can imagine yourself working with a designer two or three homes from now, keep interviewing.

You may wish to hire a designer for one room before making a commitment to do the whole house.

Some designers maintain a high degree of confidentiality regarding their clients, but if possible, get references and contact them, especially clients with whom they've worked on more than one home. Be sure to ask about the quality of follow-up service.

Be prepared to talk in specific terms about your project, and to honestly assess your lifestyle. For a home or a room to work well, function must be considered along with the evolving style. Designers ask many questions; some of them may be:

- What function should each room serve? Will a living room double as a study? Will a guest room also be an exercise area?

- Who uses the rooms? Growing children, adults, business associates? Which are shared and which are private?

- What safety and maintenance issues must be addressed? A growing family or a family pet may dictate the degree of elegance of a home.

- What kind of relationship do you want to establish between the interior and the landscape?

- Style: Formal, casual or a bit of both?
Are you comfortable with color?
Are you sentimental, practical?
Are you naturally organized or disorganized?

- What kind of art do you like? Do you own art that needs to be highlighted or displayed in a certain way? Do you need space for a growing collection?

- Do you feel at home in a dog-eared, low maintenance family room or do you soothe your soul in an opulent leather chair, surrounded by rich cabinetry and Oriental rugs?

- What kind of furniture do you like? Queen Anne, contemporary, American Arts and Crafts, casual wicker, or eclectic mixing of styles?

- What words describe the feeling you want to achieve? Cheerful, cozy, tranquil, elegant, classic?

COMPUTING THE INTERIOR DESIGN FEE

Designers use individual contracts, standard contracts drawn up by the American Society of Interior Designers (ASID), or letters of agreements as legal documents. The ASID contract outlines seven project phases – programming, schematic, design development, contract documents, contract administration, project representation beyond basic services, and additional services. It outlines the designer's special responsibilities, the owner's responsibilities, fees, and payments to the designer, including reimbursement of expenses.

Payments may be due at the completion of each project phase, monthly or quarterly, or as orders are made. You can usually expect to pay a retainer, or a 50 percent deposit on goods as they are ordered, 40 percent upon the start of installation, and the balance when the job is completed.

Design fees, which may be based on "current market rate," are computed as a percentage of a job, on a flat fee or hourly basis, or may be tied to retail costs. Expect hourly fees of approximately $100 an hour, varying by experience, reputation and workload.

PROFESSIONAL DESIGNATIONS

ASID (American Society of Interior Designers)/
South Florida
1855 Griffin Rd.
Ste B-485
Dania, Florida
(954) 926-7555
Offers referrals to homeowners

National Headquarters
IIDA (International Interior Design Association)
341 Merchandise Mart
(312) 467-1950
www.iida.org
Email:
IIDAhq@iida.org
Provides referrals to homeowners.

Designers who add ASID or IIDA after their names are certified members of the organization.

265

EMBRACE THE MASTER PLAN

Gone are the days when Florida area homeowners felt the need to move into a "finished" interior. They take their time now, letting the flow of their evolving lifestyle and needs guide them along the way.

MAKE LIGHTING A PRIORITY

The trend toward a comprehensive lighting programs as part of good interior design is catching on in Chicago area luxury homes. Appropriate light and well designed accent lighting are very important to the overall comfort and functionality of a home. Neither the stunning volume ceiling nor the cozy breakfast nook can reach their potential if the lighting is wrong. Ask your interior designer for his or her lighting ideas. These choices need to be made in coordination with the building timeline, so plan and place orders early.

CAN YOU WEAR WHITE AFTER LABOR DAY?

There are colors and emotions for every season. Let your designer know if you want to be able to change the look and feel of your home to reflect the seasons.

If an hourly rate is being used, ask if there is a cap per day, and if different rates are charged for an assistant's or drafter's time. Percentages may be figured as a certain amount above the retail or trade price, and can range from 15 to 100 percent. Separate design fees may be charged by the hour, room, or entire project. It is imperative to trust your designer and rely on his or her reputation of delivering a top quality project in an honest, reliable fashion. You must feel you're being given a valuable service for a fair price.

If you work with a designer of staff at a retail store, a design service fee ranging from $100 to $500 may be charged and applied against purchases.

FROM THE MIND'S EYE TO REALITY

Once you've found a designer whom you like and trust, and have signed a clear, specific agreement, you're ready to embark on the adventure.

A designer who knows his or her way around the masses of products and possibilities will guide you through upscale retail outlets, and to craftsmen and women known only to a fortunate few in the trade. You can be a "kid in a candy store."

Just as you've allowed time to carefully consider and reconsider architectural blueprints, temper your enthusiasm to rush into decisions regarding your interiors. Leave fabric swatches where you see them day after day. Look at paint samples in daylight, evening light and artificial light. If possible, have everyone in the family "test sit" a kitchen chair for a week before ordering the whole set, and play with furniture placement. This small investment of time will pay handsomely in an end result that suits you perfectly.

Be prepared to wait for your interiors to be installed. It's realistic to allow eight months to complete a room, and eight to 12 months to decorate an entire home.

Decide if you want your interiors to be installed piecemeal or all at once. Many designers recommend waiting for one installation, if you have the patience. Homeowners tend to worry and try to outthink their original decisions when pieces are brought in as they arrive. By waiting for one installation, they treat themselves to a stunning visual and emotional thrill. ■

A'VARE DESIGN GROUP ....**(561) 741-4010**
337 E. Indiantown Rd., Suite 6, Jupiter
See Ad on Page: 144, 314
Principal/Owner: Lorraine Alwaise
Website: www.avare.com
Additional Information: Award-winning design group. Making your vision a reality!

Fax: (564) 741-4011
800 Extension: 1001

AGOSTINO'S DESIGN GROUP ....**(941) 430-9108**
3078 North Tamiami Trail, Naples
See Ad on Page: 322, 323
Principal/Owner: Gus Sciacqua
Website: www.agostino's.com email: ADGNaples@aol.com

Fax: (941) 430-9135
800 Extension: 1009

BONACCI DESIGN GROUP ....**(954) 581-6869**
6600 NW 16 Street, Suite 12, Plantation
See Ad on Page: 299 - 306
Principal/Owner: Thomas J. Bonacci
Additional Information: Manufacture custom furniture, upholstery, drapery &
full design firm. Full showroom with many ready made lines show at DCOTA.

Fax: (954) 581-6865
800 Extension: 1038

BROOKS INTERIOR DESIGN, INC. ....**(407) 539-2655**
670 N. Orlando Avenue, Suite 1001, Maitland
See Ad on Page: 346, 347
Principal/Owner: Angela Brooks
email: brooksintd@aol.com
Additional Information: Inspired by the uniqe character and personality of each
client, Brooks Interior Design begins as early as blueprint stage when architectural details can be specified to enhance an interior's one-of-a-kind flair. FL lic
#00002930, Allied ASID Member.

Fax: (407) 539-0973
800 Extension: 1045

CM INTERIORS ....**(954) 783-9191**
800 N. Federal Highway, Pompano Beach
See Ad on Page: 313
Principal/Owner: Lyn Burrell
Additional Information: We are a "complete decorating" service.

Fax: (954) 943-1247
800 Extension: 1058

267

DENNIS CONNEL INTERIORS ....**(954) 564-8999**
3020 N. Federal Highway #5, Ft. Lauderdale
See Ad on Page: 308, 309
Principal/Owner: Dennis Connel

Fax: (954) 564-9155
800 Extension: 1069

L. REESE CUMMING INTERIORS, INC. ....**(941) 263-9104**
5100 N. Tamiami Trail, Suite 204, Naples
See Ad on Page: 318, 319
Principal/Owner: L. Reese Cumming

Fax: (941) 263-8682
800 Extension: 1158

CVRZON DESIGNS ....**(561) 997-7228**
6192 N. Federal Highway, Boca Raton
See Ad on Page: 336, 337
Principal/Owner: Grenville Pulien
email: cvrzon@bellsouth.net
Additional Information: This company offers a full - service turnkey service
backed by thirty years of International experience.

Fax: (561) 997-6282
800 Extension: 1063

DIANNE DAVANT & ASSOCIATES ....**(561) 287-2872**
41 West Seminole Street, Stuart
See Ad on Page: 340
Principal/Owner: Dianne Davant
Website: www.davant-interiors.com email: ddi@boone.net

Fax: (561) 287-3211
800 Extension: 1073

continued on page **298**

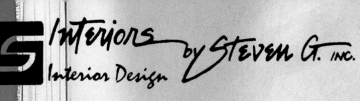

"Expressing Interior Excellence is our Specialty"

IN THE DETAILS...

Interior Architecture
Interior Design
Decoration

MARC-MICHAELS
INTERIOR DESIGN, INC.

Harmony by Design

The ancient art of Feng Shui is built upon the principles of living in harmony with our environment. Feng Shui is a 4,000-year-old science that translates to "Wind" and "Water." This translation opens up one's insights to the understanding that there is a seen world, the "Water" aspect, and the unseen world, the "Wind" aspect. Ancient scholars studied how the unseen world of energy affected the seen world of matter, and deduced that this duality existed in everything. Nothing exists without its equal opposite. Known as Yin and Yang, these two opposites encompass heaven and earth, body and soul, and the physical and psychological. When these are in balance, harmony and inner peace will be reflected in your life.

One doesn't have to believe in Feng Shui to experience the benefits. Utilizing the methods used in Feng Shui, the ability to manifest your intended reality increases. Specific colors, incorporating the five elements, and the use of mundane and transcendental solutions are incorporated to cure, or enhance the energy in any one of the eight life areas existing in all environments. Utilizing Feng Shui at any stage in the design process sets the energetic foundation for creating an environment that will support your well-being.

Elyse M. Santoro

Elyse M. Santoro, *Feng Shui Designs*

Frederiksen Design International Inc.

Creators of the Unique
- *Elegant Interiors*
- *Custom Kitchens & Baths*
- *Interior Architecture*
- *Display & Exhibition*

7378 West Atlantic Boulevard, Suite 230, Margate, Florida 33063
954/974-2038   Fax: 954/974-7811
E-mail: FrederiksenDesign@Hotmail.com

H. ALLEN HOLMES, INC.

INTERIOR DESIGN ■ SPACE PLANNING

STATE LICENSE #IB0000008   TELEPHONE: 561.747.4443

H. ALLEN HOLMES, INC.

INTERIOR DESIGN ■ SPACE PLANNING

STATE LICENSE #IB0000008   TELEPHONE: 561.747.4443

Photos: Sargent Architectural Photography

MARGAUX,

Margarita Courtney:

"Living in South Florida allows us the perfect opportunity to create a spectacular tropical atmosphere in our homes. For my own home, the abundance of light and lush greenery made it natural to decorate in warm woods and light, textured fibers of cotton, linen and sisal. I used touches of vibrant color to bring the outdoors inside and took advantage of South Florida's international heritage by using antiques and hand-crafted furnishings and accessories from all over the world."

282

Photo by Roy Quesada

Desi

ONYX DESIGN,

Maria I. Flores:

"Our client is a single man who loves to entertain. He desired a high level of comfort for himself and his guests, and wanted a different look and feel in each room of his island home. We designed this Florida room in relaxing, neutral tones because it was to be used for casual, lounge-style entertaining. Our client tested every sofa and chair for comfort and as a result, the custom designed furniture is down-filled to his specifications. The sofa and chairs also face windows to take advantage of the fabulous view."

DISTINCTIVE INTERIORS,

Jeffrey S. Adler:

"As exotic and textural as his world travels, the master retreat for an international make-up artist reflects his complex personality. His varied collections are woven against a background of colorful silks, velvets, linens, and sumptuous chenille."

INTERIORS BY STEVEN G., INC.,

Steven Gurowitz:

"'He who panders to the trend of the day is tomorrow's obsolescence.' What we created in this powder room shows just how Old World design can make the boldest of statements. Our use of natural materials, along with hand-crafted corbels, create a rich feel that will be elegant for years to come. Beautiful sconces create warmth, and the use of lighting under the vanity show a timeless elegance that our clients require and expect."

285

Interiors by Steven G. Inc.

hoto by Brantley

Photo by Peter Morpurgo

CM INTERIORS,

Lyn Burrell:

"This high-profile client wanted the finest and most elegant surroundings. The bedroom displays an Asian influence by combining suede and African tapestry for the bed dressing, and using an animal applique in each of the window swags. To complete this eastern flair we used a velvet leopard rope throughout all of the window treatments. My client loves the allure as he steps into his private quarters."

Desi

STRAUSS & WASSNER, INC.,

Madelyn Strauss:

"Our client was moving from a large home with cathedral ceilings to a slightly smaller condominium with flat 10-foot ceilings. Our challenge was to transform a sterile backdrop into a warm environment and showcase her magnificent possessions. We accomplished our goal by removing solid wing walls between the great room and dining room and replacing them with two pairs of columns topped by Corinthian Capitals. We used Jerusalem Stone flooring laid on the diagonal, oriental rugs, Acanthus Dentil moldings and a warm paint palette to achieve an overall ambiance."

287

Photo by Barry Grossman

ners

DANIEL DUBAY INTERIOR DESIGN, INC.,

Daniel DuBay:

"This library was designed as a retreat, a place for the wife to escape from the outside world, read, write and converse via her lap top. The room is paneled in mahogany, incorporating numerous bookshelves. The desk is French, circa 1920, in the Louis XVI style and made of amboyna and burl with inlays of ivory. The inset desktop is of tooled leather. The window treatment consists of pleated shades, which were made from a sheer casement fabric of woven metallic bronze threads with cotton sateen, and tied back draperies abundantly trimmed and tasseled for an opulent effect. A most elegant retreat."

288

Photo by Craig Dugan/Hedrich-Blessing

Desi

LA MAISON FLEURIE, INC.,

Annick Presles:

"The challenge was to transform a conventional contemporary house into a warm and cozy residence blending furniture and artifacts from several cultures to compose rooms tinged with exotic mystery. My intention was to create a 'chic' and casual look that I thought would translate well for a young family. For the master bedroom, I chose a printed toile fabric and a statement-making Mexican bed to make the room both feminine and exotic."

Photos by Robert Branley

jners

DENNIS CONNEL INTERIORS,

Dennis Connel:

"Good design always begins with an appreciation of a client's lifestyle and taste. This is reflected in the bedroom where my clients wanted to combine their love of modern furnishings with the look of their home's 1920's architecture and design. To give the space a more modern feeling, I moved the bed away from the wall so it seems to float. In designing the custom entertainment unit, I selected classic elements and used them in a streamlined manner, covering the molding with contemporary reflective brass."
Photos by Adam Chinitz

Desi

SARUSKI DESIGN,

Michael Saruski:

"Sometimes even the most luxurious residence has a room that seems cold and impersonal. This large living area with its 20-foot ceiling was a good example. By using rich earth tones on the furniture and walls, I warmed-up the area, making it seem smaller and more inviting. The beautifully executed rosettes kept the window treatment elegant but not overwhelming, and the placement of the draperies helped to lower the ceiling by directing the eye downward. Superimposing custom designed leaded glass over the existing small glass-block windows made them less predominant and a more integrated part of the overall design."

Photo by Buxton Photography

SUMMERHOUSE DESIGN GROUP,

Michael Beamish:

"I was commissioned by the client to create a soft, whimsical, romantic master bedroom suite with a Mediterranean flavor. The room was octagonal with an 18-foot vaulted ceiling and a wonderful Juliet balcony overlooking the entire bedroom. It also featured a large oversized stone-carved fireplace. As much as these wonderful features made the room vibrant and interesting, it was a design challenge to create a concept encompassing the room's natural drama. I began with a dramatic canopy over the ornate crested iron bed that I double draped in wonderful soft white sheer linen. I then hung ornate iron rods over the two tiered windows and draped them using grapevine and ivy as well as the same sheer fabric. This brought natural sunlight into the room. I dressed the bed with white eyelet bed linen and pillows. I added an antique Aubusson rug on the cobblestone floor, which brought comfort and elegance into the room with a rich warm color palette. An oversized antique French crystal chandelier with beeswax candles was suspended from the vaulted ceiling to give sparkle to the room. We further reflected the sunlight into the room by adding a large wood framed platinum rubbed mirror. The finished room radiates a wonderful atmosphere of tranquility and intimacy with a timeless romantic flavor."

A'VARE DESIGN GROUP,

Gloria Tian:

"Our mission was to disguise an ordinary butler's pantry, visible from the formal estate living room, into an elegant focal point. The metamorphosis began with the Mediterranean colonnade inspired trompe l'oeil. To complete the illusion, we designed the entrance gate to the colonnade, creating a magnificent distraction from the original design."

Photo by Sargent

Photography: Michael Garland

312 787 7766 P
312 787 7743 F

D A N I E L   D U B A Y   I N T E R I O R   D E S I G N

Los Angeles | Chicago | Palm Beach

Photography: Michael Garland

Summerhouse
DESIGN GROUP

1328 SE 17th Street   Fort Lauderdale, FL 33316
Tel 954.728.9400   Fax 954.728.9544
email summerde@bellsouth.net www.summer-house.com
Worldwide CNN TEXT

Interior Designers

Interior Designers

(continued from page 267)

D. DEPERRO DESIGN, INC ....**(561) 392-5051**
110 E. Boca Raton Road, Boca Raton — Fax: (561) 392-3031
See Ad on Page: 341 — 800 Extension: 1064
Principal/Owner: Danielle DePerro
email: all4design@aol.com
Additional Information: Licensed, ten years in operation.

DANIEL DU BAY INTERIOR DESIGN, INC. ....**(312) 787-7766**
1512 North Fremont Street, Chicago — Fax: (312) 787-7743
See Ad on Page: 294, 295 — 800 Extension: 1067
Principal/Owner: Daniel Du Bay
Additional Information: Interior Architectura and Design.

FENG SHUI DESIGNS ....**(305) 674-1408**
5600 Collins Avenue, Suite 4P, Miami Beach — Fax: (305) 861-6973
See Ad on Page: 345 — 800 Extension: 1097
Principal/Owner: Elyse Santoro

FREDERIKSEN DESIGN INTERNATIONAL, INC. ......**(954) 974-2038**
7378 West Atlantic Blvd. #230, Margate — Fax: (954) 974-7811
See Ad on Page: 277 — 800 Extension: 1106
Principal/Owner: Richard Frederiksen

MARIA FREEDMAN INTERIORS, INC. ....**(561) 487-3000**
8320 Twin Lake Drive, Boca Raton — Fax: (561) 883-0022
See Ad on Page: 280, 281 — 800 Extension: 1172
Principal/Owner: Maria Freedman

H. ALLEN HOLMES INC. ....**(561) 747-4443**
1001 S. US Highway One, Suite 102, Jupiter — Fax: (561) 747-0942
See Ad on Page: 278, 279 — 800 Extension: 1117
Principal/Owner: H. Allen Holmes, ASID
email: haholmes20@aol.com
Additional Information: Complete design services & consulting, project management, conception, design development, budgeting and implementation.

HOWARD DESIGN GROUP ....**(305) 446-4088**
2801 Florida Avenue, Coconut Grove — Fax: (305) 446-4428
See Ad on Page: 342, 343 — 800 Extension: 1126
Principal/Owner: Jeffrey Howard
email: hdgroup@aol.com

INTERIOR DESIGN CENTER AND MFG ....**(954) 725-6480**
1100 S. Powerline Road, Deerfield Beach — Fax: (954) 725-6485
See Ad on Page: 348, 500 — 800 Extension: 1135
Principal/Owner: Rami Argov
Website: www.idcmfg.com email: idcmfg@earthlink.net

INTERIORS BY STEVEN G ....**(954) 735-8223**
1608 NW 23 Avenue, Ft. Lauderdale — Fax: (954) 735-7546
See Ad on Page: 268 - 271 — 800 Extension: 1138
Principal/Owner: Steven Gurowitz
Website: www.interiorsbysteveng.com email: szelman@interiorsbysteveng.com

INTERNATIONAL INTERIORS ASSOCIATES............**(800) 840-7780**
1900 Purdy Avenue, Suite 1105, Miami — Fax: (305) 673-3637
See Ad on Page: 272, 273, 625 — 800 Extension: 1141
Principal/Owner: Rebecca Tedder
Website: www.interiors-inc.com email: info@interiors-inc.com
Additional Information: Award winning designs & services for over 4 decades. Full service interior design and architectural renovations with an eclectic array of unique handcrafted furnishings from around the globe, achieves the utmost in creation, values & client satisfaction.

298

continued on page 316

From concept to Bonacci Design expertise in custom

Design, with a
Difference...

Your Full-Service Design Group

With a staff of creative designers, expert cabinetmakers, remarkable finishers and gifted upholsterers,"BDG" offers a creative blend between

(954) 581-6869

6600 NW 16 Street
Suite 12
Plantation, FL

The Bonacci Design Group & Manufacturing Inc.

DESIGN

nacci

N GROUP

completion, the Group offers designing and manufacturing.

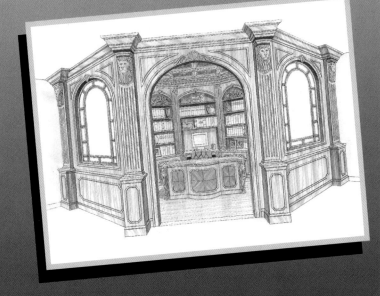

Scaled floor plans and detailed renderings are provided after our initial consultation, along with complete fabric and furniture finish boards. Whether you desire a single item or a full interior, the Bonacci Design Group can custom create for your individuality.

(954) 581-6869

IslandHouse
INTERIORS

2424 S.E. Indian Street • Stuart, Florida 34997
561-286-1394 • fax: 561-220-2345
www.islandhouse.com

DENNIS CONNEL INTERIORS, INC.

561.748.3911   FAX: 561.748.7515

**DENNIS CONNEL
INTERIORS, INC.**

Perla Lichi Design

Specialists in mid to
high-end residential
design and turnkey
model merchandising
for builders and
developers

Lifestyles for the 21st Century

7127 North Pine Island Road
Tamarac, FL 33321
Tel: 954-726-0899 Fax: 954-720-5828
FL ID. No.1727 • FL IB. No. 1037 • FL IB. No. 1039
www.perlalichi.com

Susan Morgan Interiors

*When you simply deserve
the best for your home, yacht,
or business...*

Susan Morgan ASID, ALID
31 East Ocean Blvd. Stuart, FL 34994
Stuart: (561) 286-5967
Jupiter: (561) 746-0029
Fax (561) 286-7716
www.SusanMorganInteriors.com
Lic.#IB0001083

La Maison Fleurie, Inc.
Palm Beach

Interiors
Annick Presles · Sophie-Eve Hacquard
561.833.1083

Interiors

A complete and unique interior decorating concept.

800 North Federal Highway Pompano Beach, Florida 33062 (954) 783-9191 Fax (954) 943-1247

a 'Vare design group

Award winning Architectural and Interior Design.

a 'Vare design group

MCWHORTER/ROSS

DESIGN GROUP

INTERIOR
&
ARCHITECTURAL DESIGN

BEVERLY HILLS

MCWHORTERDESIGN.COM · TELEPHONE 323.930.2113

Interior Designers

continued from page **310**

ISLAND HOUSE INTERIORS ....**(561) 286-1394**
2424 S.E. Indian Street, Stuart   Fax: (561) 220-2345
See Ad on Page: 307   *800 Extension:* 1144
Principal/Owner: Chris Cornell & Alexis Cornell

LA MAISON FLEURIE, INC. ....**(561) 833-1083**
139 N. County Road, Suite 25, Palm Beach   Fax: (561) 833-9313
See Ad on Page: 312   *800 Extension:* 1159
Principal/Owner: Annick Presles / Sophie-Eve Hocquard
email: lmfinc2@aol.com
Additional Information: Annick Preles & Sophie-Eve Hocquard are specialized in residential and commercial, and they have established a fine clientele all over the world

MARC-MICHAELS INTERIOR DESIGN, INC..............................**(561) 362-7037**
850 E. Palmetto Park Road, Boca Raton   Fax: (561) 362-4226
See Ad on Page: 274, 275   *800 Extension:* 1169
Principal/Owner: Michael J. Abbott / S. Marc Thee
email: marc-michaels.com
Additional Information: In its 15 year history, Marc-Michaels Interior Design has garnered over 350 prestigious design awards.

MARC-MICHAELS INTERIOR DESIGN, INC..............................**(407) 629-2124**
720 W. Morse Blvd., Winter Park   Fax: (407) 629-0910
See Ad on Page: 274, 275   *800 Extension:* 1170
Principal/Owner: Michael J. Abbott / S. Marc Thee
Website: marc-michaels.com
Additional Information: In its 15 year history, Marc-Michaels Interior Design has garnered over 350 prestigious design awards.

MCWHORTER/ ROSS DESIGNS.......................................**(323) 930-2113**
269 S. Beverly Drive #123, Beverly Hills, CA   Fax: (323) 936-4198
See Ad on Page: 315   *800 Extension:* 1179
Principal/Owner: Matthew Ross

SUSAN MORGAN INTERIORS ....**(561) 286-5967**
31 East Ocean Blvd., Stuart   Fax: (561) 288-7716
See Ad on Page: 311   *800 Extension:* 1255
Principal/Owner: Susan Morgan

ERIC MULLENDORE, ARCHITECT AND
INTERIOR DESIGNER ....**(305) 604-5673**
1500 Ocean Drive, Penthouse 4, Miami Beach   Fax: (305) 604-5674
See Ad on Page: 351   *800 Extension:* 1085
Principal/Owner: Eric Mullendore
email: emullendor@aol.com
Additional Information: As licensed Architects and Interior Designers, we have the ability to meet all of your design needs.

ONYX DESIGN GROUP ....**(305) 758-5388**
660 Grand Concourse, Miami   Fax: (305) 758-9256
See Ad on Page: 320, 321   *800 Extension:* 1194
Principal/Owner: Maria Flores / Susana Henriquez
Website: www.onyxdesign.com email: onyx@onyxdesign.com

PERLA LICHI DESIGN ....**(954) 726-0899**
7127 N. Pine Island Road, Tamarac   Fax: (954) 720-5828
See Ad on Page: 258, 259, 310   *800 Extension:* 1205
Principal/Owner: Perla Lichi
Website: www.perlalichi.com
Additional Information: Specializing in mid to high-end residential designs for home buyers and turnkey model merchandising for builders and developers.

316

continued on page **344**

With Eyes of

Let your Ho

Color .....

L. Reese Cumming Interiors, Inc.
5100 N. Tamiami Trail · Suite #204
Naples · Florida · 34103

Tel. 941·263·9104
Fax. 941·263·8682

Offering
exclusive
architectural
interiors &
furnishings
for the
discriminating
homeowner.

...ne come Alive !

INTERIOR DECORA
Remodeling &

II Tequesta Point

Atlantic III

660 Grand Concourse/
Tel: (305) 758-5388 /
E-mail: onyx
www.onyx

Santa Maria

Hibiscus Island

Miami Shores, FL 33138

Fax : (305) 758 - 9256

@ onyxdesign.com

design.com

TAMARA TENNANT INTERIOR DESIGN,

Tamara Tennant:

"Working with a smaller room can be a design challenge when the requirements include a sleep sofa, computer desk, large TV and storage. But in this project, these requirements were achieved in an organized and aesthetically pleasing way. The height was maximized by running the built-ins to the ceiling. The use of the relief painting, leather sofa and ottoman, and Oriental rug create a wonderful masculine den that our client loves."

324

Photo by Brantley Photography

Desi

INTERIOR DESIGN CENTER,

Rami Argov:

"Beginning with an empty room then filling it with completely new furnishings is an exciting experience for an interior decorator and requires a close partnership with clients. Here, my clients wanted a room that was formal yet warm and inviting, contemporary yet traditional. After extensive consultation, I created a comfortable area that is delightfully eclectic in style. The colors are relaxing and neutral. The contemporary area rug, sofa, and chair are paired with the more traditional lamps, coffee table and end table. The flower arrangement was used to echo those in the picture on the wall and bring it all together. An empty room was transformed into a gracious setting for entertainment and conversation."

Photo by Interior Design Center

S & B INTERIORS, INC.,

Sandi Samole:

"The challenge for this home was to create defined yet open spaces with natural materials in a living sculpture. I began by placing a two-sided glass sculpture over a dual-purpose floating console/buffet. The use of 'functional art' in furnishings and accessories is an important factor in our design schemes as seen in the functional and artistic area achieved by creating a second column opposite the structural one and adding a light soffit. Reflecting the concept of a 'living sculpture' that utilizes all natural materials, the countertop in the dining room is durable Black Galaxy granite, while the foyer side is elegant Portoro Gold marble. Continuing this theme in the great room is a fireplace/media wall made of stone, marble, wood and glass. Even the wall sculpture mixes these mediums."

Photos by Robert Stein

Desi

Photo by Oscar Thompson

AGOSTINO'S DESIGN GROUP,

Kit Mathews:

"Our clients wanted an elegant, dynamic bedroom. The bedding is a luxurious blend of silk, chiffon and brushed fringe. We used neutral tones throughout the room to accentuate the unique faux harlequin design on the walls. Above the silk window treatments are two fabulous carved cornice boards glazed with burnt umber and antiqued with silver and gold leaf. The ceiling is glazed in silver and gold, and is a spectacular finish to this impressive room."

ners

Photo by Dan Forer

L. REESE CUMMING INTERIORS, INC.,

L. Reese Cumming:

"We were challenged to create a truly authentic Southwest residence in a contemporary seaside condominium. Walls were modified with rounded corners and an adobe finish. Moldings, corbels, rough-hewn beams, jambs, doors and wonderful spiral-carved pine columns were crafted and shipped from New Mexico. An intense search for great furnishings and accessories set the final mood, leaving us all exhausted and very excited over the results."

Desi

Photo by Kim Sargent

MARC-MICHAELS INTERIOR DESIGN,

Cree Lewis:

"Our primary focus in designing this dining room involved capturing the elegant synergy that exists between architectural detailing and refined furnishings. Highlighted by antique stone sculptures and an intricate mosaic-tile inlay instead of a rug beneath the table, this room exudes a tangible warmth. Varied eras and mediums were successfully blended into a pan-cultural collection of moments defining a uniquely intimate mood. The overall atmosphere is one of confident sophistication and eclectic charm."

ners

Photo by Everett & Soulé

BROOKS INTERIOR DESIGN,

Angela Brooks:

"The client's wish list included a home theatre. An unusual bonus space over the garage proved to be the perfect location to create a theatre that reflects an air of drama and elegance. The 'lobby area' has black granite flooring inlaid with a marble star pattern. A gold leaf ceiling above reflects the light of a crystal chandelier. To the left is a Corinthian columned concession stand complete with a popcorn maker and lighted candy shelves. Just beyond the stand is a wet bar area that overlooks the screening room. The audio/video equipment is housed along the back wall. The sloped ceiling is faux finished with a celestial night sky. To gain admittance to the 'theater seats', you must pass through an archway guarded by two 14K gold lions head rings that suspend a velvet rope. A sofa, two chairs and ottomans upholstered in suede and leather offer comfortable seating to view the wide screen television. The screen is revealed by motorized black velvet drapes flanked by stationary panels of burgundy velvet and gold fringe. An antique tufted ottoman serves as a cocktail table. The sloped walls are trimmed in burl walnut panels and walnut moldings inset with suede covered acoustical panels. Starfire lighting accents the ceiling and base boards."

H. ALLEN HOLMES, INC.,

Allen Holmes:

"Interior design should reflect the interest and personalities of the people who live there. My clients were long-time South Florida residents who moved from a ground floor condo to a penthouse. They asked me to design an environment that would showcase their antique treasures — many of which had been passed down over generations. I created a room with old Florida accents. To highlight their antique rugs and treasured collections, we created a pecky cypress ceiling, found a reproduction of an antique West Indies pattern for the drapes, and covered the chairs in neutral fabrics. We displayed their collection of crystal on a table so the morning sun would play off the pieces."

ners

FENG SHUI DESIGNS,

Elyse M. Santoro:

"Designing with Feng Shui is creating your environment from the inside out. A consultation begins with furniture placement, color recommendations and proper element balancing. This maximizes energy flow to achieve personal and professional goals. In this room, I looked at how I could bring the elements of nature closer. I added symbols including the empty vessels, which signified the client's openness to being filled with new inspiration. All objects tell a story and give us subliminal messages; surrounding oneself with natural beauty and art allows you to live in a sanctuary that expresses your creative soul."

CVRZON DESIGNS,

Grenville Pullen:

"Interior design should be sympathetic to the architecture of a building, and, in many ways, is predicated by its details, be it period or contemporary. In this home, the clients were anxious to preserve a magnificent African Mahogany tree. We determined that the house should have transparency, both to enjoy the intimate courtyard and to see the foyer display of two wonderfully elegant staircases with a view through to the Intracoastal Waterway beyond. This is where the interior designer can radically influence the architecture, achieving breathtaking ambience by affecting a perfect harmony with nature and the essential element of surprise — the measure of any successful design."

Photo by Kim Sargent

ıners

INTERNATIONAL INTERIORS ASSOCIATES,

Rebecca Tedder:

"All designs should capture the personality and spirit of the client along with the character and essence of the space. The finishing touches can send a well-designed area soaring. This room has touches of classic transitional and contemporary styles creating a warm, rich eclectic setting. Opulent wood, luxurious fabrics and ambient lighting combined with unique art and accessories are what makes this room so special, and it's the signature of my design style."

Photo by Barry Grossman

PERLA LICHI DESIGN,

Perla Lichi:

"Two penthouse units in a high-rise were combined into one spectacular residence. My client asked us to create interiors with such impact that a buyer would love everything and want to move right in. He specified elegant overall styling with a slight masculine flavor. Custom built-ins and architectural millwork helped delineate the spaces and multi-coffered ceiling soffits were highlighted with mahogany moldings to add just the right dramatic 'punch.' Custom cabinetry to house audio/video equipment wraps an odd wall shape, and a custom sofa mirrors this shape affording an unobstructed view. Other built-ins match the rich cherry color of the custom unit in its Neoclassical, carved wood styling."

CVRZON
DESIGNS

GRENVILLE PULLEN ASID
dedicated to excellence in interior design

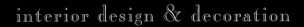

t a m a r a 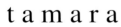 t e n n a n t

INTERIOR DESIGN, INCORPORATED

2499 Glades Road, Suite 202 • Boca Raton, Florida 33431

561. 394. 7882

IB0000657

Designer's unlimited style captures the individuality of each client.

COMMERCIAL
Web Site
www.howarddesigngroup.com

RESIDENTIAL
Email
hdg@aol.com

continued from page **316**

ROMANZA ARCHITECTURAL INTERIORS ....**(407) 228-0997**
2900 N. Orange Avenue, Orlando   Fax: (407) 228-0977
See Ad on Page: 350   800 Extension: 1224

ROSS DESIGN ASSOCIATES ....**(941) 261-8951**
995 Eighth Avenue South, Naples   Fax: (941) 261-0502
See Ad on Page: 317   800 Extension: 1226
Principal/Owner: Tim Ross

S & B INTERIORS, INC. ....**(305) 661-1577**
11270 NW 59th Ave, Pinecrest   Fax: (305) 661-2722
See Ad on Page: 296   800 Extension: 1232
Principal/Owner: Sandi Samole
Website: www.sandbinteriors.com email: sandi@sandbinteriors.com
Additional Information: Complete Interior Design Services for residential and commercial clients nationwide from conception to completion, we design and build your dreams.

SARUSKI DESIGN STUDIO ....**(305) 573-6900**
4141 NE Second Avenue, Suite 106C, Miami   Fax: (305) 573-9888
See Ad on Page: 349   800 Extension: 1234

SUMMERHOUSE DESIGN GROUP ....**(954) 728-9400**
1328 SE 17th Street, Ft. Lauderdale   Fax: (954) 728-9544
See Ad on Page: 297   800 Extension: 1253
Principal/Owner: Michael Beamish
Website: www.summer-house.com email: summerde@bellsouth.net
Additional Information: DCOTA: Designer on call, worldwide context.

TAMARA TENNANT INTERIOR DESIGN, INC............................**(561) 394-7882**
2499 Glades Road, Suite 202, Boca Raton   Fax: (561) 394-2584
See Ad on Page: 338, 339   800 Extension: 1258
Principal/Owner: Tamara Tennant
Additional Information: This national award winning design firm has earned a reputation for integrity, superior craftsmanship and a meticulous attention to detail.

344

Feng Shui Designs

Create a sanctuary for your soul

www.elysesantoro.com
tel: 305.674.1408 fax: 305.861.6975

BROOKS INTERIOR DESIGN
INCORPORATED

Whether the desired look is traditional, eclectic or contemporary, Brooks Interior Design combines unique design elements with expertise to create the perfect ambiance for you home.

As we approach each project, we focus on the goals of our client, making them the central axis of our design solutions. We believe that designing your home should be an exciting process for you. Creating a living environment that reflects your taste, style and personality is our top priority.

Photo: Everett & Soulé

670 North Orlando Avenue, Suite 1001
Maitland, Florida 32751
Telephone 407-539-2655 Fax 407-539-0973
E-mail Brooksintd@aol.com

Just Imagine What If...

Designers and Manufacturers of

*Wall Units, Entertainment Centers, Window Treatments,
Area Rugs, Upholstery, Art and more.*

Family business owned and operated since 1985.
A Professional Team of designers to serve you at our 30,000-square-foot showroom and factory.

INTERIOR DESIGN CENTER
& MANUFACTURER

SARUSKI DESIGN STUDIO

Commercial and Residential Interior Design

4141 Northeast Second Avenue, Suite 106C • Miami, Florida 33137
305.573.6900 • fax: 305.573.9888

ROMANZA

Photography © Laurence Taylor

Photography © Christopher Doncsecz

Photography © Laurence Taylor

Interior Design

Interior Detailing

Luxury Models

Custom Residential

Commercial

ROMANZA
INTERIOR DESIGN

2900 N. Orange Avenue
Orlando, FL 32804
407.228.0997

2016 Trade Center Way • Suite F
Naples, FL 34109
941.596.1613

www.romanza.com

ERIC MULLENDORE

A R C H I T E C T

INTERIOR DESIGNER

1500 OCEAN DRIVE

MIAMI BEACH, FL 33139

305.604.5673 • FAX 305.604.5674

Only If You Want the Very Best...

www.floridahomebook.com

www.chicagohomebook.com

www.lahomebook.com

www.dcmetrohomebook.com

The
Ashley
Group

1350 E. Touhy Ave., Des Plaines, Illinois 60018
888.458.1750   Fax 847.390.2902

Ashleybooksales@Cahners.com

LANDSCAPING

Photo courtesy of:
Enviroscapes
Photo by:
David Sose

LANDSCAPING

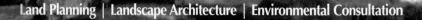

Land Planning | Landscape Architecture | Environmental Consultation

LAND
DESIGN
SOUTH

Congress Business Center
1280 N. Congress Avenue | Suite 215
West Palm Beach | Florida 33409
561.478.8501 | general@landdesignsouth.com

"I trust in *nature* *for the* stable laws of *beauty.*"

Robert Browning

Natural Selection

photo courtesy of:
Morgan Wheelock, Inc.

Landscaping is the only design area that is by nature intended to evolve over time. The philosophy behind landscape design has evolved as well. From traditional European formality to the naturalism of Prairie Style, to the simplicity and order of Far Eastern influences, your landscape should be as unique a design statement as your home itself.

More and more people are blurring the divisions between inside and outside environments, with expanses of windows, patios designed to act as "outdoor rooms," and various types of glass and screened enclosures to enjoy the outdoors whatever the weather. Landscape becomes almost an architectural element at times, creating an interplay and synthesis of indoors and outdoors.

Water gardens are growing in popularity as people learn that they are ecosystems in their own right, requiring little additional time or attention once they are established. Think of it: the soothing splash of a waterfall or babbling brook right in your own backyard!

VIEWS AND VISTAS

First you choose your views, then you build your home. To create a harmonious balance between your home and its surroundings, your architect should be invited to visit the site of your new home, and to meet with your landscape architect. The site can often serve as a catalyst, inspiring a design that responds to the uniqueness of the site. When all the team members arc included, important details (like the location of your air conditioning units) can be discussed and settled, making for the best results for you and your family.

THE LANDSCAPE BUDGET

**Basic:
10% of the cost of your home & property
In-depth:
The 10 to 25% rule of thumb applies to your landscapes too. Starting at $90,000:**
- **Finish grading**
- **Sodded lawns**
- **Foundation plantings (all around the house) including some smaller trees**
- **Walkways of pavers or stone
City Dwellers!**

GETTING BACK TO THE GARDEN

Think of the land as a canvas for a work of environmental art. Think of the landscape professional as an artist who uses nature to translate your needs and desires into a living, breathing reality. A formal English garden or seemingly artless arrangements of native plantings, a winding cobblestone walkway leading from a hand-laid brick driveway or dramatically lit oak trees above a steaming spa – these are the kinds of possibilities you can explore. When you work with a professional who is personally committed to superior work and service, designing a landscape is full of creativity, new ideas and satisfying results.

GETTING A LANDSCAPE STARTED

Selecting a landscape professional to create and maintain a distinctive landscape is one of the most important decisions you'll make as a homeowner. In making your decision, consider these questions:

• Are you landscaping a new construction home? There are critical decisions to be made early in the home building planning process that concern the landscape. Interview and work with professionals who have considerable experience in doing excellent work with new construction projects. Make them part of your team and have them meet with your architect, interior designer and builder early in the project.

• Do you want to hire a landscape architect or a landscape designer? Landscape architects have met the criteria to be registered by the state. Many hold university degrees in landscape architecture. A landscape designer generally has had training and/or experience in horticulture and landscaping and may also have a background in art.

• Do you want full service? If you want to work with one source, from design through installation to maintenance, only consider those who offer comprehensive service.

Allow time to interview at least two professionals before making a decision. Start early, especially if you plan to install a swimming pool, which should be dug the same time as the foundation of a new home.

Invite the professional to your home to acquaint him or her with your tastes and personality through observing your choices in interior design as well as the current landscape. Have a plat of survey available. Be prepared to answer questions like:

• Do you prefer a formal or informal feel? The formality of symmetrical plantings or the informal look of a natural area?

• Is there a place or feeling you'd like to recreate? Summers spent in Arizona? Your childhood home in New England?

• What colors do you like? This will impact the flowers chosen for your gardens.

• Are you a gardener? Would you like to be? If you're fond of flower, herb or vegetable gardening, your landscape professional will build the appropriate gardens.

• How will you use the space? Will children use the backyard for recreation? Will you entertain outdoors? If so, will it be during the day or at night? Do you envision a pool, spa, gazebo or tennis court?

• Are you fond of lawn statuary, fountains, or other ornamental embellishments?

• What architectural features must be considered? A wrap-around porch, large picture windows? Brick or stone exteriors?

• To what extent will you be involved in the process? Most landscape architects and designers are happy to encourage your involvement in this labor of love. There is a great deal of pleasure to be derived from expressing your personality through the land. A lifelong hobby can take root from this experience. Landscapers say their clients often join garden clubs after the completion of their project, and that many of their rehabbing projects are done for clients who are already avid gardeners.

Landscape professionals expect that you will want to see a portfolio, inquire about their styles, and their experience. You may wish to request permission to visit sites of their installed landscapes. If you have special concerns, such as environmental issues, ask if the landscape professional has any experience in such areas.

COMPUTING LANDSCAPE FEES

It's important to create a workable budget. It's easy to be caught off guard when you get a landscape proposal – it is a significant investment.

To make sure you give the outside of your home the appropriate priority status, plan to invest ten to 25 percent of the cost of a new home and property in the landscaping. Although landscape elements can be phased in year after year, expect that the majority of the cost will be incurred in the first year. Maintenance costs must also be considered. Billing practices vary among professionals and depend on the extent of the services you desire.

• Soft atmospheric lighting up to the front door and in the back yard
• Asphalt driveway
• Concrete unit pavers or stone patio, or deck
• Perimeter plantings of trees and shrubs for privacy and finished look

OUTDOOR DECOR

As Chicago area homeowners get more involved in their yards and gardens, they learn to "see" outdoor rooms and take deep pleasure in decorating them. Arbors, sculpture, tables, benches, water features, or any piece of whimsy add delightful decorating. Hedges or fences create natural partitions. The results are appealing, comfortable and richly rewarding.

359

A PARTY OF GARDENS

As gardening attracts more devotees, people are re-discovering the satisfaction of creating imaginative gardens. Some ideas: One-color gardens, Fragrance gardens, Native plant gardens, Japanese gardens.

LIGHTING YOUR LOT

"Less is more" is the best philosophy when designing an outdoor lighting system. Today's beautiful, functional fixtures are themselves worthy of admiration, but their purpose is to highlight the beauty of your home while providing safe access to your property. Well established lighting companies and specialty companies offer extensive landscape lighting product lines.

THE FINAL EVALUATION

When the landscape is installed, conduct a final, on-site evaluation. You should evaluate the finished design, find out what elements will be installed later and learn more about how the plan will evolve over time. You, the landscape designer or architect, project manager, and maintenance manager should be involved.

Some charge a flat design fee up front, some charge a one-time fee for a contract that includes everything, some charge a design fee which is waived if you select them to complete the project, and some build a design fee into the installation and/or maintenance cost.

A PROFESSIONAL DEVELOPS AN ENVIRONMENT

While you're busy imagining glorious flowers waving a welcome at you from your expertly designed tiered gardens, or snow-laden pine trees seen through your kitchen window, your landscaper will be out walking around your property, assessing practical issues like grading and drainage, the location of sewers, utility lines, and existing trees, where and when the sun hits the land, and the quality of the soil.

This important first step, the site analysis, should take place before construction has even begun, in the case of a new house. Site work helps ensure that the blueprints for your house won't make your landscape dreams impossible to achieve, and vice versa. If you've told your builder you want a breakfast nook, you'll probably get one regardless of the fact that it requires taking out a tree you value.

If you're considering installing a custom driveway or sidewalk, this early stage is the time to inform your builder. Ask your builder not to do construction outside the building envelope. You and your landscape professionals will design and build your driveway and walkways.

Expect the design process to take at least six weeks. During this time, the designer is developing a plan for the hardscape, which includes all of the man-made elements of your outdoor environment, and the many layers of softscape, which are the actual plantings. You can expect to be presented with a plan view that is workable and in harmony with your home, as well as your budget.

Hardscape elements, like irrigation systems and pavements, will be installed first, before a new house is completely finished. Softscape will go in later.

During this landscape project, you most likely have begun to appreciate the special nature of landscape and will not be surprised if your completed project does not look "complete." A landscape should be given time in the hands of nature to come to maturity: three years for perennials, five years for shrubs, and 15 years for trees.

LUXURY LIVING WITH A CUSTOM-DESIGNED POOL

The beauty and value of a custom-designed swimming pool are unmatched. A welcome design element to the landscape, a pool adds to the overall property value of the residence, and creates greater use and enjoyment of the yard. As area families spend more and more of their leisure time at home, a pool answers their dreams of living well at home.

Deciding to build a swimming pool is best done as a new home is being designed so the pool can enhance the home and landscape architecture. By integrating the pool into the overall scheme, you'll be able to establish a realistic budget. One of the biggest mistakes homeowners make when purchasing a pool is not initially getting all the features they want. It's difficult and costly to add features later.

The design process is time consuming. You may have four or more meetings with your pool professional before finalizing the design. Pool projects can be started at almost any time of year, so avoid getting caught in the busy season, spring to summer. Start getting approvals in January if you want to be enjoying your pool in the summer. The building process takes about two months, after obtaining permits. You should plan to have your pool dug at the same time as the home foundation. Pool construction is integrated with surrounding decking, so make sure your landscape architect, pool builder, or hardscape contractor is coordinating the effort.

OUTDOOR LIVING

Today's homeowners, having invested the time and resources to create a spectacular environment, are ready to "have it all" in their own backyards.

Decks, gazebos, and increasingly, screened rooms, are popular features of today's upscale homes. The extended living space perfectly suits our "cocooning" lifestyle, offering more alternatives for entertaining, relaxation, and family time at home. Many new homes tout outdoor living space as a most tantalizing feature.

Decks and terraces offer extra living space which can be utilized seven months a year and are functional enough to host almost any occasion. With thoughtful and proper design, it fulfills our dreams of an outdoor getaway spot. A multi-level deck built up and around mature trees can feel like a treehouse. A spa built into a cedar deck, hidden under a trellis, can make you believe you're in a far-off paradise.

With so many options available, building a new deck provides a unique opportunity for homeowners to give their creativity free rein.

EVERY KID'S FANTASY

In a yard with plenty of flat area: A wood construction expandable play system with: Several slides, including a spiral slide, crawl tunnels and bridges to connect fort and structures, a tic-tac-toe play panel, three swings, climbing ropes, fire pole, gymnastics equipment (trapeze, turning bar), sandbox pit, and a built in picnic table with benches. Price Tag: Around $12,000

In a smaller yard: A wood construction expandable play system with: A small fort, two swings and a single slide. Price Tag: Around $1,400

DREAM POOLS

Yours for $60,000: Custom-designed mid-sized pool with a deep end, spa, custom lighting, cleaning system, remote control functions, cover, deck.

Yours for $200,000: A custom-designed Roman style pool with bar stools, a small wading pool, elevated spa, and elaborate waterfall. Specialized lighting, built-in planters, automated hydraulic cover, top of the line automated cleaning system, all with remote control functions.

Landscaping

A TYPICAL LANDSCAPE DESIGN TIMETABLE

• One to two weeks to get the project on the boards

+

• One to two weeks to do the actual site and design work and prepare plans

+

• One week to coordinate calendars and schedule presentation meeting

+

• One to two weeks to leave the plans with client and get their feedback

+

• One week to incorporate changes, create and get approval on a final design

=

FIVE TO EIGHT WEEKS

THE TIGHT SQUEEZE. When homes get bigger, back yards get smaller. A landscape architect will be attentive to keeping all aspects of your plan in proper balance.

THINKING ABOUT OUTDOOR LIVING

An on-site meeting with a licensed contractor who is an expert in landscape building or a landscape architect is the first step in designing and building a deck, patio, or any outdoor structure. An experienced professional will guide you through the conceptualization by asking questions like these:

• Why are you building the structure? For business entertaining, family gatherings, child or teen parties, private time?

• Do you envision a secluded covered area, a wide open expanse, or both?

• Do you want a single level, or two or more levels (the best option for simultaneous activities)?

• Will it tie in with current or future plans?

• How do you want to landscape the perimeter?

• Do you want benches, railings, trellises, or other stylish options, like built-in counters with gas grills, or recessed lighting under benches or railings?

Don't let obstacles block your thinking. Your gas grill can be moved. Decks are often built around trees and can convert steep slopes into usable space.

Once a design has been settled upon, expect three to four weeks to pass before a deck or gazebo is completed. In the busy spring and summer months, it most likely will take longer. The time required to get a building permit (usually two to four weeks) must also be considered.

If you're landscaping during this time, be sure to coordinate the two projects well in advance. Building can wreak havoc on new plantings and your lawn will be stressed during construction.

DISTINCTIVE OUTDOOR SURFACES

Driveways, walkways, patios, decks, and wood terraces, hardscape features once relegated to "last minute" status, with a budget to match, are now being given the full and careful attention they deserve. A brick paver driveway can be made to blend beautifully with the color of the brick used on the house. Natural brick stairways and stoops laid by master crafters add distinctive detail and value. Custom-cut curved bluestone steps, hand selected by an experienced paving contractor, provide years of pride and pleasure.

Hardscape installation doesn't begin until your new home is nearly complete, but for your own budgeting purposes, have decisions made no later than home mid-construction phase.

To interview a paving or hardscape contractor, set up an on-site meeting so you can discuss the nature of the project and express your ideas. Be ready to answer questions like:

• Will the driveway be used by two or three cars, or more? Do you need it to be wide enough so cars can pass? Will you require extra parking? Would you like a circular driveway? A basketball court?

• Will the patio be used for entertaining? Will it be a family or adult area, or both? How much furniture will you use? Should it be accessible from a particular part of the house?

• Do you have existing or future landscaping that needs to be considered?

• Would you like to incorporate special touches, like a retaining wall, a small koi pond, or a stone archway?

If you're working with a full service landscape professional, and hardscape is part of the landscape design, be certain a hardscape expert will do the installation. A specialist's engineering expertise and product knowledge are vital to the top quality result you want.

SOURCES

Florida Chapter American Society of Landscape Architects
306 Summerwood Drive
Crawfordsville, FL 32327
fsasla@greenwork.com

WHY YOU NEED AN ARBORIST.

It's not just your kids, dogs, and the neighborhood squirrels trampling through your yard during construction. Excavation equipment, heavy trucks, and work crews can spell disaster for your trees. Call an arborist before any equipment is scheduled to arrive, and let him develop a plan that will protect the trees, or remove them if necessary.

363

Landscape
Architects

BLAKELY AND ASSOCIATES ....**(561) 627-6145**
4099 Burns Road, Palm Beach Gardens   Fax: (561) 627-5837
See Ad on Page: 372   800 Extension: 1035
Principal/Owner: Jeff Blakely, A.S.L.A.
Additional Information: An Award - Winning, third generation firm, specializing
in the creation of custom spaces for significant commercial and residential
clients.

ENVIROSCAPES, INC...**(305) 279-9914**
PO Box 160703, Miami   Fax: (305) 655-2958
See Ad on Page: 366, 367   800 Extension: 1084
Principal/Owner: Mark Drew Martin
Website: www.enviroscape.com email: design@enviroscape.com
Additional Information: Designers of high-end, high profile residential and com-
mercial landscape projects. Video tape of completed projects.

GENTILE HOLLOWAY O'MAHONEY & ASSOC, INC. ....**(561) 575-9557**
1907 Commerce Lane, Suite 101, Jupiter   Fax: (561) 575-5260
See Ad on Page: 373   800 Extension: 1108
Principal/Owner: George Gentile
Website: www.landscape-architects.com

GEOMANTIC DESIGNS INC...**(305) 665-9688**
6800 SW 81st Street, Miami   Fax: (305) 668-8426
See Ad on Page: 375   800 Extension: 1109
Principal/Owner: Robert A. Parsley III
Website: www.geomanticdesigns.com email: g_design@bellsouth.net

KURISU INTERNATIONAL ....**(561) 638-5797**
P.O. Box 480067, Del Ray Beach   Fax: (561) 638-8336
See Ad on Page: 368, 369   800 Extension: 1156
Principal/Owner: Hoichi Kurisu
Website: www.kurisu.com email: hoichi@kurisu.com

LAND DESIGN SOUTH ....**(561) 478-8501**
1280 N. Congress Ave, Suite #215, West Palm Beach   Fax: (561) 478-5012
See Ad on Page: 354, 355, 371   800 Extension: 1161
Principal/Owner: Bob Bentz
email: general@landdesignsouth.com

ROY-FISHER ASSOCIATES, INC. ....**(561) 747-3462**
381 Tequesta Drive, Tequesta   Fax: (561) 747-0281
See Ad on Page: 368, 369   800 Extension: 1227
Principal/Owner: Connie Fisher
Website: www.roy-fisher.com email: design@roy-fisher.com

STEPHEN J. TRUDNAK LANDSCAPE..**(941) 495-6464**
3461 Bonita Bay Blvd., Suite 224, Bonita Springs
See Ad on Page: 374   800 Extension: 1249
Principal/Owner: Stephen J. Trudnak

**MORGAN WHEELOCK INCORPORATED LANDSCAPE
ARCHITECTS** ....**(561) 585-8577**
444 Bunker Road, Suite 201, West Palm Beach   Fax: (561) 585-0720
See Ad on Page: 365   800 Extension: 1186
Principal/Owner: Morgan Wheelock
Website: www.morganwheelock.com email: mwheelockfl@prodigy.net

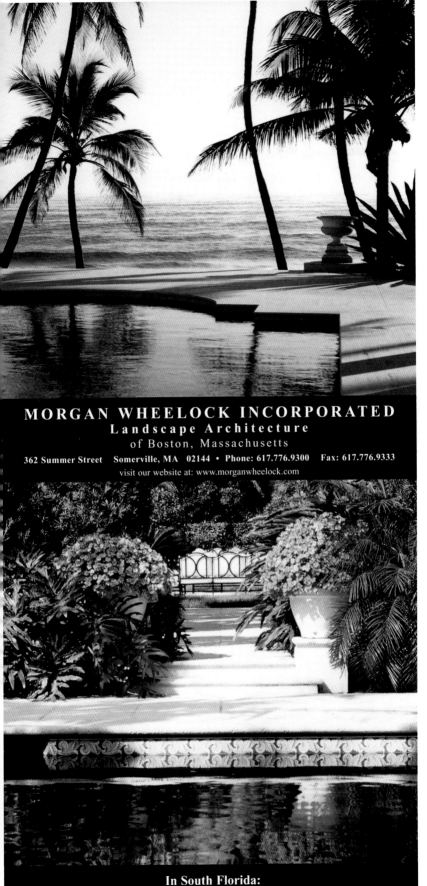

LANDSCAPE ARCHITECTURE   INTERIOR DESIGN
DESIGN MAINTENANCE   MANUALS

"Where art & the landscape become one…"

Innovation

Joie de vivre

Vision

*Najimi: a unifying balance of
life and nature*

Tropical paradises
to
Zen meditation gardens

Restore, invigorate

Inspired spaces for passionate lives.

and

PO Box 480067
Delray Beach, FL 33448

Tel: 561-638-5797
Fax: 561-638-8336
www.kurisu.com

381 Tequesta Drive
Tequesta, FL 33469

Tel: 561-747-3462
Fax: 561-747-0281
www.roy-fisher.com

Prioritizing Happiness

As we enter the millennium, we have started to reevaluate our priorities. As a nation, we are constantly striving to discover what really makes us happy. Thus far, our journey has shown us that investments and material possessions are simply tools to aid in our comfort and happiness. As we discover ourselves and hopefully become wiser, we have begun to focus our attention on our environment. A well-designed environment that addresses our visual pleasures with gardens, water-features, themes and vistas can serve to sooth our overwhelmed psyches and tired bodies.

Part of this discovery reminds us why we select exotic places in which to vacation. We are searching for visual pleasure, diversity and our unique interpretation of paradise. We can also create our own paradise at home if we choose the right professional to work with. The right professional knows when to listen, but he is also an adept communicator. Communication comes from listening to the client and answering their needs, as well as knowing the budget and being realistic about what can be achieved. And finally, the completion of a project can be the beginning of a harmonious relationship with the client.

Mark Drew Martin, *Environscapes, Inc.*

Design Excellence

Land Planning | Landscape Architecture | Environmental Consultation

BLAKELY AND ASSOCIATES
Landscape Architects and Planners, Inc.
4099 Burns Road, Palm Beach Gardens, Florida 33410
561.627.6145
Specializing in spaces reflecting the personal,
the distinctive and the memorable

Gentile
Holloway
O'Mahoney
& Associates, Inc.

Landscape Architects
Planners and
Environmental Consultants

1907 Commerce Lane
Suite 101
Jupiter, Florida 33458
561-575-9557
561-575-5260 FAX
www.landscape-architects.com

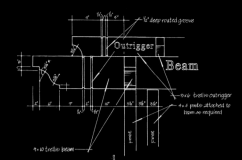

Nature By Design

STEPHEN J. TRUDNAK, P.A.

LANDSCAPE ARCHITECTURE AND LAND PLANNING

3461 Bonita Bay Boulevard • Bonita Springs, Florida 34134
(941) 495-6464

LANDSCAPE ARCHITECTURE

LANDSCAPE MAINTENANCE

LANDSCAPE CONSTRUCTION

GEOMANTIC DESIGNS
ROBERT A. PARSLEY, A.S.L.A.
305-665-9688
www.geomanticdesigns.com
6800 S.W. 81 Street, Miami, Florida 33143

Landscape
Contractors

ARMSTRONG LANDSCAPE GROUP, INC. ....**(561) 747-1689**
Palm Beach, Jupiter Island   Fax: (561) 743-5826
See Ad on Page: 384   *800 Extension:* 1023
<u>Principal/Owner:</u> Bruce Armstrong
<u>Additional Information:</u> During our 27 years in business we have earned an
excellent reputation for our Integrity in Landscape design and installation.

BLUE SKY LANDSCAPING, INC. ....**(954) 327-0777**
5870 South Davie Road, Davie   Fax: (954) 327-0888
See Ad on Page: 378, 379   *800 Extension:* 1036
<u>Principal/Owner:</u> Robert Braddy
<u>Website:</u> artscapesbybluesky.com <u>email:</u> braddy@artscapesbybluesky.com

EARTH WORKS, INC. ....**(954) 321-9222**
5020 SW 70th Avenue, Davie   Fax: (954) 321-9655
See Ad on Page: 380, 381   *800 Extension:* 1076
<u>Principal/Owner:</u> Michael Cournoyer
<u>Additional Information:</u> South Florida's largest pond and waterfall specialist.

ENVIRO-DESIGN INC....**(305) 758-8032**
252 NE 87th Street, Miami   Fax: (305) 756-1787
See Ad on Page: 385   *800 Extension:* 1082
<u>Principal/Owner:</u> John Tomczak
<u>Additional Information:</u> Creative landscapes. Creating beautiful communities.

GREEN GATE LANDSCAPE DESIGN ....**(561) 832-5393**
224 Datura Street Suite 602, West Palm Beach   Fax: (561) 832-5395
See Ad on Page: 383   *800 Extension:* 1113
<u>Principal/Owner:</u> Andrew H. Allen
<u>email:</u> specimens@msn.com

PACIFIC BEACH LANDSCAPING INC. ....**(305) 969-8978**
11304 SW 112th Circle Lane East, Miami   Fax: (305) 969-8978
See Ad on Page: 377   *800 Extension:* 1197
<u>Principal/Owner:</u> Nick Dietel

T.E.C. TUCKER ENVIRONMENTAL CONTRACTORS, INC. ......**(561) 750-5510**
7040 West Palmetto Park Road, Suite 279, Boca Raton   Fax: (561) 750-5408
See Ad on Page: 382   *800 Extension:* 1257
<u>Principal/Owner:</u> Bruce Tucker

Photo courtesy of Armstrong Landscaping

Photo Courtesy of Haus Associates, ASLA

EXTREME LANDSCAPING

LANDSCAPING ARCHITECTURE * LANDSCAPING CONSTRUCTION
WATERFALLS * JAPANESE GARDENS * TROPICAL RAINFORESTS
LANDSCAPE LIGHTING

*SPECIALIZING IN OCEANFRONT RESIDENCES REQUIRING
EXPERTISE IN SALT-TOLERANT PLANT MATERIALS.*

Pacific
BEACH INC.
LANDSCAPE DESIGN, INSTALLATION & LIGHTING

11304 SW 112th Circle Lane East * Miami, FL 33176
Tel: (305) 969-8978

Blue Sky Landscaping, Inc.

SPECIALIZING IN DESIGN
AND INSTALLATION OF
CREATIVE ENVIRONMENTS

- *Design Services*

- *Unique Landscaping*

- *Pool Construction
  & Tranformation*

- *Formal & Natural
  Water Features*

- *Spas & Lagoons*

- *Serenity Gardens & Atriums*

- *Decks & Pathways*

- *Life-like sculptures*

***CREATING MASTERPIECES
WORLDWIDE***

Blue Sky Landscaping, Inc.

5870 S. David Road, Davie, FL 33314 • Toll Free: 1-800-794-4163
Dade: 305-770-1110 • Broward: 954-327-0777 • Fax: 954-327-0888
www.artscapesbybluesky.com • braddy@artscapebybluesky.com

Earth Works, Inc.
LANDSCAPE CONTRACTORS

At **Earth Works** we...
Design your surroundings...
with you, your home and your
lifestyle in mind.
We not only consider how it
will look now...
but how it will look five years
from now.

Call us today for a FREE consultation.

BROWARD:
(954) 321-9222

STATEWIDE:
(800) 518-4523

INTERIOR/EXTERIOR   COMMERCIAL/RESIDENTIAL

5020 S. W. 70th AVENUE   DAVIE, FL 33314

Knowing how...doing it right!

Comprehensive Landscape, Irrigation & Maintenance Services.

Tucker Environmental Contractors has dedicated years of service to an ever changing South Florida lifestyle. Adapting to these changes—has allowed TEC to become a versatile and invaluable resource to numerous homeowners, developers, and municipalities.

TUCKER
ENVIRONMENTAL
CONTRACTORS, INC.

GREEN GATE

Landscape & Design
Specimen Palm Specialists
224 Datura St., #602
Harvey Building
West Palm Beach, FL 33401

Andrew H. Allen
561.832.5393
Fax 561.832.5395
Mobile 561.722.5458
E-mail SPECIMENS@MSN.COM

"I have traveled world-wide observing and studying all types of landscapes. Our company offers many types of personalized designs and we install with many years of professional experience. I have 41 years in the landscape industry and still learn something new every day."

Armstrong
Landscape Group
• Palm Beach •

Bruce Armstrong
561-747-1689

Enviro Design

Landscape Design & Contracting
252 NE 87th Street
El Portal, Florida 33138
305.758.8032
305.756.1787 (Fax)

Our services include:

- Design
- Landscape Construction
- Ponds & Waterfalls
- Fences
- Arbors
- Landscape Lighting
- Irrigation

Creating beautiful communities.
Personalized attention for your home.

Hardscape, Masonry & Water

ANTHONY'S ....**(941) 594-5847**
1406 Rail Head Blvd., Naples   Fax: (941) 594-5178
See Ad on Page: 388, 389   *800 Extension:* 1017
Principal/Owner: D. Vichot

BOSS PAVING, INC. ....**(866) 267-7728**
1130 S. Powerline Road, Suite 103, Deerfield Beach   Fax: (954) 421-1714
See Ad on Page: 387   *800 Extension:* 1041
Principal/Owner: Phillip Joseph
Website: www.bosspaving.com
Additional Information: Boss Paving specializes in interlocking brick & old Chicago pavers for driveways, pool decks, and pathways.

RUCK BROTHERS BRICK, INC...**(941) 334-8022**
2902 Warehouse Road, Fort Meyers   Fax: (941) 334-0870
See Ad on Page: 390, 391   *800 Extension:* 1230
Principal/Owner: Skip Ruck
Additional Information: Our branch yard is located at: 2700 12 Street, Sarasota, FL 34237

Photo courtesy of Roy Fisher Associates, Inc.

Shape your world.

Tile ■ **Marble** ■ **Architectural Precast**

1406 Railhead Blvd.
Naples, FL 34110
Phone: (941) 594-5847
Fax: (941) 594-5178

RUCK BROTHERS BRICK INC.

Established in 1974

2902 Warehouse Road, Fort Meyers, FL 33916
941-334-8022 • Fax 942-334-0870

2200 12th Street, Sarasota, FL 34237
941-957-3933 • Fax 941-366-1343

OVER SIX ACRES STOCKED WITH:

- Clay Brick of All Kinds
- Landscape Boulders
- Flagstones
- Landscape Aggregates
- Natural Stone Columns, Ballustrades, Fireplaces, and Fountains
- Marble and Granite Fabrication
- Glass Blocks

Swimming Pools,
Spas & Sport

CERTIFIED POOL MECHANICS/
CERTIFIED ENVIROSCAPES ....**(941) 992-9096**
  24280 S. Tamiami Trail, Bonita Springs   Fax: (941) 992-7153
  See Ad on Page: 402, 403   800 Extension: 1052
  <u>Principal/Owner:</u> S. Knight

GREENBROOK POOLS ....**(305) 661-0707**
  1550 Madruga Ave, Suite 408, Coral Gables   Fax: (305) 661-7610
  See Ad on Page: 404, 405   800 Extension: 1114
  <u>Principal/Owner:</u> Ira Grabow
  <u>Website:</u> greenbrookpools.com <u>email:</u> grnbrook@bellsouth.net
  <u>Additional Information:</u> Marathon, FL location: phone number is: (305) 289-8090

HACKL POOL CONSTRUCTION CO., INC. ....**(561) 588-7493**
  1331 Central Terrace, Lake Worth   Fax: (561) 585-7929
  See Ad on Page: 398, 399   800 Extension: 1118
  <u>Principal/Owner:</u> Doug Hackl
  <u>Additional Information:</u> Hackl Pool Construction is a third generation family
  business that has always strived for perfection. We love the challenges of
  unique water features.

HITCHING POST ....**(561) 499-0077**
  4013 W. Atlantic Avenue, Delray Beach   Fax: (561) 632-8462
  See Ad on Page: 408   800 Extension: 1123
  <u>Principal/Owner:</u> Marianne & Michael Skiera
  <u>Additional Information:</u> We sell outdoor wooden products; playsets, gazebos, arbors and
  trellise; porch swings, furniture and decorative items. Serving South Florida since 1979.

JACKSON POOLS INC. ....**(941) 495-6700**
  24017 Production Circle, Bonita Springs   Fax: (941) 495-8151
  See Ad on Page: 401   800 Extension: 1147

PLAY NATION ....**(305) 597-3800**
  7680 NW 63 Street, Miami   Fax: (305) 597-3777
  See Ad on Page: 393   800 Extension: 1208
  <u>Principal/Owner:</u> Allen Blenden
  <u>Website:</u> www.playset.com <u>email:</u> playsetmia@aol.com
  <u>Additional Information:</u> Play Nation offers the specialty of playground and recreation areas for your enjoyment.

POOL TECH OF MIAMI ....**(305) 226-7510**
  9002 SW 40th Street, Miami   Fax: (305) 226-2205
  See Ad on Page: 396, 397   800 Extension: 1210

RAINBOW PLAY SYSTEMS OF S. FLORIDA, INC. ....**(954) 455-7878**
  2516 SW 30th Avenue, Hallandale   Fax: (954) 455-7879
  See Ad on Page: 394, 395   800 Extension: 1216
  <u>Principal/Owner:</u> Terry Lott
  <u>Website:</u> www.rainbowplay.com <u>email:</u> rpsofl@aol.com

Photo courtesy of Greenbrook Pools

"We use the strongest
and most durable
lumber available
to create your
play set or
gazebo"

© 2000 Liz Ordoñez

PlayNation Play
Systems of
Miami, Inc.
7680 NW 63rd St.
Miami, FL 33166
(305) 597-3800

RAINBOW
PLAY SYSTEMS, INC.®

Fine Residential
Play Equipment

Rainbow Play Systems
of South Florida, Inc.
2516 SW 30th Avenue
Hallandale, FL 33009
800-RAINBOW • 954.455.7878 • FAX 954.455.7879
www.rainbowplay.com

9002 S.W. 40 STREET
MIAMI, FLORIDA 33165

PHONE:
(305) 226-7510
FAX:
(305) 226-2205

Hackl
POOL
CONSTRUCTION CO

The office of Thierry W. Despont, Ltd., was the designer as protected by a copyright law.

Doing it Right the First Time

"Do it right the first time." This is a very straightforward statement with no subliminal meanings. Unfortunately, when it comes to swimming pool design and construction, many homeowners fail to approach their project with this simple philosophy. However, with proper guidance and planning, this can be painlessly achieved, and the pool of your dreams can become a reality.

Before deciding upon a pool design, ask this very basic question, "What swimming pool design would best suit my needs and my lifestyle?" Certainly you know your lifestyle requirements, but you may know very little about the endless possibilities available to you regarding swimming pool design and construction.

The first step in the process of owning the wet and wonderful masterpiece you seek is to consult with a professional designer, preferably one with a reputation for fine water shape design. After performing a thorough site analysis and inventory, and by asking a series of basic questions, this individual can compile the program criteria necessary to "do it right the first time." Once the program is set, concepts are generated and presented to the client. Upon review of the basic concept, any necessary revisions, or modifications are made so that the concept is 'tweaked' to perfection.

No homeowner ever wants to face the regrettable reality of building a pool or spa that they are just not happy with — it can be expensive and frustrating. Yet, by embracing the knowledge and guidance of designers and contractors whose ultimate goal is your satisfaction, you can have the waterscape of your dreams, and, you will never second-guess the decisions you have made.

R. Grant Wilbanks

Steven Knight, *Certified Pool Mechanics, Inc.*

Jackson Pools, Inc.

Commercial ⏵ *Residential* ⏵ *Rock* ⏵ *Features*

24017 Production Circle
Bonita Springs, Florida 34135
Phone: 941-495-6700
Fax: 941-495-6151
E-mail: jcksnsales@aol.com

*Serving South Florida
and the Caribbean*

MEMBER

NATIONAL
SPA & POOL

Dreams by you...
we do the rest!!!

Aquatic & Hardscape Specialists

Design, Consultation, & Construction
24280 South Tamiami Trail
Bonita Springs, Florida 34134
Tel. (941) 992-9096
Fax (941) 992-7153

Only Perfection Will Do

Greenbrook Pools

1550 Madruga Avenue, Suite 408
Coral Gables, FL 33146
305.661.0707
Fax 305.661.7610

greenbrookpools.com

11500 Overseas Highway
Marathon, FL 33050
305.289.8090

grnbrook@bellsouth.net

Decks, Conservatories &
Architectural Elements

CAST IN STONE ....**(954) 458-7706**
970 Pembroke Road, Hallandale   Fax: (954) 458-7707
See Ad on Page: 407   800 Extension: 1047
<u>Principal/Owner:</u> Matthew Van de Mark
<u>Additional Information:</u> Specializing in customizing the interior & exterior of your home with quality period details. Bringing you the beauty & old world charm inspired by Europe.

HITCHING POST...**(561) 499-0077**
4013 W. Atlantic, Delray Beach   Fax: (561) 637-8462
See Ad on Page: 408   800 Extension: 1122
<u>Principal/Owner:</u> Marianne & Michael Skiera
<u>Additional Information:</u> We sell outdoor wooden products; playsets, gazebos, arbors and trellise; porch swings, furniture and decorative items. Serving South Florida since 1979.

Photo courtesy of The Hitching Post

- **Redwood Playsets**

- **Gazebos**

- **Arbors**

- **Weather-vanes**

- **Storage Sheds**

- **Country Furniture**

The Hitching Post

4013 West Atlantic Avenue
Delray Beach, Florida
561-499-0077

Lighting

DAN ALLEN LANDSCAPE LIGHTING ....**(941) 514-0803**
760 104th Ave N., Naples   Fax: (941) 514-0803
See Ad on Page: 413   800 Extension: 1066
<u>Principal/Owner:</u> Dan Allen

WERNER DIETEL AND ASSOCIATES ....**(305) 661-8489**
Box 562136, Miami
See Ad on Page: 411   800 Extension: 1271
<u>Principal/Owner:</u> Werner Dietel

FARREY'S LIGHTING & BATH..**(305) 947-5451**
1850 NE 146 Street, North Miami   Fax: (305) 940-0157
See Ad on Page: 410, 458, 511, 643   800 Extension: 1093
<u>Principal/Owner:</u> Bud Farrey
<u>Website:</u> www.farreys.com <u>email:</u> info@farreys.com
<u>Additional Information:</u> Largest selection of lighting, decorative hardware, plumbing, furniture and accessories. Branch location at 4101 Ponce de Leon Blvd in Coral Gables.

PALM BEACH LIGHTING & FAN CO., INC. ....**(561) 575-6878**
880 Jupiter Park Drive, Suite 12, Jupiter   Fax: (561) 744-8551
See Ad on Page: 412, 644, 645   800 Extension: 1198
<u>Principal/Owner:</u> Walter Miller

409

"A lake is the landscape's most beautiful and expressive feature. It is earth's eye, looking into which the beholder measures the depth of his own nature."

Henry David Thoreau

WERNER DIETEL AND ASSOCIATES

Landscape Architecture and Lighting

Werner Dietel, ASLA

Fla Reg. No. 76

Phone: (305) 661-8469
Fax: (305)661-6562

South Florida Landscape Architecture of unmatched experience. We blend your dreams with our talent and knowledge to create gardens of everlasting beauty.

CONSULTATIONS, HARDSCAPE (POOLS, PATIOS), IRRIGATION, PLANTING PLANS, LIGHTING AND JOB ADMINISTRATIONS.

Landscape lights are by Hanover Lantern Incorporated and are Handcrafted in Pennsylvania. They are available at Palm Beach Lighting and Fan Co.

**Palm Beach
Lighting & Fan Co.**
Professional Custom Lighting Consultants

880 Jupiter Park Drive, Suite 12
Jupiter, FL 33458

(561) 575-6878
Fax: (561) 744-8551

"IT STARTS
WITH IDEAS...
BIG OR SMALL, IN
WORDS OR PICTURES,
IN COLORS OR SHAPES....
CRYSTAL CLEAR
OR BARELY THERE.
THAT'S HOW IT STARTS."

Paul A Casper & Carolyn Nichols

The
Ashley
Group

Publishers of Fine Visual Reference for the Discerning Connoisseur
1350 Touhy Ave. • Des Plaines, Illinois 60018
888.458.1750 • FAX 847.390.2902
ashleygroup@cahners.com

DAN ALLEN
LANDSCAPE LIGHTING

DESIGN - INSTALLATION - MAINTENANCE

760 104TH AVE. NORTH
NAPLES, FLORIDA 34108

941-514-0803

Casual
Outdoor Furnishings

CASUAL ENVIRONS ....**(954) 923-2811**
DCOTA- 1855 Griffin Road, Suite B-200, Dania Beach   Fax: (954) 925-2454
See Ad on Page: 415   800 Extension: 1048
Principal/Owner: Kip Paulen
Additional Information: Fine casual furnishings for indoors and outdoors.

Photo courtesy of ResourceASIA

Cast Classics Landgrave

Casual ENVIRONS

DCOTA 1855 Griffin Road / Suite B-200 / Dania, Florida 33004

(800) 789-0825
(954) 923-2811
FAX (954) 925-2454

Finally...
South Florida's Own
Home & Design
Sourcebook

The SOUTH FLORIDA HOME BOOK, a comprehensive hands-on Design Sourcebook to building, remodeling, decorating, furnishing and landscaping a luxury home in South Florida is a "must-have" reference for the South Florida homeowner. At over 700 pages, this beautiful, full-color hard cover volume is quite simply the most complete, well-organized reference to the South Florida home industry. It covers all aspects of the process, with hundreds of listings of local home industry professionals, accompanied by hundreds of inspiring photographs. You will also find articles to assist in planning and completing a project. The SOUTH FLORIDA HOME BOOK tells you how to find what you need when you need it.

Order your copy today!

SOUTH FLORIDA
HOME
BOOK

Published by
The Ashley Group
3440 Hollywood Blvd., Suite 460 • Hollywood, Florida 33021
Toll Free 888.458.1750   Fax 847.390.2902
E-mail: ashleybooksales@cahners.com

Photo courtesy of:
Rynone Kitchen & Bath Centre Inc.

KITCHEN & BATH

Ferguson

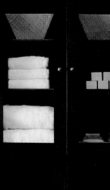

" A thing of
beauty
is a joy
forever

It's *loveliness*
increases;
it will never pass into
nothingness. "

John Keats

Form, Function... Fabulous!

421

Once designed merely for efficiency with little attention to beauty, today's kitchens and baths have become paramount to a home's comfort and style, places to nurture body and spirit.

Without a doubt, today's larger kitchen is the real family room, the heart and soul of the home. Some kitchens serve as the control center in "Smart Houses" wired with the latest technology. With the kitchen as a focal point of the home, good design means the room must be both functional and a pleasure to be in, while reflecting the "feel" of the rest of the home. From the European "unfitted" look to super-high tech, there are styles and finishes to make every taste, sophisticated to simple, feel at home in the kitchen. The bath has evolved into a truly multipurpose "cocooning" area as well. Sufficient room for exercise equipment, spacious master closets, and spa features are all in high demand, creating master suites to allow you to escape from the world. The emphasis on quality fixtures and luxury finishes remains, whatever the size of the room.

FIVE WAYS TO SPOT A TOP QUALITY KITCHEN OR BATH

1. **A feeling of timelessness:** Sophisticated solutions that blend appropriately with the home's overall architecture & smoothly incorporate new products and ideas.
2. **A hierarchy of focal points:** Visual elements designed to enhance – not compete with – each other.
3. **Superior functionality:** Rooms clearly serve the needs they were designed to meet, eliminate traffic problems and work well years after installation.
4. **Quality craftsmanship:** All elements, from cabinets, counters, and floors, to lighting, windows and furnishings, are built and installed at the highest level of quality.
5. **Attention to detail:** Thoughtful planning is evident – from the lighting scheme to the practical surfaces to the gorgeous cabinet detailing.

PLANNED TO PERFECTION
THE CUSTOM KITCHEN & BATH

In many ways, the kitchen and bath define how we live and dictate the comfort we enjoy in our everyday lives. Families continue to design their kitchens to be the heart of the home – in every way. It's the central gathering place. It's a work space. It's a command center for whole house electronic control systems. Bathrooms become more luxurious, more multi-functional. Having experienced the pleasures of pampering on vacations, in spas, beauty salons, and health clubs, sophisticated area homeowners are choosing to enjoy a high degree of luxury every day in their own homes.

Homeowners building a new home, or remodeling an existing one, demand flexible and efficient spaces, custom designed to fill their needs. Reaching that goal is more challenging than ever; as new products and technologies race to keep up with the creative design explosion, the need for talented, experienced kitchen and bath designers continues to grow.

The kitchen/bath designer will be a member of your home building team, which also includes the architect, contractor, interior designer and in new home construction, the landscape architect.

Professional kitchen and bath designers, many of whom are also degreed interior designers, possess the education and experience in space planning particular to kitchens and baths. They can deliver a functional design perfectly suited to your family, while respecting your budget and your wishes. Their understanding of ergonomics, the relationship between people and their working environments, and a familiarity with current products and applications, will be invaluable to you as you plan.

SEARCH OUT AND VALUE
DESIGN EXCELLENCE

Designing a kitchen or bath is an intimate undertaking, filled with many decisions based on personal habits and family lifestyle. Before you select the kitchen/bath professional who will lead you through the project, make a personal commitment to be an involved and interested client. Since the success of these rooms is so important to the daily lives of your family, it's a worthwhile investment of your time and energy.

Choose a designer whose work shows creativity and a good sense of planning. As in any relationship, trust and communication are the foundations for success. Are they open to your ideas, and do they offer information on how you can achieve your vision?

If you can't express your ideas freely, don't enter into a contractual relationship, no matter how much you admire his or her work. If these rooms aren't conceived to fulfill your wishes, your time and resources will be wasted.

What also is true, however, is that professional designers should be given a comfortable degree of latitude to execute your wishes as best as they know how. Accomplished designers earned their reputation by creating beautiful rooms that work, so give their ideas serious consideration for the best overall result.

Many homeowners contact a kitchen or bath designer a year before a project is scheduled to begin. Some come with a full set of complete drawings they simply want to have priced out. Some take full advantage of the designer's expertise and contract for plans drawn from scratch. And some want something in between. Be sure a designer offers the level of services you want – from 'soup to nuts' or strictly countertops and cabinetry.

Designers charge a design fee which often will be used as a deposit if you choose to hire them. If you expect very detailed sets of drawings, including floor plans, elevations, and pages of intricate detail, such as the support systems of kitchen islands, the toe kick and crown molding detail, be specific about your requirements. All contracts should be written, detailed, and reviewed by your attorney.

TURNING DREAMS INTO DESIGNS - GET YOUR NOTEBOOK OUT

The first step toward getting your ideas organized is to put them on paper. Jot down notes, tape photos into your Idea Notebook, mark pages of your Home Book. The second step is defining your lifestyle. Pay close attention to how you use the kitchen and bath. For example, if you have a four-burner stove, how often do you cook with all four burners? Do you need a cook surface with more burners, or could you get by with less, freeing up space for a special wok cooking module or more counter space? How often do you use your bathtub? Many upper-end homeowners are forgoing the tub in favor of the multi-head shower surround and using bathtub space for a dressing or exercise area or mini-kitchen. As you evaluate your lifestyle, try to answer questions like these:

THINKING ABOUT KITCHEN DESIGN

• What feeling do you want to create in the kitchen? Traditional feel of hearth and home? The clean, uncluttered lines of contemporary design?

THE LATEST APPLIANCES

There's a revolution in kitchen appliances, guaranteed to make your life simpler and more enjoyable: High performance stainless steel cook-top ranges with a commercial level of performance; Cook-tops with interchangeable cooking modules (like woks, griddles); Down draft ventilation on gas cook-tops; Convection ovens with oversize capacity, and electronic touchpad controls; Refrigeration products and systems you can put wherever you could put a cabinet or drawer; Flush-design appliances; Ultra-quiet dishwashers with lifelong stainless steel interiors; Refrigerators that accept decorative door panels and handles to match your cabinets; State-of-the-art warming drawers.

423

WHAT DESIGNERS OFFER YOU

1. Access to the newest products: With their considerable knowledge of products and solutions, your remodeling or budget limitations can be more easily addressed.
2. Ergonomic design for a custom fit: Designers consider all the measurements – not just floor plan space – but also how counter and cabinet height and depth measure up to the needs of the individual family members.
3. A safe environment: Safety is the highest priority. As kitchens and baths serve more functions, managing traffic for safety's sake becomes more crucial.
4. Orderly floor plans: When an open refrigerator door blocks the path from the kitchen to the breakfast room, or you're bumping elbows in the bathroom, poor space planning is the culprit.
5. Smart storage: Ample storage in close proximity to appropriate spaces is essential.

• Is meal preparation the main function of the kitchen? Gourmet cooks and gardeners want a different level of functionality than do homeowners who eat out often or want to be in and out of the kitchen quickly.

• How does the family use the kitchen? How will their needs change your requirements over the next ten years? (If you can't imagine the answer to this question, ask friends who are a few years ahead of you in terms of family life.)

• Do you want easy access to the backyard, dining room, garage?

• Is there a special view you want preserved or established?

• Do you want family and friends to be involved and close to the action in the kitchen?

• What appliances and amenities must be included? Do some research on this question. Warming drawers, refrigeration zones, wine coolers, ultra-quiet dishwashers that sense how dirty the dishes are, cooktops with interchangeable cooking modules, convection ovens with electronic touchpad controls, are all available.

• What are your storage needs? If you own a lot of kitchen items, have a relatively small kitchen, or want personally tailored storage space, ask your kitchen designer to take a detailed inventory of your possessions. Top quality cabinets can be customized to fit your needs. Kitchen designers, custom cabinet makers, or space organization experts can guide you. Consider custom options such as:

- Slotted storage for serving trays
- Pull-out recycling bins
- Plate racks and wine racks
- Cutlery dividers
- Angled storage drawer for spices
- Pivoting shelving systems
- Pull-out or elevator shelves for food processors, mixers, televisions or computers

• Is the kitchen also a work area or home office? Do you need a location for a computerized home management or intercom system?

THINKING ABOUT BATH DESIGN

• What look are you trying to create? Victorian, Colonial, contemporary, whimsical?

• What functions must it fill? Exercise area, sitting room, dressing or make-up area?

• Who will use the bath? Children, teens, guests, (and how many)?

• What is the traffic pattern? How do people move in and around a bathroom? (Set up your video camera in the corner one morning to get a realistic view.)

• What amenities are desired? Luxury shower systems, whirlpool tub, ceiling heat lamps, heated towel bars, spa, heated tile floors, audio and telephone systems

• What are your storage needs? Linen or clothes closets? Stereo and CD storage? Professionals will customize spaces for your needs.

• Do you want hooks for towels or bathrobes? Heated towel bars or rings?

THE SKY'S THE LIMIT

New high-end kitchen budgets can easily reach the $100,000 range, so it's important to identify your specific needs and wishes. The sky's the limit when designing and installing a luxury kitchen or bath in the 2000s, so don't get caught by surprise by the cost of high quality cabinetry, appliances and fixtures. Know what you're willing to spend and make sure your designer is aware of your budget. Projects have a way of growing along the way. If you've established a realistic budget, you have a solid way to keep the project moving forward and prioritizing your wishes. As you establish your budget, think in terms of this general breakdown of expenses:

Cabinets	40%
Appliances	15%
Faucets and Fixtures	8%
Flooring	7%
Windows	7%
Countertops	8%
Labor	15%

THE NEW KITCHEN – THE FLAVOR OF THE PAST – A TASTE OF THE FUTURE

Many of the fabulous new kitchens being built now don't look "new." The desire for a inviting, lived-in look that encourages friends and family to linger over coffee and conversation is leading homeowners to embrace European design ideas of furniture-quality cabinetry, and dedicated work zones. Consumers are investing in restaurant-quality appliances, gorgeous imported natural stone countertops and floors, and luxury options like dedicated wine coolers, stem glass holders, and plate racks. Tastes are turning to more classical, traditional detailing in cabinetry, with Georgian, Greek and Roman influence in its architecture.

"WHAT ABOUT RESALE?"

This is a question designers hear when homeowners individualize their kitchens and baths. It's only prudent to consider the practical ramifications of any significant investment, including investing in a new custom kitchen and bath.

Beautiful upscale kitchens and baths will only enhance the value of your home. Indeed, these two rooms are consistently credited with recouping much of their original cost. Research by professional builders' organizations and real estate companies bears this out year after year. The greatest return, however, is in the present, in the enjoyment of the space.

YOUR KITCHEN. COM

Technology has arrived in the kitchen. On-line grocery shopping, computers, multiple phone lines, intercom, security system & "smart house" controls. Right by the breakfast table.

425

A STEP UP

Custom counter height is an idea whose time has arrived in new and remodeled homes in South Florida. Multiple heights, appropriate to the task or the people using the particular area, are common. When one permanent height doesn't work as a solution to a problem, consider asking for a step to be built in to the toe kick panel of the cabinetry.

GET TWO DISHWASHERS

**Homeowners today are installing extra dishwashers:
1. To make clean up after a party a one-night affair.
2. To serve as a storage cabinet for that extra set of dishes.
They're also installing dishwashers at a more friendly height to eliminate unnecessary bending.**

That's not to say that homeowners no longer demand state-of-the-art features; quite the contrary. New, smart ideas play an ever more important role in a kitchen's daily life. Kitchens are often equipped as a central hub in a computer automated home, with everything from ovens and entertainment systems accessible by remote control. Home office or homework areas equipped with telephones, computers, printers, and fax machines are included in most every new project. With advances in refrigeration technology, homeowners now have separate integrated refrigerators and freezer drawers installed near the appropriate work zone – a refrigerated vegetable drawer near the sink, a freezer drawer by the microwave, dedicated refrigerators to keep grains or cooking oils at their perfect temperatures. Ultra-quiet dishwashers, instant hot water dispensers, roll-out warming drawers and versatile cooktops are just some of the products that meet the demands of today's luxury lifestyle.

THE "UN-FITTED" KITCHEN

As homeowners today snuggle deeper into their nests, kitchens that look generations old are more and more appealing. To achieve that look, designers are installing "unfitted" cabinetry, and countertops that look like well-coordinated, complementary furniture. Cabinets of different styles, different finishes, or from altogether different manufacturers are put together to create distinctive environments. Character-lending ledges and shelves hold ceramic canisters, bottle collections, cookbooks, or ultra-chic frosted stemware. Plate racks, European dish-drying racks and wicker basket drawers all add to the open, Old World feel.

Homeowners continue to include an island in their kitchen plan, not so often as a cooking zone but usually with a sink. Today's island helps define the work areas, directs people in the right directions and offers the perfect setting for socializing. Islands linking the kitchen to the breakfast or family room can be built with two or three levels for simultaneous use by a cook, a child busy with homework, and a friend stopping in for a chat and a snack. An extra microwave oven or small refrigerated space is often installed in the base of the island for ultimate convenience, especially when the kitchen is used for entertaining.

The classic "work triangle," with the refrigerator, sink and stove forming the points of an unobstructed traffic pattern, is no longer the automatic rule of thumb. The European concept of zones allows much more individualized, workable floor plans.

The commitment to quality extends to choosing the best appliances available. In addition to contributing top quality function, these kitchen workhorses dress up the kitchen with great style and design. Imported appliances are priced up to $20,000 for a European range, plus freight and installation.

THE NEW BATH – PRACTICALITY DRENCHED WITH PANACHE AND POLISH

Imagine it's a Thursday night at the end of a very busy week. You come home, have a great work out while listening to your favorite CDs over the loudspeakers in your private exercise room, then jump into an invigorating shower where multiple shower heads rejuvenate your tired muscles, and a steaming, cascading waterfall pulls all the stress from your body. You wrap yourself in a big fluffy bath sheet, toasty from the brass towel warmer as you step onto the ceramic tile floor that's been warmed by an underfloor radiant heating unit. You grab something comfortable from your lighted, walk-in closet, and then head out of your luxurious bathroom to the kitchen to help with dinner.

A master bath such as this, built in custom luxury homes fills a growing demand for private retreats replete with nurturing indulgences.

Master bathrooms are being rethought, with the emphasis shifting from form to function. These baths are still large, up to 400 square feet, but the space is organized differently. The newly defined master bath is actually an extension of the master suite, often including his and her walk-in closets, mirrored exercise space, (in remodeling projects, carved out of a spare bedroom) and separate areas for dressing, applying make-up, listening to music or making phone calls, or making coffee.

Large whirlpool tubs are often replaced with custom shower systems with built-in seats and steam capabilities, stylish alternatives like Victorian style claw-foot tubs, or smaller whirlpool tubs.

THE LUXURIOUS POWDER ROOM

A small space like a powder room can easily exude style, grace and superior quality. Stunning perfection shows in the details, like floors and counters of cultured marble, hand painted tile, or deeply colored solid surfacing, carefully placed lighting and gorgeous plumbing fixtures, and lots of distinctive accessories – decorative hardware, fancy soaps and towels and silk flowers.

Lighting is a major component of a successful bath, especially in a powder room. Consult with a lighting professional or your interior designer or bath designer, about appropriate lighting for the best results.

TAKING A TEST DRIVE

You wouldn't invest in a new car without taking it out for a test drive, so take the opportunity up front to test the individual fixtures and elements of a new kitchen or bath. Don't be hesitant to grab a magazine and climb into a bathtub, or to test sit a number of possible toilet choices or shower seats. Take your family to a showroom to evaluate counter heights and faucets. The more involved you can be in the planning, the more fun you'll have, and the better the end result will be.

427

UNIVERSAL DESIGN

One trend in the South Florida luxury home market is "Universal Design." This term, interchangeable with accessible design or barrier-free design, refers to an emphasis on designing spaces for easy access and the utmost safety for everyone. As homeowners look forward in their lives, to the possibilities of starting a family, opening their home to aging parents, and staying in place as they themselves age, universal design concepts answer some of the concerns that come with these life changes. Some universal design concepts – wider door openings, varying vanity and countertop heights, lighting at appropriate height and strength, non-slip floors, and easy to use light switches and door, drawer, or window hardware.

THE REALITY OF REMODELING

Upscale kitchen and bath renovations are most often undertaken by homeowners who decide to invest in making their home aesthetically and functionally pleasing; or those who are so attracted to a particular part of town that they buy a home fully intending to update to meet their needs. As the median age for existing area homes reaches 30+ years, nowhere is the need for renovation and the desire for updating more obvious than in these two rooms.

These dollar smart homeowners know that in cost versus value surveys, kitchen renovations and bath additions or renovations yield a very high return on the original investment. Although these homeowners rarely embark on such remodeling projects with resale in mind, knowing their investment is a wise one gives them the freedom to fully realize their dreams of the ultimate sybaritic bath or the friendliest family kitchen that accommodates them now and well into the future.

Remodeling projects present a number of challenges and limitations to be addressed by your kitchen or bath designer.

Existing plumbing, electrical and ventilation systems will define what is and is not easily accomplished. Existing plumbing may not support luxury bath features, and ventilation systems dictate where cabinetry can be installed. The integrity of the original architecture is also an important defining parameter of the project.

Take your time in the planning stages. Decide if your budget will support raising floors to change plumbing or rewiring for refrigeration drawers in the kitchen, or luxury shower system in the bath. An extra few weeks at this point can save months and thousands of extra dollars, at the other end.

As soon as your contractor calls and says he's coming out to turn off your water and utilities to begin the remodeling process, your home life will be turned upside down. If possible, find alternate living quarters, and remove or carefully cover your furniture. In a kitchen remodel, set up a makeshift kitchen in a lower level family room or guest bedroom and expect to be using it for at least three or four months. Ask your contractor to schedule the work in the least disruptive way possible. Ask for a flowchart which allows you to understand the sequence of work to be done and the relationship of one trade to another's work schedule.

CONTEXTUALISM IN THE KITCHEN AND BATH

Like any other rooms in the home, continuity and contextualism in the kitchen and bath are important to the overall appearance of the home. This is an important point to consider in a remodeling project, especially in an historic home. There often are restrictions on the materials and structural changes that may be made in historic buildings. Your kitchen or bath designer should be aware of these kinds of restrictions.

A REMODELING CONTINGENCY FUND

Kitchen and bath remodeling projects are well known for unexpected, unforeseen expenses, so put a contingency fund in your budget from the beginning. This fund can cover anything from structural changes that need to be made to meet current building codes to your sudden desire to buy (and have installed) skylights in the kitchen or a little chandelier in the bathroom.

THE BEAUTY OF TOP QUALITY SURFACES

Luxury surfaces continue to add astonishing beauty to kitchens and baths in new and remodeled homes throughout the area. Solid surfaces now are available in a ever-widening range of colors, including a granite look, with high degrees of translucence and depth. Granite and stone add a beautiful, natural look, with an abundance of choices and finishes. Tile, stainless steel, laminates, and wood – even concrete – are other possibilities. Each surface has its benefits, beyond the inherent beauty it can add to your design. Your kitchen designer will advise you on the best choices for your project, based on overall design and budget. Use the professionals showcased in these pages to find the best quality materials and craftsmanship.

WHY EUROPEAN PRODUCTS COST MORE

1. European appliances and cabinets are built for a lifetime. When European families put their homes on the market, there's no question about whether the appliances are staying or going. They're going. So are the cabinets. These products are designed and built to be purchased and kept forever; therefore, the initial cost is higher.

2. Shipping tends to be more expensive, as are service parts.

429

KEEPING IT CLEAN

The beauty of high end fixtures, hardware, appliances, flooring and countertops can blind you from the practical considerations of maintenance and upkeep. Many new products are actually easier to keep clean. But before installing deeply colored countertops, ceramic tile backsplashes, or marble floors, make sure you're aware of the time and effort required to keep them in top condition.

LEAN AND LAVISH

The trend toward flush-mounted appliances and cabinetry is here. With built-in refrigerators, ovens and cooktops, kitchens gain a sleek, space-saving look. It's rich, elegant, smart design.

THE LUXURY OF BEAUTIFUL FIXTURES

Sinks, showers, tubs, faucets and hardware, are now top contributors to the true luxury and craftsmanship that homeowners are striving for in their new kitchens and baths. Today's sophisticated homeowners can be pampered by a wide variety of upgraded, special fixtures that offer luxury without sacrificing efficiency and function. Whirlpool tubs, unique surround spray shower enclosures and glamorous custom-designed vanities are in demand. Beautiful wall mounted faucets, float glass bathroom sinks and sleek industrial designs are hallmarks of high tech fixture style. Stainless steel sinks, and faucets are enjoying immense popularity in the kitchen, along with stainless steel appliances. But choices range into many unique colors of solid surface or quartz sinks, paired with elegant, multi-featured faucets and unusual drawer and cabinet hardware crafted from any number of materials.

To avoid construction delays, order your kitchen or bath fixtures according to the schedule on the contractor's timeline for your project. Allow yourself at least one month for shopping. There is such a wide variety of possibilities that you'll want to be able to give careful consideration to them all. You'll also want to have enough time to coordinate fixture colors and styles with the other design elements of the room. Don't hesitate to "test-drive" the fixtures, particularly bathroom fixtures. If a tub isn't a comfortable fit for your body, find out before you have it installed in your home. Once you've made your decision, plan on eight weeks between order and delivery. If you're building a new home, that means placing your fixtures order about the time when the roof goes on the house.

Establish your priorities and then set a good, working budget for your kitchen and bath fixtures and hardware, keeping an eye on your builder's allowance for these elements. Focus on the installed, not the retail cost. And remember, according to value versus cost studies, kitchens and bathrooms yield returns of over 100 percent at resale. ∎

Kitchen & Bath
Designers

ARCHITECTURAL GLASS ARTS, INC....**(305) 284-8621**
7414 SW 48th Street, Miami   Fax: (305) 667-3355
See Ad on Page: 446   800 Extension: 1020
Principal/Owner: Paul Snyder
Website: www.framelessshowers.com email: www.frameless-shower.com

COLETTE DESIGN, INC. ....**(561) 367-9626**
2142-2150 N. Federal Highway, Boca Raton   Fax: (561) 367-9606
See Ad on Page: 441, 596   800 Extension: 1059
Principal/Owner: Jurgen Muller, MBA
Website: www.colettedesign.com
Additional Information: Designers and direct importers of the German brand
names.

DESIGNER KITCHEN OF S. FLORIDA ....**(305) 252-0008**
13570 SW 129 Street, Miami   Fax: (305) 252-9909
See Ad on Page: 449   800 Extension: 1072
Principal/Owner: Rita Perez
Website: www.designer-kitchens.com
Additional Information: Custom woodworking. Miami's best kept secret!

FEBAL USA ....**(954) 522-8805**
350 East Las Olas Blvd., Suite 140, Ft. Lauderdale   Fax: (954) 522-1476
See Ad on Page: 454   800 Extension: 1096

INNOVATIVE INC. ....**(561) 241-8877**
6590 West Rogers Circle #7, Boca Raton   Fax: (561) 989-8865
See Ad on Page: 452, 453, 499   800 Extension: 1132

431

continued on page **444**

Photo courtesy of Snaidero Miami

New in the

NAPLES LUMBER & SUPPLY CO., INC.

Rocky Mountain Hardware:
This unique line of door, cabinet and bath hardware compliments a broad range of architectural styles. It is handmade and sand-cast of solid bronze.

FARREY'S LIGHTING & BATH

The Hastings Bath Collection:
This innovative collection of imported Italian bath designs features pedestal sinks, mirrors and decorative hardware. Hastings' unique contemporary styles incorporate glass, chrome, steel and porcelain in delightful combinations to create the ultimate bath experience.

432

FERGUSON BATH AND KITCHEN GALLERIES

MasterShower by Kohler:
MasterShower is the ultimate showering experience, with showerheads, handshowers, and body spray options that let you customize your shower with pulsating, full flow and soft aerated sprays. Trim is available in polished brass, polished chrome and white.

ARCHITECTURAL GLASS ARTS, INC.

Shower Enclosure:

Wide-open spaces give a sense of freedom in the privacy of today's master baths. This freestanding circular shower enclosure by Architectural Glass Arts is 100% frameless! Its simple lines clearly add understated elegance and charm. Each shower enclosure is custom-designed and installed to enhance existing architecture.

433

COLETTE DESIGN

ALNO Kitchens:

The latest kitchen trends concentrate on classy and sleek design: aluminum, glass and stainless steel elements give the modern kitchen a cool look with clear lines. Bringing lifestyle enhancing functions in the design of a kitchen are what appeals to clients today. The simplicity and natural sunlight of this kitchen design keeps energy efficiency in mind. ALNO kitchens from Europe offer an impressive portfolio of design choices.

FEBAL USA

Italian Kitchen Cabinets by Febal USA:

Custom made in Italy, Febal USA brings Italian quality solutions to your kitchen living space. Innovative size drawers, superior technical design, and lasting materials define Febal USA kitchen and bathroom cabinets.

SUB-ZERO DISTRIBUTORS

Wolf Gourmet Grill:

This is a state-of-the-art grill from the top name in gourmet ranges that has an infrared rear burner and a 115-volt rotisserie for slow roasting or intense vertical heat. Like all Wolf products, this 52-inch high, 18-gauge stainless steel grill is built to commercial industry standards. It is available in four different models for your choice of 4 to 8 burners, a width of 36 inches to 48 inches, a broiling area of 450 to 950 square inches and a total BTU of 69,000 to 101,000.

ELEGANT HARDWARE

Porcher Zen Above-Counter Basin:

Let Elegant Hardware's experienced staff help transform your bath into a peaceful retreat with the Porcher Zen Above-Counter basin. Measuring 20 by 14 inches and 2 3/4 to 3 inches high, it is available in all 20 Porcher colors and the faucet can be wall- or deck-mounted. Add your own unique table or countertop. We also work with the trade.

SUB-ZERO DISTRIBUTORS

ASKO Laundry Care System:

Built to last an eternity, this unique, high-performance washer and dryer team offers superior cleaning power and reliability. Made with stainless steel inner and outer drums to resist chipping, rusting or staining, the washer features a spin cycle that's about twice as fast as other brands, and the microprocessor-controlled dryer uses precise heat and humidity sensors to prevent over drying and reduce wrinkles.

Showroom

SUB-ZERO DISTRIBUTORS

Wine Storage System:

It's like a health spa for fine wines and champagnes, with settings that range from 38 to 65 degrees, two separate temperature zones — one for storage and another for serving — and a constant 60% humidity to keep corks moist and labels dry. This innovative wine storage system comes in a variety of sizes to hold from 46 to 147 bottles and can be customized with panels and hardware to fit any décor.

ANDREA'S LAS OLAS LINENS & BATH

Peacock Chair:

Shown here with our coordinating gold finish rope and tassel bath accessories is our peacock chair, featuring gold-leaf finish, an authentic rope and tassel design and neutral gold damask jacquard upholstery.

435

SNAIDERO USA

Gioconda Kitchen:

Italian Contemporary kitchen trendsetter Snaidero launches a traditional-styled masterpiece. Gioconda, their newest kitchen, incorporates the stylish innovations of renowned Italian designer Massimo Iosa Ghini to achieve the perfect blend of traditional and contemporary design. Gioconda takes the past and makes it new and exciting for the present.

irpinia
KITCHENS

- excellence by design -

www.irpinia.com

Show Rooms

Oaktree Plaza
11585 U.S. Highway One
Suite 306
North Palm Beach, Florida 33408
Tel: (561) 627•5400
Fax (561) 627•0629

Boca Bay Plaza
7600 N. Federal Highway
Suite 103
Boca Raton, Florida 33487
Tel: (561) 998•9933
Fax: (561) 998•0990

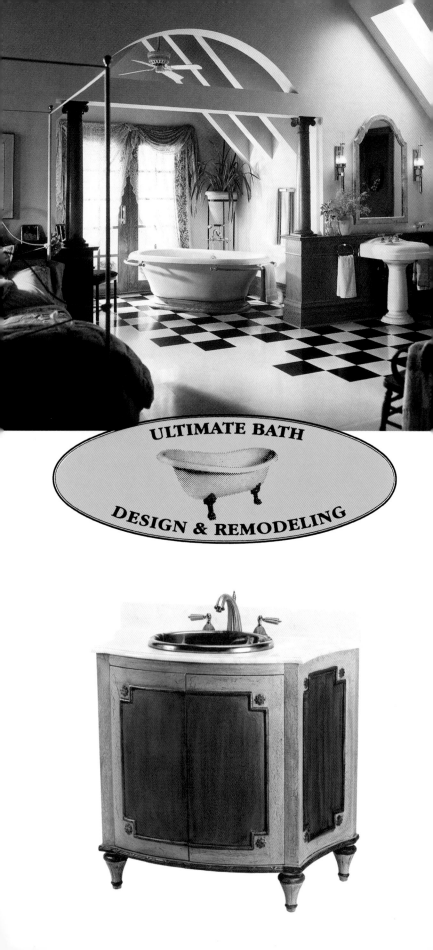

ULTIMATE BATH

DESIGN & REMODELING

1209-A South Military Trail, West Palm Beach, FL 33415
West Palm Beach 561. 357. 0801 ● Delray/Boca 561. 265. 2257
Fax: 561. 357. 5831

WE'LL HELP YOU

THROUGH THE KITCHEN

REMODELING PROCESS.

EVEN THE STAGE WHEN YOU

MIGHT PULL YOUR HAIR OUT.

Everyone goes through a tribulation or two when doing a new kitchen. Which is why as Wood-Mode design professionals we do more than create a kitchen that uniquely reflexts who you are. We go to great lengths to make the entire process, from concept to installation, go as smoothly as possible. So you're confident every step along the way.

All Wood-Mode cabinetry comes with a lifetime limited warranty.

Wood·Mode
INCORPORATED

Rynone Kitchen & Bath Centre, Inc.

7740 Byron Drive, West Palm Beach, FL 33404

PHONE 561.845.7337 FAX 561.848.7572

www.rynonekitchens.com

email rynone@gate.net

RYNONE

ALNOSOFT Birch Cognac

ALNORANCH Vanilla

colette design, inc.

direct importers of german brand names
2142-2150 North Federal Highway
Boca Raton, FL 33431
Phone 561-367-9626 Fax 561-367-9606
web site: http//www.colettedesign.com

GRUCO ROSARIO

I M A G E   I S   E

kitchens

V E R Y T H I N G

extraordinary
c u l i n a r y
e n v i r o n m e n t s

SERVING SOUTH FLORIDA SINCE 1968

KITCHEN CENTER, INC.

3968 CURTISS PARKWAY   MIAMI SPRINGS, FL 33166
TEL: 305.871.4147   FAX: 305.871.5332
E - M A I L :   K I T C H E N C @ G A T E . N E T
W E B S I T E :   W W W . K I T C H E N C E N T E R S . C O M

continued from page **431**

IRPINIA KITCHENS ....**(561) 627-5400**
   11585 US Highway One, Suite 306, North Palm Beach   Fax: (561) 627-0629
   See Ad on Page: 436, 437   *800 Extension:* 1143

KITCHEN CENTER INC...**(305) 871-4147**
   3968 Curtiss Parkway, Miami   Fax: (305) 871-5332
   See Ad on Page: 442, 443, 495   *800 Extension:* 1152
   Principal/Owner: A. Lee Paron
   Website: kitchencenter.com email: kitchenc@gate.net
   Additional Information: Serving South Florida for over 30 years! Where excellence is our middle name.

KITCHENS & BATHS BY NEAL, INC. ....**(561) 338-7171**
   3350 NW Boca Raton Blvd, Suite B22, Boca Raton   Fax: (561) 338-8788
   See Ad on Page: 448   *800 Extension:* 1153
   Principal/Owner: Neal Nowend

NAPLES LUMBER ....**(941) 643-7000**
   3828 Radio Road, Naples
   See Ad on Page: 445, 510   *800 Extension:* 1189

CHRISTOPHER PEACOCK CABINETRY ....**(561) 833-3232**
   234 South County Road, Palm Beach   Fax: (561) 833-7570
   See Ad on Page: 451   *800 Extension:* 1056
   Principal/Owner: Felton Pervier / Werner Ziegerer
   Website: www.peacockcabinetry.com
   Additional Information: Handcrafted furniture for kitchen, bedroom, bath and library.

PIEDRAS INTERNATIONAL...**(305) 666-8555**
   4760 SW 72nd Avenue, Miami   Fax: (305) 666-2113
   See Ad on Page: 455, 548, 549   *800 Extension:* 1206
   Principal/Owner: Justo Parada
   Website: www.piedras.com email: piedras@piedras.com

RYNONE KITCHEN & BATH CENTRE INC. ....**(561) 845-7337**
   7740 Byron Drive, West Palm Beach   Fax: (561) 848-8518
   See Ad on Page: 440   *800 Extension:* 1231

SNAIDERO MIAMI...**(954) 923-9860**
   2860 Pershing Street, Hollywood   Fax: (954) 923-9981
   See Ad on Page: 447   *800 Extension:* 1240

TRADITIONS CUSTOM WOODWORKING, INC. ....**(954) 946-5552**
   400 SW 12th Ave., Pompano Beach   Fax: (954) 946-5554
   See Ad on Page: 450   *800 Extension:* 1267
   Principal/Owner: Glenn Ranucci
   Additional Information: Full service custom furniture/cabinet facility with every job personally built and controlled by owner.

ULTIMATE BATH DESIGN & REMODELING ....**(561) 357-0801**
   1209- A South Military Trail, West Palm Beach
   See Ad on Page: 438, 439   *800 Extension:* 1268

TAKE A FRESH LOOK AT OUR HARDWARE.

ARCHITECTURAL GLASS ARTS INC.

Frameless Shower and Steam Enclosures
Featuring the Patent Pending
"100% Truly Frameless System"

- *Each enclosure is a work of art, custom-designed to enhance existing architecture or to serve as a focal point.*

- *The only "100% Truly Frameless System" in the industry.*

- *The strongest, safest frameless enclosures available.*

- *Virtually maintenance free — nothing to corrode or mold.*

- *No channels, tracks, clips, or caulk-filled gaps.*

- *Each enclosure is field-measured, custom-fabricated, and precisely installed by licenced, certified craftsmen.*

- *We guarantee the highest quality standards, workmanship, and service.*

Standard components include solid polished brass or chrome-plated brass double-acting hinges with spring-assist close and hold-open features, 3/8" clear tempered safety glass with custom mitered joints and clear polycarbonite seals on the doors. Bent tempered glass enclosures or floor-to-ceiling steam or free-standing enclosures can be custom-fit to existing surfaces. Options include 1/2" tempered, textured, bronze, or gray glass; custom plating; powder coat colors; and designer door pulls.

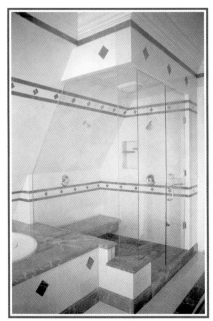

CERTIFIED
★ *Truly* ★
FRAMELESS
SYSTEM
INSTALLER

Architectural Glass Arts, Inc.
7414 SW 48 Street
Miami, Florida 33155
Phone: 305.284.8621
Fax: 305.667.3355
www.framelessshowers.com

The kitchen you want designed for the space you have

• Internationally Known • Specializing in Remodeling
• Accredited Kitchen Designers • Professional Kitchen & Bath Space Planners

*Where Design, Function &
Quality Come Together*

Kitchens & Baths By Neal, Inc.

561.338.7171 • Fax 561.338.8788
Plumtree Centre, 3350 N.W. Boca Raton Blvd. B22, Boca Raton, FL 33431

Bremtown
FINE CUSTOM CABINETRY

SOKEE

KITCHENCRAFT

ELMWOOD

Custom Woodworking.

TRADITIONS CUSTOM WOODWORKING INC.
Fine Custom Furniture and Cabinetry

400 SW 12th Ave.
Pompano Beach, FL 33069
Tel: 954-946-5552
Fax: 954-946-5554

ChristopherPeacockCabinetry

designs by

Innovative

6590 West Rogers Circle
Studio 7
Boca Raton, FL 33487
561 241.8877 tel
561 989.8865 fax
KitchenEd@mail.com

QUALITY ITALIAN KITCHENS

Fixtures & Hardware

ELEGANT HARDWARE INC. ....**(561) 994-4393**
6600 West Rogers Circle, Boca Raton   Fax: (561) 994-9693
See Ad on Page: 513   800 Extension: 1079
Principal/Owner: Genie Alonso
email: eleganthdwe@aol.com
Additional Information: Serving Boca Raton and beyond for 15 years.
Specialist in high-end bath and kitchen fixtures, hardware and accessories.

FARREY'S LIGHTING & BATH..**(305) 947-5451**
1850 NE 146 Street, North Miami   Fax: (305) 940-0157
See Ad on Page: 410, 458, 511, 643   800 Extension: 1094
Principal/Owner: Bud Farrey
Website: www.farreys.com email: info@farreys.com
Additional Information: Largest selection of lighting, decorative hardware,
plumbing, furniture and accessories. Branch location at 4101 Ponce de Leon
Blvd in Coral Gables.

FERGUSON BATH & KITCHEN GALLERY ....**(954) 726-3951**
9439 W. Commercial Blvd., Tamarac   Fax: (954) 720-1554
See Ad on Page: 418, 419, 457   800 Extension: 1099
Additional Information: High-end bath and kitchen showrooms with 6 locations
in South Florida.

MILLER'S FINE DECORATIVE HARDWARE, INC.......................**(954) 584-0200**
4244 Peters Road, Ft. Lauderdale   Fax: (954) 584-0233
See Ad on Page: 459   800 Extension: 1182
Principal/Owner: Debbie Miller
Website: millerssouth.com email: info@millerssouth.com
Additional Information: In business for 25 years. Family operated dealing in
high end plumbing, door hardware, cabinet hardware, and bath accessories.

MILLER'S FINE DECORATIVE HARDWARE, INC.......................**(561) 746-4800**
226 Center Street , Suites 3,4 & 5, Jupiter   Fax: (561) 743-0233
See Ad on Page: 459   800 Extension: 1183
Principal/Owner: Victoria Pfeil-Findley
Website: millershardware.com email: info@millershardware.com
Additional Information: A family owned and operated high-end plumbing and door
hardware business for over 10 years, with the finest selection in Palm Beach County.

Photo courtesy of Chambriar

Ferguson is polished.

Finding the right kitchen appliances can be a challenge. But not at a Ferguson Bath and Kitchen Gallery. In addition to offering the latest designs by KitchenAid®, our highly trained consultants are as polished as they come. They'll help you select from a long line of the world's most unique and innovative products to add shine to any décor. Come see Ferguson today!

FERGUSON
Bath 🐘 Kitchen Gallery 🎗FERGUSON
Products You Know. _People You Trust._℠

Proud Sponsor of
Habitat for Humanity® International

Fort Lauderdale/Tamarac, 9439 W. Commercial Boulevard, (954) 726-3951
Boca Raton, 1041 South Rogers Circle, (561) 997-8735
Miami, 7480 N.W. 48th Street, (305) 716-2766
West Palm Beach, 2636 Old Okeechobee Road, (561) 697-3434
North Miami Beach, 2983 N.E. 163rd Street, (305) 944-2474
Fort Lauderdale - East, 641 South Andrews Ave., (954) 524-3322

www.ferguson.com

KitchenAid™

Miller's Fine Decorative Hardware offers

the latest trends in fixtures and faucets, as

well as, door and cabinet hardware.

No matter the style – traditional –

contemporary – or old world –

we carry jewelry for the home

to meet every clients taste.

Miller's Fine Decorative Hardware

4244 Peters Road
Ft. Lauderdale, FL 33317
Ph. 954.584.0200
Fax. 954.584.0233
e-mail. info@millerssouth.com
www.millerssouth.com

226 Center Street, #3, 4 & 5
Jupiter, FL 33458
Ph. 561.746.4800, 561.286.4810
Fax. 561.743.0233
e-mail. mfdh@shadow.net
www.millershardware.com

Kitchen & Bath
Surfaces

PIEDRAS INTERNATIONAL..**(305) 666-8555**
   4760 SW 72nd Avenue, Miami   Fax: (305) 666-2113
   See Ad on Page: 455, 548, 549   800 Extension: 1207
   Principal/Owner: Justo Parada
   Website: www.piedras.com email: piedras@piedras.com

RAINBOW TILE OF POMPANO INC....**(954) 972-8001**
   1800 N. Powerline Road, Pompano Beach   Fax: (954) 960-1325
   See Ad on Page: 461, 542, 543   800 Extension: 1217
   Principal/Owner: Michel Sztanski
   Website: www.rainbowtile.com email: info@rainbowtile.com

"Outside of the chair,

the *teapot* is the most

ubiquitous and important

design element in

the domestic environment."

David McFaddon

SICIS

Poussin Stone Mosaic
"The Unique and Rare Mosaic"
Rug Collection "

Rainbow Tile, Paul Young:

The trend in tiles and stone is definitely moving toward old world looks. Clients are seeking materials that resemble centuries old stones, mosaics and tiles. Many of our newer items meet these demands with stone and glass mosaics taking center stage. The ability for limitless design patterns and colorcombinations has broadened the imaginations of designers, architects and homeowners. The rise in internet activity and the use of www.rainbowtile.com has helped to make the creative ideas more accessible and usable.

Appliances

BELL'S APPLIANCES BUILDERS, DIST. ....**(888) 883-3369**
1900 West 4th Avenue, Hialeah   Fax: (305) 883-3388
See Ad on Page: 468   800 Extension: 1031
email: sambellc@aol.com
Additional Information: Servicing builders, designers and architects for forty
four years.

CHAMBRAIR USA, INC ....**(305) 573-5120**
4100 NE 2nd Avenue Suite 102, Miami   Fax: (305) 573-5121
See Ad on Page: 469   800 Extension: 1053
Principal/Owner: Michael Reinhart
Website: www.chambrairusa.com email: mlr@chambrairusa.com
Additional Information: We design and build custom walk-in wine cellars - turn
key - commercial/ residential refrigeration wine rack manufacturing/contruction
services. **New location — Chambrair West, Inc: Las Vegas 702-435-3305 or
702-461-0988   (f) 702-435-3313.

IMPEL APPLIANCES GALLERY ....**(305) 887-8576**
5461 NW 72nd Avenue, Miami   Fax: (305) 885-0524
See Ad on Page: 472, 473   800 Extension: 1129
Website: www.impelamerica.com email: impelgal@bellsouth.net

OPEN HOUSE, INC. ....**(305) 594-3464**
8353 NW 36th Street, Miami   Fax: (305) 594-1771
See Ad on Page: 470, 471   800 Extension: 1195

SUB-ZERO DISTRIBUTORS, INC..**(800) 782-0013**
9777 Satellite Blvd, Suite 200, Orlando   Fax: (407) 856-1719
See Ad on Page: 463 - 467   800 Extension: 1252
Principal/Owner: James Donlin

Photo courtesy of Sub-Zero Distributors

Gourmet ranges,
cooktops,
convection ovens
and outdoor grills

Over 70 years of
experience

The connoisseur's
choice

Call for an
appointment
and experience
the difference

WOLF *Gourmet*

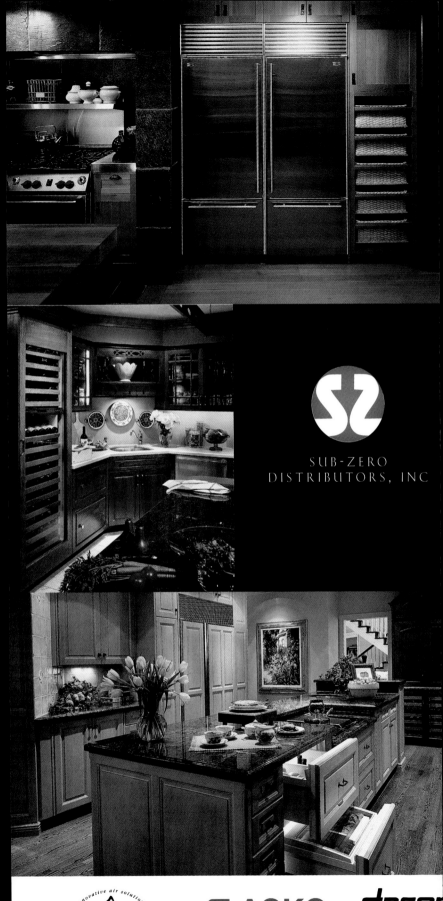

SUB-ZERO
DISTRIBUTORS, INC

"THE SIGNIFICANT
DIFFERENCE IN KITCHEN
APPLIANCES."
DESIGNER DECORATED
SHOWROOMS
HOLLYWOOD · ORLANDO
1 800 782-0031
WWW.SZDFL.COM

BELL'S APPLIANCES

1900 West 4th Avenue
Hialeah, Florida 33010
Tel: 305-883-3377
Fax: 305-883-3388
1-888-883-3369

The Wine Care System

4100 NE Second Ave., Suite 102 • Miami, Florida 33137
(305) 573-5120 (305) 799-5223 fax (305) 573-5121
e-mail: mlr@chambrairusa.com www.chambrairusa.com

We design and construct custom walk-in wine cellars.
Complete residential and commercial refrigeration.

✳ We carry all major brands. ✳
Subzero • Eurocave • Haier • Vinotheque

New location!
Chambrair West Inc. Las Vegas, Nevada (702) 435-3303

MONOGRAM

SUBZERO

MIELE

DACOR

WOLF

VIKING

FABER

KITCHEN AID

GE

IMPEL APPLIANCES GALLERY

5461 N.W. 72nd Ave. Miami, FL 33166
(305) 887-8576 • Fax: (305) 887-0524
www.impelamerica.com
Email: impelgal@bellsouth.net

The Ashley Group Luxury Home Resource Collection

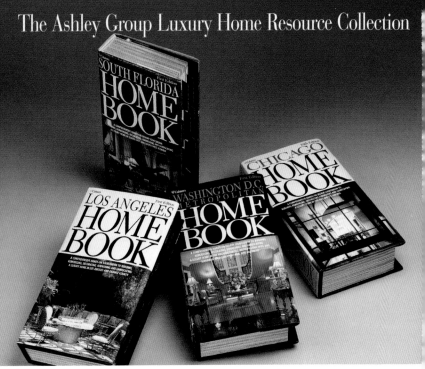

Call Toll Free at 888-458-1750

The Ashley Group is pleased to offer as your final destination when searching for home improvement and luxury resources the following Home Books in your local market: Chicago, Washington DC, South Florida and the Los Angeles area. These comprehensive, hands-on design source books to building, remodeling, decorating, furnishing, and landscaping luxury a home, is required reading for the serious and selective homeowners. With over 600 full-color, beautiful pages per market, these hard cover volumes are the most complete and well-organized reference to the home industry. The Home Books in each market, cover all aspects of the building and remodeling and design process, including listings of hundreds of industry professionals, accompanied by informative and valuable editorial discussing the most recent trends. Ordering your copy of any of the *Home Books* now can ensure that you have the blueprints to your dream home, in your hand, today.

Order your copies today and make your dreams come true!

O R D E R   F O R M

CUSTOM WOODWORKING, METALWORKING, HARDWARE & GLASS

We take pride in
our craftsmanship
and our attention
to the finest
detail

Kitchens
bookcases
bars, paneling
display cases
stairways etc...

"God is in the details."

Ludwig Mies van der Rohe

479

Elegant
Touches

F ine, handcrafted interior architectural elements are
the details that distinguish the highest quality custom-
designed and -built luxury homes and remodeling projects
from all others. They lend richness and elegance, infusing
a home with character and originality. Even an empty
room can speak volumes about the personal taste and style
of its owners with cabinetry, moldings, ceiling medallions,
chair rails, staircases, mirrors and mantels created and
installed by the best in the business. Windows, doors, and
hardware must endure the rigors of regular use,
synthesizing beauty and function into high quality design
statements made to stand the test of time. Bring your eye
for detail as you explore the finest in architectural elements
on the following pages.

Custom Woodworking Metal & Glass

PRICING A POWER LIBRARY

480

WALL TO WALL ELEGANCE

Nowhere is the commitment to elegant living through quality materials more apparent than in the selection of cabinets and millwork. Representing a significant percentage of the overall cost of a new or renovated home, sophisticated homeowners use this opportunity to declare their dedication to top quality.

Architectural millwork, made to order according to a set of architectural drawings, is becoming an increasingly popular luxury upgrade in new and remodeled homes. Creating a richly nostalgic atmosphere that reminds homeowners of the comfort and security of a grandparents' home, or the elegance of a club they've been in, the traditional styling of architectural features leads them to request drawings heavy on moldings and other fancy embellishments.

Elegant libraries, dens or sitting rooms dressed with fashionable raised panel cabinetry and special moldings are often included in the plans for new homes and remodeling projects. As a homeowner considering how and where to install millwork, ask yourself questions like these:

• How is the room used? Will a study be used for work or for solitude? Entertaining or a second office? Will it have to function as both a working office and an elegant room?

• How are the cabinets and shelves used? Books, collectibles, audio-video equipment, computer, fax or copy machines?

• What look do you want? You may want to consider "dressing" your rooms in different woods. You may like the rich look and feel of cherry paneling in your library, mahogany in the foyer, oak in a guest room and plaster in a dining room.

• Will the interior millwork choices work with the exterior architecture? A colonial home reminiscent of Mount Vernon should be filled with authentic details, like "dog-ear" corners, that create classic luxury. Using millwork inside a modern home can add interest and warmth to one or many rooms.

TIME IS OF THE ESSENCE

Hand-crafted high quality woodwork cannot be rushed. Millwork specialists encourage clients to contact them as early as possible with a clear idea of what kind of architectural statement they wish to make. The earlier you plan these details, the more options you'll have. Wainscoting with raised panels has to be coordinated with electrical outlets, window and door openings; beamed ceilings with light fixtures, and crown moldings with heating vents.

Hold a preliminary meeting before construction begins while it's early enough to incorporate innovative or special requirements into your plans. The more time you can devote to design (two to three weeks is recommended), the better your result will be. You're creating a custom millwork package that's never been designed for anyone before. Investments made on the front end are the most valuable. Ask about design fees, timelines and costs per revision. Keep your builder up to date on all of your millwork plans.

Drawings can be as detailed as you require. If you want to see the intricacies of a radius molding before you contract for it, let the millwork specialist know your requirements. Ask to see wood samples, with and without stain or paint.

Try to visit installed projects to get a firsthand feel for the quality of a specialist's work and to develop clearer ideas for your own home.

Changes made after an order is placed are costly. Therefore, if you're unsure, don't make a commitment. Add accessory moldings and other details as you see the project taking shape.

Expect a heavily laden room to take at least five to eight weeks to be delivered, about the time from the hanging of drywall to the installation of flooring. Installation takes one to three weeks, depending on the size and scope of the project.

THE ELEGANT REFINEMENT OF CUSTOM CABINETRY

Handcrafted custom cabinets are a recognizable standard of excellence which lend refinement and beauty to a home. Built in a kitchen, library, bathroom, or closet, or as a free-standing entertainment system or armoire, custom cabinets are a sophisticated signature statement.

There are no limits on the possibilities of custom cabinets. The requirements of any space, no matter how unusual, can be creatively met. The endless combinations of style and detail promise unique cabinetry to homeowners who are searching for an individual look, while the first class craftsmanship of experienced, dedicated woodworkers promises unparalleled quality.

DESIGNING HANDSOME CABINETRY

Cabinetry is a major element in your dream home, so let your imagination soar. Collect pictures of cabinets, noting the particular features you like. Cabinet makers appreciate visual examples because it's easier to interpret your desires from pictures than from words. Pictures crystallize your desires.

HOW TO RECOGNIZE CUSTOM CABINET QUALITY

1. Proper sanding which results in a smooth, beautiful finish.
2. Superior detail work, adding unexpected elegance.
3. Classic application of design features and architectural details.
4. Beautiful, functional hardware selections.
5. High quality hinges and drawer glides.
6. Superior overall functionality.

WHY YOU WANT A PROFESSIONAL DESIGNER

481

• They rely on experience to deliver you a custom product. Computer tools are great, but nothing replaces the experienced eye.
• They have established relationships with other trades, and can get top quality glass fronts for your cabinets, or granite for a bar top.
• Their design ability can save you significant dollars in installation.
• They know how to listen to their clients and help them get the results they dream of.

PRICING OF CUSTOM KITCHEN CABINETS

• **Deluxe Kitchen –Face frame style cabinets or oak, maple or pine, with raised panel doors; crown molding on upper cabinetry, decorative hardware, wood nosing (cap) around counter tops: $10,000 - $20,000**
• **Upgrade To – Shaker inset-style cabinets in cherrywood, painted finish: $20,000 additional.**

When you first meet with a cabinet maker, take your blueprints, and if possible, your builder, architect or designer. Be prepared to answer questions like:

• What is the exterior style of your home and do you want to continue that style inside?

• How will you the use the cabinets? Cutlery trays, pull-out bins? Shelves for books, CDs, computer software, collections?

• What styles and embellishments do you like? Shaker, Prairie, Country English, contemporary? Fancy moldings, wainscoting, inlaid banding? Use your Idea Notebook to communicate your preferences.

• Do you prefer particular woods? Cherry, oak, sycamore, or the more exotic ebony, Bubinga or Swiss pearwood? (Species must be selected on the basis of the finish you want.)

• Will cabinetry be visible from other rooms in the house? Must it match previously installed or selected flooring or countertops? (Take samples.)

MANAGING THE LENGTHY PROCESS OF A CUSTOM CABINET PROJECT

W ith plenty of unhurried time, you can be more creative, while allowing the woodworkers the time they need to deliver a top quality product. Take your blueprints to a cabinet maker early. Although installation occurs in the latter part of the construction, measuring usually takes place very early on.

If your project is carefully thought out, you won't be as likely to change your mind, but a contingency budget of ten to 15 percent for changes (like adding radiuses or a lacquered finish) is recommended.

Custom cabinets for a whole house, (kitchen, butler's pantry, library, master bath, and three to four additional baths) may take ten to 15 weeks depending on the details involved (heavy carving adds significant time). Cabinets for a kitchen remodeling may take two months.

THE DRAMATIC EFFECT OF EXCEPTIONAL STAIRCASES

T ake full advantage of the opportunity to upgrade your new or remodeled home with a spectacular staircase, by contacting the stairmakers early in the design phase. Their familiarity with products, standards and building codes will be invaluable to you and your architect, contractor, or interior designer.

Visit a stair showroom or workroom on your own or with your architect, interior designer or builder, during the architectural drawing phase of your project. Discuss how you can achieve what you want at a cost conscious price. Choosing a standard size radius of 24 inches, in place of a custom 25 1/2 inch radius, for example, will help control costs.

Although your imagination may know no bounds in designing a staircase, hard and fast local building codes may keep your feet on the ground. Codes are not static, and stairmakers constantly update their files on local restrictions regarding details like the rise and run of a stair, and the size and height of rails.

THE STAIR-BUILDING PROCESS

The design of your stairs should be settled in the rough framing phase of the overall building project. If you work within this time frame, the stairs will be ready for installation after the drywall is hung and primer has been applied to the walls in the stair area.

Stairs can be built out of many woods. The most popular choice is red oak, but cherry, maple, walnut and mahogany are also used. If metal railings are preferred, you'll need to contact a specialist.

A top quality stair builder will design your stairs to your specifications. Consider the views you want of the house while on the stairs, and what kind of front entrance presentation you prefer. You may want to see the stairs from a particular room. An expert also can make suggestions regarding comfort and safety, and what styles will enhance the overall architecture.

Plans which are drawn on a computer can be changed with relative ease and can be printed at full size. This is very helpful to homeowners who want to see exactly what the stairs will look like in their home. The full-size plans can be taken to the job site, and tacked to the floor to be experienced firsthand

THE POLISHED ARTISTRY OF CUSTOM GLASS AND MIRROR

A room can be transformed through the use of custom decorative glass and mirrors. Artists design intricately patterned, delicately painted glass to add light and architectural interest in all kinds of room dividers and partitions. Glass artistry can be based on any design, playing on the texture of carpet, the pattern of the brick, or repeating a fabric design. A glass block wall or floor panel can add the touch of distinction that sets a home above the others. Stained glass, usually associated with beautiful classic styling, can be designed in any style – from contemporary to art deco to traditional.

USING PLASTER DETAILING

Plaster architectural detailing and trim add a distinctive look to any home. Most often used in out of the way places, like in ceiling medallions or crown moldings, the high relief detailing is especially impressive.

PRICES OF CUSTOM STAIRS

Stairs can cost anywhere from $200 to $95,000, depending on size, materials and the complexity of design:

483

- Red Oak spiral staircase, upgraded railing: $10,000
- Red Oak circle stairs, standard railings on both sides and around upstairs landing: $13,000
- Six flights of Red Oak circle stairs stacked one atop the next, with landings at the top of each stair: $95,000
- Walnut or mahogany adds 50 percent to the overall cost.

DOOR #1, #2, OR #3?

• **Door #1 – Six panel oak door with sidelights of leaded glass: $1,700-$2,000**

• **Door #2 – Six panel oak door with lead and beveled glass: $3,000**

• **Door #3 – Oversized, all matched oak, with custom designed leaded glass and brass, sidelights, elliptical top over door: $15,000**

• **Allow $500 to $1,500 for doorknobs, hinges and other hardware.**

Top specialists, like those presented in the following pages, take great care in designing and delivering unique, top quality products. They work with top quality fabricated products, with the highest quality of beveling and edge work.

THE ARTISTIC PROCESS

Glass specialists will visit your home or building site to make recommendations and estimate costs and delivery time. Study their samples and if they have a showroom, go take a look. Perhaps you could visit an installed project. Seeing the possibilities can stimulate your imagination and open your eyes to new ideas in ways pictures simply cannot.

Allow a month to make a decision and four weeks for custom mirror work delivery, and ten to 14 weeks for decorated glass.

In order to have the glass or mirror ready for installation before the carpet is laid, decisions must be made during the framing or rough construction phase in a new home or remodeling job. Mirrored walls are installed as painting is being completed, so touch-ups can be done while painters are still on site.

Expect to pay a 50 percent deposit on any order after seeing a series of renderings and approving a final choice. Delivery generally is included in the price.

THE DRAMATIC EFFECT OF CUSTOM WINDOWS AND DOORS

Just as we're naturally drawn to establish eye contact with each other, our attention is naturally drawn to the "eyes' of a home, the windows, skylights and glass doors.

These very important structural features, when expertly planned and designed, add personality and distinction to your interior while complementing the exterior architectural style of your home.

After lumber, windows are the most expensive part of a home. Take the time to investigate the various features and qualities of windows, skylights and glass doors. Visit a specialty store offering top of the line products and service and take advantage of their awareness of current products as well as their accumulated knowledge.

Visit a showroom with your designer, builder or architect. Because of the rapidly changing requirements of local building codes, it's difficult for them to keep current on what can be installed in your municipality. In addition, the dizzying pace of energy efficiency improvements over the past five years can easily outrun the knowledge of everyone but the window specialist. Interior designers can help you nderstand proper placement and scale in relation to furnishings and room use.

As you define your needs ask questions about alternatives or options, such as energy efficiency, ease of maintenance, appropriate styles to suit the exterior architecture, and interior.

Top quality windows offer high energy efficiency, the best woodwork and hardware, and comprehensive service and guarantees (which should not be pro-rated). Good service agreements cover everything, including the locks.

Every home of distinction deserves an entry that exudes a warm welcome and a strong sense of homecoming. When we think of "coming home," we envision an entry door first, the strong, welcoming look of it, a first impression of the home behind it. To get the best quality door, contact a door or millwork specialist with a reputation for delivering top quality products. They can educate you on functionality, and wood and size choices and availability, as well as appropriate style. Doors are also made of steel or fiberglass, but wood offers the most flexibility for custom design.

Since doors are a permanent part of your architecture, carefully shop for the design that best reflects the special character of your home. Allow two to three weeks for delivery of a simple door and eight to 12 weeks if you're choosing a fancy front door. Doors are installed during the same phase as windows, before insulation and drywall.

FABULOUS HARDWARE ADDS DESIGN FLAIR

Door and cabinet hardware, towel bars and accessories add style and substance to interiors. Little things truly do make the difference – by paying attention to the selection of top quality hardware in long-lasting, great-looking finishes, you help define your signature style and commitment to quality in a custom home. There are hundreds of possibilities, so when you visit a specialty showroom, ask the sales staff for their guidance. They can direct you towards the products that will complement your established design style and help you stay within the limits of your budget. When a rim lock for the front door can easily cost $500, and knobs can be $10 each, the advice of a knowledgeable expert is priceless.

Most products are readily available in a short time frame, with the exception of door and cabinetry hardware. Allow eight weeks for your door hardware, and three to four weeks for cabinetry selections. Since accessory hardware is usually in stock, changing cabinet knobs, hooks and towel bars is a quick and fun way to get a new look. ∎

LUXURY GLASS & MIRROR

• **Mirrored Exercise Room:** Floor to ceiling, wall to wall mirrors, on two or three walls. Allow at least a month, from initial measuring, to squaring off & balancing walls, to installation. Price for polished mirror starts around $9 per square foot. Cut-outs for vents outlets cost extra.
• **Custom Shower Doors:** Frameless bent, or curved shower doors are popular luxury upgrades. Made of clear or sandblasted heavy glass–1/2" to 3/8" thick. $2,000 and up.
• **Stained Glass Room Divider:** Contemporary, clear on clear design, with a hint of color. Approximately 4' X 6', inset into a wall. $4,500.
• **Glass Dining Table:** Custom designed with bevel edge, 48" X 96" with two glass bases. $1,200.

THREE TIPS FOR DOOR HARDWARE

1. Use three hinges to a door–it keeps the door straight.
2. Match all hardware–hinges, knobs, handles, all in the same finish. use levers or knobs–don't mix.
3. Use a finish that will last.

Custom Woodworking, Metal, Hardware & Glass

Millwork

ARREDO ITALIANO ....**(305) 445-7780**
4018 Aurora Street, Coral Gables — Fax: (305) 445-7780
See Ad on Page: 490 — 800 Extension: 1024
Principal/Owner: Enrico Cavaciocchi
Website: www.arredoitaliano.com email: arredoitaliano@worldnet.att.net
Additional Information: Fifty years old company in Italy - for the first time in U.S.A. Our philosophy: door as furniture just something to open and close.

F.P.G. WHOLESALE INC ....**(305) 266-2296**
7190 Coral Way, Miami — Fax: (305) 261-6540
See Ad on Page: 487, 512 — 800 Extension: 1089
Principal/Owner: Gustavo Eguaras
Website: fpghomedesign.com email: fpgmiami@aol.com
Additional Information: Specializing in fancy doors, hardware and kitchen cabinets (Condoor , Entergy, Baldwin, Schlage, Kwikset, Omnia, Emteck, Bouvet).

HANSEN GROUP, LC ....**(954) 929-2121**
DCOTA 1855 Griffin Road, Suite C336, Dania Beach — Fax: (954) 929-2109
See Ad on Page: 488, 515 — 800 Extension: 1120
Principal/Owner: Denise S. Reyna
Additional Information: German manufacturers of specialty woodwork whose focus is on handcrafted built-ins and custom made doors and windows in solid mahogany.

RENAISSANCE PLASTER USA LLC......................**(941) 591-8002**
6166 Taylor Road #102, Naples — Fax: (941) 591-2283
See Ad on Page: 491 — 800 Extension: 1221
Principal/Owner: Nicholas Evans
Website: www.renaissanceplaster.com email: info@renaissanceplaster.com

S & P ARCHITECTURAL PRODUCTS ....**(954) 968-3701**
1721 Blount Road, Pompano Beach — Fax: (954) 968-9953
See Ad on Page: 493 — 800 Extension: 1233

SUN SALES & INSTALLATION, INC.......................**(941) 261-6530**
3754 Arnold Ave, Naples — Fax: (941) 261-2538
See Ad on Page: 489 — 800 Extension: 1254
Principal/Owner: Ronald Sundblad

ZELUCK INC. ....**(800) 233-0101**
5300 Kings Highway, Brooklyn, NY — Fax: (718) 209-8273
See Ad on Page: 492, 730, 731 — 800 Extension: 1277
Principal/Owner: Roy Zeluck

486

Photo courtesy of F.P.G. Wholesale Inc

F.P.G.
WHOLESALE INC.

7190 Coral Way, Miami, Florida 33155
305.266.2296
Fax 305.261.6540

HANSEN

U.S.A. ■ GERMANY

MILLWORK ■ WINDOWS ■ DOORS

US SALES OFFICE

DCOTA
1855 Griffin Road C336
Dania Beach, FL 33020

Phone: (954) 929-2121
Fax: (954) 929-2109

HEADQUARTERS ■ FACTORY

Cologne Germany

SUN

4135 15th Ave SW • Naples, FL 34116
tel: (941) 354-3112 • fax: (941) 455-4660

ARREDO ITALIANO

Italian Interior Doors & Architectural Glass

A unique collection of interior doors and
architectural glass created by the most famous
italian designers. For the first time available in the U.S.

Show room: 4018 Aurora Street
Coral Gables, FL 33146
ph/fax 305 - 445 7780
www.arredoitaliano.com

Renaissance Plaster USA, LLC
Authentic Plaster Mouldings and Architectural Trim
Specialists in Bespoke Ceilings and other Plasterwork designs

6166 Taylor Road, Naples FL 34119
Tel: 941 591 8002 Fax: 941 591 2283
Email: info@renaissanceplaster.com
Website: renaissanceplaster.com

When we sent our new Weather Shield Legacy Series™ tilt and casement windows to the test lab, we expected them to test well. And they did. Our casements withstood 65 mph driving rain and 205 mph winds – well beyond the hurricane standards for most residential applications. High Performance windows and doors in the South Florida market are serious business and Weather Shield is the market leader that offers a complete line of Dade County Impact approved products with a rainbow of exterior colors complimented by pine, oak, maple, cherry, and mahogany interiors. Weather Shield products are not only tough but also beautiful. So punishing weather isn't a problem. If Legacy Series Windows can stand that kind of abuse in a test lab, just imagine how they'll perform in the home you build.

Weather Shield
Windows & Doors

There's more to see in a Weather Shield *window.*™

S & P ARCHITECTURAL PRODUCTS, INC.

WINDOWS & DOORS • RESIDENTIAL & COMMERICIAL

1721 Blount Road • Pompano Beach, FL 33069
Main Office (954) 968-3701 • Fax (954) 968-9953
Toll Free in Florida (800) 992-8959 • Miami Area (305) 266-2635

Custom Cabinets

HP DESIGN INC...**(954) 609-5866**
   3845 Pembroke Road, Bay 1-R, Hollywood   Fax: (954) 349-5438
   See Ad on Page: 497   800 Extension: 1127
   <u>Principal/Owner:</u> Helmut Paffrath

INNOVATIVE INC. ....**(561) 241-8877**
   6590 West Rogers Circle #7, Boca Raton   Fax: (561) 989-8865
   See Ad on Page: 452, 453, 499   800 Extension: 1133

INTERIOR DESIGN CENTER AND MFG ....**(954) 725-6480**
   1100 S. Powerline Road, Deerfield Beach   Fax: (954) 725-6485
   See Ad on Page: 348, 500   800 Extension: 1136
   <u>Principal/Owner:</u> Rami Argov
   <u>Website:</u> www.idcmfg.com <u>email:</u> idcmfg@earthlink.net

KITCHEN CENTER INC....**(305) 871-4147**
   3968 Curtiss Parkway, Miami   Fax: (305) 871-5332
   See Ad on Page: 442, 443, 495   800 Extension: 1151
   <u>Principal/Owner:</u> A. Lee Paron
   <u>Website:</u> kitchencenter.com <u>email:</u> kitchenc@gate.net
   <u>Additional Information:</u> Serving South Florida for over 30 years! Where excellence is our middle name.

PRESTIGE INTERIORS ....**(800) 206-6289**
   1951 Whitfield Pakr Drive, Sarasota   Fax: (941) 755-2141
   See Ad on Page: 476, 477, 501   800 Extension: 1212
   <u>email:</u> enwus@gte.net

QUIET TIME INC...**(561) 274-3950**
   240 SE Second Avenue, Delray Beach
   See Ad on Page: 498   800 Extension: 1213
   <u>Principal/Owner:</u> Stuart Surfer

TECNO WOOD ....**(954) 971-4141**
   4100 N. Powerline Road, Suite J3, Pompano Beach   Fax: (954) 971-4144
   See Ad on Page: 496   800 Extension: 1259
   <u>Principal/Owner:</u> Roger Ahmadi
   <u>Website:</u> www.tecnowood.com <u>email:</u> sales@tecnowood.com
   <u>Additional Information:</u> Tecno Wood specializes in creating fine custom cabinetry, including childrens rooms, home offices, wall units, closets, libraries, kitchens, and bathrooms. Call 1-877-WOOD-DESIGN.

TRADITIONS CUSTOM WOODWORKING, INC. ....**(954) 946-5552**
   400 SW 12th Ave., Pompano Beach   Fax: (954) 946-5554
   See Ad on Page: 450   800 Extension: 1267
   <u>Principal/Owner:</u> Glenn Ranucci
   <u>Additional Information:</u> Full service custom furniture/cabinet facility with every job personally built and controlled by owner.

Photo courtesy of Kitchen Center Inc

WE'LL HELP YOU THROUGH THE KITCHEN REMODELING PROCESS. EVEN THE STAGE WHEN YOU MIGHT PULL YOUR HAIR OUT.

Everyone goes through a tribulation or two when doing a new kitchen. Which is why as Wood-Mode design professionals we do more than create a kitchen that uniquely reflects who you are. We go to great lengths to make the entire process, from concept to installation, go as smoothly as possible. So you're confident every step along the way.

Wood·Mode®
FINE CUSTOM CABINETRY

Kitchen Center Inc.

3968 Curtiss Parkway • Miami, FL 33166 • Tel: 305-871-4147 • Fax: 305-871-5332
E-mail: Kitchenc@gate.net • www.kitchencenters.com

Just Imagine What If...

Designers and Manufacturers of
Wall Units, Entertainment Centers, Window Treatments,
Area Rugs, Upholstery, Art and more.

Family business owned and operated since 1985.
A Professional Team of designers to serve you at our 30,000-square-foot showroom and factory.

INTERIOR DESIGN CENTER
& MANUFACTURER

1100 SOUTH POWERLINE ROAD • DEERFIELD BEACH, FLORIDA 33442
954.725.6480 • FAX 954.725.6485 • E-MAIL: idcmfg@earthlink.net • WEBSITE: www.idcmfg.com

"IMAGINATION IS MORE IMPORTANT THAN KNOWLEDGE. "

Albert Einstein

Custom wood interiors
- yachts
- residential
- commercial

PRESTIGE INTERIORS

Sarasota • Fort Lauderdale
1-800-205-6289

Decorative
Glass & Mirrors

AMCOA GLASS CO...**(305) 751-2202**
    6454 NE 4th Ave., Miami   Fax: (305) 751-0672
    See Ad on Page: 504, 505   *800 Extension:* 1013
    <u>Principal/Owner:</u> Ron Katz
    <u>Website:</u> www.amcoa.com <u>email:</u> glass@amcoa.com
    <u>Additional Information:</u> The Southeast's oldest and largest manufacturer of 3/4"
    and 1" glass table tops.

ART GLASS ENVIRONMENTS, INC. ....**(561) 391-7310**
    1865 NW Boca Raton Blvd., Boca Raton   Fax: (561) 391-8447
    See Ad on Page: 506, 507   *800 Extension:* 1025
    <u>Principal/Owner:</u> Bill Klug
    <u>Website:</u> artglassage.com <u>email:</u> kluglass@bellsouth.net
    <u>Additional Information:</u> A.G.E., Inc. has been creating masterpieces in decorative architectural glass since 1983, from old world period projects to contemporary "eye openers".

OCEAN TRADING INTERNATIONAL CORP. ....**(305) 256-3190**
    12941 SW 133rd Court, Miami   Fax: (305) 256-3191
    See Ad on Page: 503   *800 Extension:* 1193

502

Photo courtesy of Art Glass Environments

What is Artistry in Glass?

RESIDENTIAL
COMMERCIAL
PUBLIC BUILDINGS
ARCHITECTURE
DESIGN
INTERIOR DECORATION
CHURCHES

PAINTED GLASS
GLASS CARVING
FUSED
CUT BRILLIANT
STAINED GLASS
SANDBLAST

SCULPTURES
LAMPS
FURNITURE
CEILINGS
BOOK ENDS
FOLDING SCREENS
BEVEL GLASS

DOORS
WINDOWS
HOME DECOR
MIRRORS
DIVIDERS
HIGH QUALITY SHOWER
DOORS
KITCHEN & CABINETS
TABLE TOPS

GLASS STAIRS
AWARDS
SIGNS
LOGOS
CONSULTING

Come visit Artistry in Glass to experience our entire collection of art in glass, accessories, and the knowledge of our informed staff. Let Atistry's timeless design be a part of your lifestyle, today and tomorrow.

 Artistry in Glass
by
OCEAN TRADING INT'L CORP

12941 S.W. 133rd Court, Miami, FL 33186
Phone: 305.256.3190 Fax: 305.256.3191
oceanvidro@cs.com
www.artsinglass.com

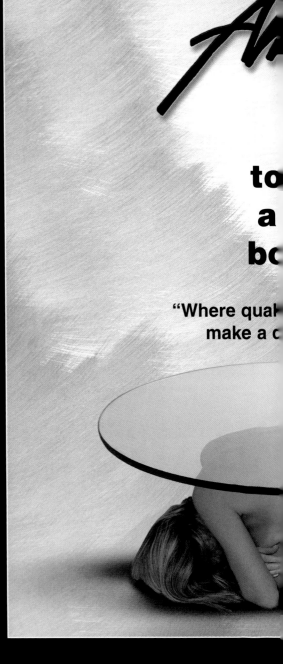

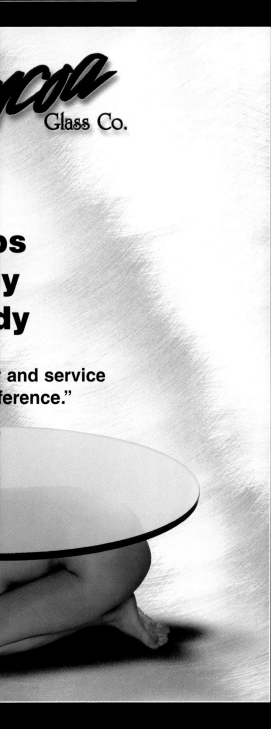

Glass Co.

...ps
...y
...dy

...r and service
...ference."

...est and largest
...glass table tops

• Miami, Florida 33138
1-800-327-7514
• www.amcoa.com

ART • GLASS • ENVIRONMENTS • Inc.

1865 NW BOCA RATON BOULEVARD, BOCA RATON, FLORIDA 33432 • website: www.artglassAGE.com

email: kluglass@bellsouth.net

(561) 391-7310 • FAX: (561) 391-8447

Photography by Photographers 2/ Jonathan Rachline

Hardware

CELLINI ARTISTIC HARDWARE CORP. ....**(561) 337-4855**
1694 SE Village Green Drive, Port St. Lucie Fax: (561) 337-3856
See Ad on Page: 509 *800 Extension:* 1051
Principal/Owner: Bill Blew
Additional Information: Unique custom wrought iron and hand-chased brass
hardware for doors, cabinets and furniture.

CELLINI ARTISTIC HARDWARE CORP. ....**(954) 920-3543**
2470 Griffin Road, Fort Lauderdale Fax: (954) 920-6949
See Ad on Page: 509 *800 Extension:* 1050
Principal/Owner: Bill Blew
Additional Information: Unique custom wrought iron and hand-chased brass
hardware for doors, cabinets and furniture.

ELEGANT HARDWARE INC. ....**(561) 994-4393**
6600 West Rogers Circle, Boca Raton Fax: (561) 994-9693
See Ad on Page: 513 *800 Extension:* 1079
Principal/Owner: Genie Alonso
email: eleganthdwe@aol.com
Additional Information: Serving Boca Raton and beyond for 15 years.
Specialist in high-end bath and kitchen fixtures, hardware and accessories.

F.P.G. WHOLESALE INC. ....**(305) 266-2296**
7190 Coral Way, Miami Fax: (305) 261-6540
See Ad on Page: 487, 512 *800 Extension:* 1090
Principal/Owner: Gustavo Eguaras
Website: www.fpghomedesign.com email: fpgmiami@aol.com
Additional Information: Specializing in fancy doors, hardware and kitchen cabi-
nets. (Condoor, Entergy, Baldwin, Schlage, Kwikset, Omnia, Emtek, Bouvet)

FARREY'S LIGHTING & BATH......................................**(305) 947-5451**
1850 NE 146 Street, North Miami Fax: (305) 940-0157
See Ad on Page: 410, 458, 511, 643 *800 Extension:* 1095
Principal/Owner: Bud Farrey
Website: www.farreys.com email: info@farreys.com
Additional Information: Largest selection of lighting, decorative hardware,
plumbing, furniture and accessories. Branch location at 4101 Ponce de Leon
Blvd in Coral Gables.

NAPLES LUMBER ....**(941) 643-7000**
3828 Radio Road, Naples
See Ad on Page: 445, 510 *800 Extension:* 1190

508

Photo courtesy of Miller's Fine Decorative Hardware

TAKE A NEW LOOK AT OUR KITCHENS.

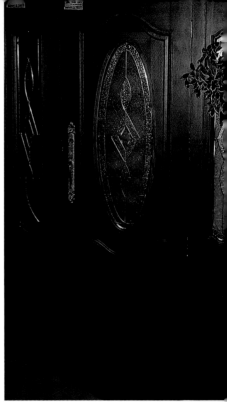

F.P.G.
WHOLESALE INC.

7190 Coral Way, Miami, Florida 33155
305.266.2296
Fax 305.261.6540

ELEGANT

From Boca With Style

HARDWARE

Windows
& Doors

ARREDO ITALIANO ....**(305) 445-7780**
4018 Aurora Street, Coral Gables · Fax: (305) 445-7780
See Ad on Page: 490 · 800 Extension: 1024
Principal/Owner: Enrico Cavaciocchi
Website: www.arredoitaliano.com email: arredoitaliano@worldnet.att.net
Additional Information: Fifty years old company in Italy - for the first time in
U.S.A. Our philosophy: door as furniture just something to open and close.

HANSEN GROUP, LC ....**(954) 929-2121**
DCOTA 1855 Griffin Road, Suite C336, Dania Beach · Fax: (954) 929-2109
See Ad on Page: 488, 515 · 800 Extension: 1120
Principal/Owner: Denise S. Reyna
Additional Information: German manufacturers of specialty woodwork whose
focus is on handcrafted built-ins and custom made doors and windows in solid
mahogany,

S & P ARCHITECTURAL PRODUCTS ....**(954) 968-3701**
1721 Blount Road, Pompano Beach · Fax: (954) 968-9953
See Ad on Page: 493 · 800 Extension: 1233

ZELUCK INC. ....**(800) 233-0101**
5300 Kings Highway, Brooklyn, NY · Fax: (718) 209-8273
See Ad on Page: 492, 730, 731 · 800 Extension: 1277
Principal/Owner: Roy Zeluck

Photo courtesy of Arredo Italiano

Surviving the Hurricane

Though it has been almost a decade since Hurricane Andrew struck South Florida in August 1992, the event ranks among the most destructive and costly natural disasters in U.S. history. As a result, there has been an increased impetus to establish new building requirements for coastal areas to address the concern of high-impact winds and the damage they can cause.

Construction experts agree that window protection represents the first line of defense in protecting a building from hurricane-force winds. On average, one to three hurricanes approach the U.S. coast each year.

Along the Hurricane Coast, commercial and residential builders need products that can maintain a building's protective "envelope." For these builders, laminated impact-resistant safety glass products are clearly a required option. To protect a building or residence, windows and doors must resist penetration by debris, and remain in place and intact throughout the storm. Tests show that specially designed laminated glass products pass windborne debris impact tests, and, when broken, the glass fragments remain integral, adhering to the plastic interlayer, thus helping to preserve the integrity of the building envelope.

To design windows that comply with Dade County, the Southern Building Code Congress International (SBCCI), and other hurricane impact requirements, many factors should be taken into consideration. These factors include the size, type, and thickness of the glass, the plastic vinyl interlayer, the design of the frame, the method by which the window or door is anchored, and the method of attaching the glass to the window frame. All of these factors must be taken into consideration to meet specifications required by future state and local municipalities. Be informed and select the proper products for your future dwelling, with safety, security and satisfaction as your goal.

John Randall, *S & P Architectural Products*

FLOORING

COUNTERTOPS

Show in Florida.
else on Earth.

"Things are *pretty*, *graceful*, rich, *elegant*, handsome, but, until they speak *to the imagination*, not yet *beautiful*."

Ralph Waldo Emerson

521

Tops 'N Bottoms

The solid surfaces of a home, the floors and countertops, are show-stopping design elements that add beauty and distinction to each room. From exquisite marble slabs, richly polished woods, and luxurious area and wall-to-wall carpets, to fabulous granites, seamless, durable solid surfaces and highly unique ceramic tiles, the possibilities for color, style and combination are unlimited.

South Florida area custom homeowners are well traveled and sophisticated in their tastes and preferences, as shop owners and craftsmen who cater to this clientele will attest. Their strong desire for quality and beauty, and their interest in understanding the benefits and unique beauty of each choice, make for educated and appropriate choices that add value and personality to the home.

The following pages will introduce you to some of the most distinguished suppliers and artisans working with these products in the South Florida area.

ORIENTAL RUGS

The decision to invest in an Oriental rug should be made carefully. Buying a rug purely for its decorative beauty and buying for investment purposes require two different approaches. If you're buying for aesthetics, put beauty first and condition second. Certain colors and patterns are more significant than others; a reputable dealer can guide you. Check for quality by looking at these features:

• **Regularity of knotting.**
• **Color clarity.**
• **Rug lies evenly on the floor.**
• **Back is free of damage or repair marks.**

522

FLOOR COVERINGS OF DISTINCTION...CARPETS & RUGS

From a room-sized French Aubusson rug to a dense wool carpet with inset borders, "soft" floor treatments are used in area homes to make a signature statement, or blend quietly into the background to let other art and furnishings grab the attention.

Selecting carpeting and rugs requires research, a dedicated search, and the guidance of a well established design plan. Because the floor covers the width and depth of any room, it's very important that your choices are made in concert with other design decisions–from furniture to art, from window treatments to lighting.

Your interior designer or a representative at any of the fine retail stores featured in the following pages is qualified to educate you as you make your selections.

Rug and carpet dealers who cater to a clientele that demands a high level of personal service (from advice to installation and maintenance) and top quality products, are themselves dedicated to only the best in terms of service and selection. Their accumulated knowledge will be a most important benefit as you select the right carpet for your home.

THE WORLD AT YOUR FEET

Today's profusion of various fibers, colors, patterns, textures, and weights make carpet selection exciting and challenging. Your search won't be overwhelming if you realize the requirements of your own home and work within those boundaries.

Begin where the carpet will eventually end up – that is, in your home. Consider how a carpet will function by answering questions like these:

• What is the traffic pattern? High traffic areas, like stairs and halls, require a stain resistant dense or low level loop carpet for top durability in a color or pattern that won't show wear. Your choices for a bedroom, where traffic is minimal, will include lighter colors in deeper plush or velvets.

• How will it fit with existing or developing decors? Do you need a neutral for an unobtrusive background, or an eye-catching tone-on-tone texture that's a work of art in itself?

• Will it flow nicely into adjoining rooms? Carpet or other flooring treatments in the surrounding rooms need to be considered.

• What needs, other than decorative, must the carpet fill? Do you need to keep a room warm, muffle sound, protect a natural wood floor?

• How is the room used? Do teenagers and toddlers carry snacks into the family room? Is a finished basement used for ping-pong as well as a home office?

THE ARTISTRY OF RUGS

Nothing compares to the artful elegance of a carefully selected area rug placed on a hard surface. Through pattern, design, texture and color, rug designers create a work of art that is truly enduring. If you have hardwood, marble or natural stone floors, an area rug will only enhance their natural beauty. From Chinese silk, to colorful Pakistanis, to rare Caucasian antiques, the possibilities are as varied as the world is wide.

If you're creating a new interior, it's best to start with rug selection. First, it's harder to find the 'right' rug than it is to find the 'right' fabric or paint: there are simply fewer fine rugs than there are fabrics, patterns or colors. However, don't make a final commitment on a rug until you know it will work with the overall design. Second, rugs usually outlive other furnishings. Homeowners like to hang on to their rugs when they move, and keep them as family heirlooms.

In recent years, many rug clients have been enjoying a bounty of beautiful, well-made rugs from every major rug-producing country in the world. As competition for the global market intensifies, rugs of exceptionally high caliber are more readily available. Getting qualified advice is more important than ever.

Fine rug dealers, like those showcased in the following pages, have knowledgeable staff members who are dedicated to educating their clientele and helping them find a rug they'll love. Through careful consideration of your tastes, and the requirements of your home, these professionals will virtually walk you through the process. They'll encourage you to take your time, and to judge each rug on its own merits. They'll insist on you taking rugs home so you can experience them in your own light (and may also provide delivery). And their companies will offer cleaning and repair service, which may well be important to you some day.

ELEGANCE UNDERFOOT: HARDWOOD

A hardwood floor is part of the dream for many custom homeowners searching for a warm, welcoming environment. Highly polished planks or fine parquet, the beauty of wood has always been a definitive part of luxurious homes and as the design "warming trend" continues, a wood floor figures prominently in achieving this feeling.

With new product options that make maintenance even easier, wood floors continue to add value and distinction in upscale homes throughout the area and the suburbs. Plank, parquet, and strip wood come in a wide variety of materials, and scores of styles and tones. Consider what effect you're trying to achieve.

FOR SUCCESSFUL CARPET SHOPPING

1. Take along blueprints (or accurate measurements), fabric swatches, paint chips, & photos.
2. Focus on installed, not retail price.
3. Take samples home to experience in the light of the room.
4. Be aware of delivery times; most carpet is available within weeks; special orders or custom designs take much longer.
5. Shop together. It saves time in the decision-making process.

523

BUDGETING FOR WOOD FLOOR*

2 1/4" strip oak—$10/sq. ft. Wider plank or parquet, glued & nailed—$15/sq. ft. Fancy parquet, hand-finished plank or French patterns (Versailles, Brittany)—$30/sq. ft. and up. *Estimates include finishing and installation; not sub-floor trim

THE NUMBER ONE WAY TO DECIDE ON A RUG

Do you like the rug enough to decorate around it? There's your answer.

DON'T GET COLD FEET

Stone and tile floors are known for their chilly feel. Electrical products are available now to help warm the surfaces of natural products. Installed in the adhesive layer under the flooring, these warming units are available at better suppliers and showrooms.

CERAMIC TILE AS STONE

With textured surfaces and color variations, ceramic tile can look strikingly like stone. You can get the tone on tone veining of marble, or the look of split stone, in assorted shapes, sizes and color.

Plank wood complements a traditional interior, while parquet wood flooring offers a highly stylized look. Designs stenciled directly on to floorboards create an original Arts and Crafts feel.

The more exotic woods used for flooring, like Brazilian cherry wood, are often harvested from managed forests.

VINYL AND LAMINATES

Vinyl or laminated floor coverings are no longer considered candidates for immediate rehab. – as a matter of fact, they're among the most updated looks in flooring. Stylish laminates are made to convincingly simulate wood, ceramic tile and other natural flooring products, and are excellent choices for heavy traffic areas. They come in hundreds of colors and patterns, and offer great compatibility with countertop materials.

THE RENAISSANCE OF CERAMIC TILE

Ceramic tile has literally come out of the back rooms and into the spotlight with its color, beauty and unique stylistic potential. As sophisticated shoppers gain a better understanding of the nature and possibilities of tile, its use has increased dramatically. Homeowners who want added quality and value in their homes are searching out hand painted glazed tiles for the risers of a staircase, quirky rectangular tiles to frame a powder room mirror, and ceramic tiles that look exactly like stone for their sun porch or kitchen. From traditional to modern, imported to domestic, ceramic tile offers a world of possibilities.

It is the perfect solution for homeowners who want floor, walls, countertops or backsplashes made of top quality, durable and attractive materials. A glazed clay natural product, ceramic tile is flexible, easy to care for, and allows for a variety of design ideas. It is easily cleaned with water and doesn't require waxing or polishing. And, like other natural flooring and counter products, ceramic tile adds visible value to a luxury home.

SELECTING CERAMIC TILE

Not all tile works in all situations, so it's imperative that you get good advice and counsel when selecting ceramic tile for your home. Ceramic tile is wear-rated, and this standardized system will steer you in the right direction. Patronize specialists who can provide creative, quality-driven advice. Visit showrooms to get an idea of the many colors, shapes and sizes available for use on floors, walls and counters. You'll be in for a very pleasant surprise.

If you're building or remodeling, your builder, architect, and/or interior designer can help you in your search and suggest creative ways to enliven your interior schemes. Individual hand-painted tiles can be interspersed in a solid color backsplash to add interest and individuality. Tiles can be included in a glass block partition, on a wallpapered wall, or in harmony with an area rug.

Grout, which can be difficult to keep clean, is now being addressed as a potential design element. By using a colored grout, the grout lines become a contrast design element – or can be colored to match the tile itself.

THE SOPHISTICATED LOOK OF NATURAL STONE

For a luxurious look that radiates strength and character, the world of natural stone offers dazzling possibilities. As custom buyers look for that "special something" to add to the beauty and value of their homes, they turn to the growing natural stone marketplace. A whole world of possibilities is now open to involved homeowners who contact the master craftsmen and suppliers who dedicate their careers to excellence in stone design, installation and refurbishing.

Marble and granite, which have always been options for homeowners are more popular than ever. With luxurious texture and color, marble is often the choice to add dramatic beauty to a grand entryway or a master bath upgrade. Granite continues to grow in popularity especially in luxury kitchens – there is no better material for countertops. It's also popular for a section of countertop dedicated to rolling pastry or dough. Rustic, weathered and unpolished, or highly polished and brilliant, granite brings elegance and rich visual texture that adds easily recognizable value to a home. Beyond marble and granite, the better suppliers of stone products also can introduce homeowners to slates, soapstone, limestone, English Kirkstone, sandstone, and travertine, which can be finished in a variety of individual ways.

MAKE IT CONCRETE

This material is a versatile and indestructible choice, available in a variety of colors and textures. Sealed concrete can be made with creative borders, scored, sandblasted or stained. A strong, natural material, it can be made to look like other materials and natural stone.

SOLID SURFACING SHOWS UP ON TILES

Durable, non-porous solid surface materials are now being used to make decorative wall tiles. Check with your countertop supplier for information and ideas.

525

ADJUSTING TO STONE PRODUCTS IN THE HOME

Like Mother Nature herself, natural stone is both rugged and vulnerable. Each stone requires specific care and maintenance and homeowners often experience a period of adjustment as they become accustomed to the requirements of caring for their floors or countertops.

Ask an expert about the different requirements and characteristics. Soapstone, for example, is a beautiful, soft stone with an antique patina many people love. Accumulated stains and scratches just add to the look. Granite, on the other hand, will not stain.

A professional can educate you about the specific characteristics of each stone product so you make an informed decision on what products will best serve the lifestyle of your family.

CHOOSING STONE – A UNIQUE EXPERIENCE

Once a decision to use a natural stone is made, begin your search right away. By allowing plenty of time to discover the full realm of choices, you'll be able to choose a stone and finish that brings luster and value to your home, without the pressure of a deadline. If you order imported stone, it can take months for delivery. Be prepared to visit your supplier's warehouse to inspect the stone that will be used in your home. Natural stone varies – piece to piece, box to box – a slab can vary in color from one end to the other. If you understand this degree of unpredictable irregularity is unavoidable, it will help you approach the selection in a realistic way.

STRONG AND ELEGANT COUNTERTOPS

The quest for quality and style does not stop until the countertops are selected. Today's countertop marketplace is brimming with man-made products that add high style without sacrificing strength and resiliency.

As the functions of kitchens become broader, the demand for aesthetics continues to increase dramatically. For lasting beauty with incredible design sensibilities, man-made solid surfaces are a very popular choice. The overwhelming number of possibilities and combinations in selecting countertops makes it vital to work with specialists who are quality-oriented. Countertops represent a significant investment in a custom home, and quality, performance and style must be the primary considerations in any decision. Established professionals, like those introduced in your Home Book, have a reputation for expert installation and service of the top quality products that define luxury.

MAKE COUNTERTOP CHOICES EARLY

Since decisions on cabinetry are often made far in advance, it's best to make a countertop choice concurrently.

Expect to spend at least two weeks visiting showrooms and acquainting yourself with design and materials. Take along paint chips, samples of cabinet and flooring materials, and any pictures of the look you're trying to achieve. Expect a solid surface custom counter order to take at least five weeks to arrive.

A WEALTH OF COUNTERTOP OPTIONS

You'll face a field of hundreds of colors and textures of solid surfacing, laminates, ceramic tile, natural stone, wood and stainless or enameled steel. Poured concrete counters also are finding their way into luxury kitchens in the area.

Laminate or color-through laminate offer hundreds of colors, patterns and textures, many of which convincingly mimic the look of solid surfacing or granite. Enjoying growing popularity in countertop application, are the natural stones, those staggeringly gorgeous slabs of granite, marble or slate, which offer the timeless look of quality and luxury. Naturally quarried stone is extremely durable and brings a dramatic beauty and texture to the kitchen or bath. For endless color and pattern possibilities, ceramic tile is a highly durable option. Man made resin-based solid surfacing materials offer many of the same benefits as stone. These surfaces are fabricated for durability and beauty, and new choices offer a visual depth that is astounding to the eye. It can be bent, carved, or sculpted. Elaborate edges can be cut into a solid surface counter and sections can be carved out to accommodate other surface materials, such as stainless steel or marble. Best known for superior durability, solid surfaces stand up to scratches, heat and water.

FINDING THE BEST SOURCE FOR MATERIALS

If you're building or remodeling your home, your designer, builder or architect will help you develop some ideas and find a supplier for the material you choose. Reputable suppliers like those featured in the Home Book, are experienced in selecting the best products and providing expert installation. Go visit a showroom or office – their knowledge will be invaluable to you. The intricacies and idiosyncrasies of natural products, and the sheer volume of possibilities in fabricated surfaces, can be confounding on your own. ∎

BEYOND TRADITIONAL

Solid surfacing is now being used to make custom faucets, decorative wall tiles, and lots of other creative touches for the home. Their rich colors (including granite), famed durability and versatility are perfect for bringing ideas to life. Check with your countertop supplier for information and ideas.

BE CREATIVE!

Mix and match counter top materials for optimum functionality and up-to-date style. Install butcher block for chopping vegetables and slicing breads, a slab of marble for rolling pastry and bakery dough, granite on an island for overall elegance, and solid surfaces for beauty and durability around the sinks and cooktop areas.

Carpeting &
Rugs

ABC CARPET & HOME ....**(561) 279-7777**
777 S. Congress (Between Linton & Atlantic), Del Ray Beach   Fax: (561) 279-4920
See Ad on Page: 530, 531, 590, 591   800 Extension: 1004
Principal/Owner: J. Weinrib
Website: www.abchome.com
Additional Information: The New York home furnishing legend, now in Del Ray
Beach. Oriental rugs, wall-to-wall antiques, linens and more.

AVAKIAN'S ORIENTAL RUGS ....**(561) 626-6455**
11940 US Highway One (Carl's Plaza), North Palm Beach   Fax: (561) 626-0277
See Ad on Page: 529   800 Extension: 1028
Principal/Owner: Paul K. Avakian
email: avakianrug@aol.com
Additional Information: Avakian's has been providing the finest oriental rugs to
clients for over 100 years.

AZHAR'S ORIENTAL RUG ....**(305) 666-3451**
Dadeland Mall, Miami   Fax: (305) 278-9725
See Ad on Page: 518, 519, 534   800 Extension: 1029
Principal/Owner: Azhar Said

FAITH ORIENTAL RUG ....**(305) 692-1940**
18759 Biscayne Blvd., Aventura   Fax: (305) 692-1942
See Ad on Page: 532, 533   800 Extension: 1091
Principal/Owner: Kevin Faith
Website: www.faithorientalrug.com email: faithrugs@aol.com
Additional Information: Importers/ retailers of traditional and designer hand
made rugs. Selling nationwide to the trade and the public since 1982.

HOFFMAN COLLECTION ....**(954) 962-7929**
2876 S. Park Road, Pembroke Park   Fax: (954) 962-1840
See Ad on Page: 535   800 Extension: 1124

528

Photo courtesy of ABC Carpet & Home

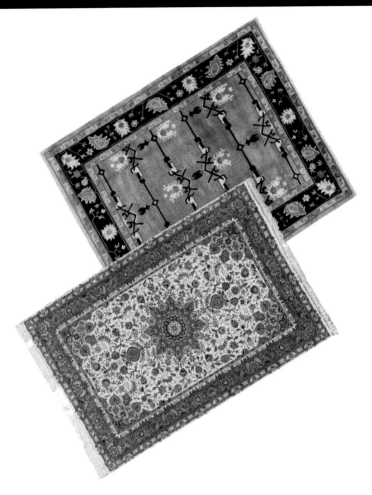

Linens

Pictured: Karastan

Broadloom

ABC Carpet & Home in Manhattan is the ultimate destination for those seeking unique and eclectic home furnishings. ABC's Florida store epitomizes the same style, originality and value. Find an exciting collection of handmade oriental carpets, innovative design rugs, rich wool carpeting, antiques and furniture, linens for bed and bath, and a wide range of decorative accessories. Open seven days a week. American Express, MasterCard, Visa accepted.

Orientals & Design Rugs

Furniture

FAITH ORIENTAL RUG
"The Strength Behind Designers"

Guaranteed Best Prices - Top Brand Names Available For Sample Viewing
Catalogs Available Upon Order
www.faithorientalrug.com

*Nominated for
2000 Retailer
the Year Award*

Faith Oriental Rug was nominated by the Atlanta exhibitors based
on their innovative business operations, demonstrated success in
sales training, store promotions, customer service, visual display
presentation and overall business credibility.

Loehmann's Fashion Island   18759 Biscayne Blvd.   Aventura, FL 33180
Phone: 305.692.1940   Fax: 305.692.1942

Nominated for 2000
Retailer of the Year Award

FAITH ORIENTAL RUG

Loehmann's Fashion Island   18759 Biscayne Blvd.   Aventura, FL 33180
Phone: 305.692.1940   Fax: 305.692.1942

Wherever in the world you live, it's worth your while to pay us a visit.

Walking into Azhar's can be something of an overwhelming experience.

Each Azhar's gallery offers values far beyond what you've seen elsewhere. The reasons are simple. Azhar's is America's leading importer, purchasing in enormous quantities directly from the weavers. There are no wholesalers and middle men to inflate the prices. So you'll save 50% or more on every rug in our inventory. At Azhar's Oriental Rugs, you'll always find the rug you want at the lowest price, in the color, fabric and size ideally suited to your particular style, taste and decor. You'll also get our guarantee as to knot count, fiber contents and country of origin. So visit one of our galleries soon and discover the incomparable glories of authentic oriental rugs.

Azhar's Oriental Rugs

Where you'll always find the world's most beautiful Oriental rugs

The **HOFFMAN**
Collection

HOFFMAN COLLECTION is a series of custom carpets made in the company's own mill in South Florida. The Hoffman Collection is the **only factory in Florida** which offers unique wool hand tufted and broadloom area rugs, lending beauty and comfort to any interior. The Hoffman Collection is now ready to provide you with **one of a kind - custom area rugs** of timeless design and uncompromising quality. Choose from our own artists' motifs or create your own design from the blueprints of your imagination.

AnycolourAnysizeAnyshapeAnydesign

HOFFMAN
Collection

Factory: 2876 S. Park Road • Pembroke Park, FL. 33009
Tel: 954-962-7929 • Fax: 954-962-1840
Website: www.Hoffmancollection.com

Flooring

ALL WOODS ....**(305) 687-2300**
    630 NW 113th Street, Miami   Fax: (305) 687-8333
    See Ad on Page: 538   *800 Extension:* 1011
RAY BARROWS WOOD FLOORS, INC.....................................**(941) 593-9388**
    5650-3 Yahl Street, Naples   Fax: (941) 593-9389
    See Ad on Page: 539   *800 Extension:* 1220
    <u>Principal/Owner:</u> Ray Barrows
NORTHERN MILLS HARDWOOD FLOORING ....**(954) 563-8474**
    3161 N. Dixie Highway, Oakland Park   Fax: (954) 563-0738
    See Ad on Page: 537   *800 Extension:* 1192

Photo courtesy of Ray Barrows Wood Floors, Inc.

Real Wood Floors
Beauty that lasts a lifetime.

There is no substitute for the durability and beauty of a real wood floor.

For every room in your home, there is a hardwood floor that can add beauty, warmth and value. Hardwood flooring has stood the test of time in durability and is easy to maintain. With its superior quality, strength and beauty, real wood flooring is one home investment that will truly last a lifetime.

Northern Mills
Hardwood Flooring Inc.

3161 N Dixie Highway • Oakland Park, FL 33334
(954) 563-8474 • (954) 563-0738 fax

MANUFACTURER OF WOOD FLOORS

"A World of Possibilities at Your Feet"

"Largest Showroom in South Florida"

*"Serving the USA, Caribbean,
Central and South America"*

ALLWOODS®
SOLID HARDWOOD FLOORS
A DIVISION OF LLOBELL BERNSTEIN CORP.

Exquisite Wood Floor From All Around The World

**ALLWOODS CONTRACTORS, SUPPLIERS AND MANUFACTURERS
OF FINE HARDWOOD FLOORS**

Office and Showroom: 630 NW 113th Street, Miami, Florida 33168
Phone 305-687-2300 Fax 305-687-8333 www.allwoods.com 1-800-wood-fla

"EVERY TIME
WE SAY LET THERE BE!
IN ANY FORM,
SOMETHING HAPPENS. "
Stella Terrill Mann

The
Ashley
Group
Publishers of Fine Visual Reference for the Discerning Connoisseur
1350 Touhy Ave. • Des Plaines, Illinois 60018
888.458.1750 • FAX 847.390.2902
ashleygroup@cahners.com

We have over 26 years of experience and offer custom and standard wood floor design and installation. Choose from any species of wood to complement or accent your home or office.

RAY BARROWS
WOOD FLOORS, INC.

5650-3 Yahl Street, Naples, FL 34109
941-591-0387

Ceramic Tile

ACCENT FLOORS ....**(561) 616-8112**
1414 Points Road, West Palm Beach   Fax: (561) 616-8113
See Ad on Page: 544   800 Extension: 1006
Principal/Owner: Blaire Ford

ANTHONY'S ....**(941) 594-5847**
1406 Rail Head Blvd, Naples   Fax: (941) 594-5178
See Ad on Page: 388, 389   800 Extension: 1018
Principal/Owner: D. Vichot

PAMI EXPORT - IMPORT, INC....**(305) 512-2836**
8004 NW 154 Street, Miami Lakes   Fax: (305) 823-3968
See Ad on Page: 541   800 Extension: 1202
Principal/Owner: Eduardo / Joan Anzola
Website: PAMIdecotile.com email: PAMIINC@attglobal.net
Additional Information: Exclusive importer of exquisite hand painted ceramic
tiles. Contact us for an appointment and directions. Showroom is located at
15203 NW 60th Avenue, Miami Lake, FL.

RAINBOW TILE OF POMPANO INC...**(954) 972-8001**
1800 N. Powerline Road, Pompano Beach   Fax: (954) 960-1325
See Ad on Page: 461, 542, 543   800 Extension: 1218
Principal/Owner: Michel Sztanski
Website: www.rainbowtile.com email: info@rainbowtile.com

RUBEN SORHEGUI TILE DISTRIBUTORS ....**(941) 643-2882**
3876 Mercantile Avenue, Naples   Fax: (941) 643-6285
See Ad on Page: 545, 561   800 Extension: 1228

Photo courtesy of Advanced Stone Technologies

Unique Hand Crafted Ceramic Tiles
Custom Made for all your Creative Design Projects

PAMI
E X P O R T

For a Showroom appointment contact:
PAMI Export-Import, Inc.
305-512-2836

TUMBLED SLATE

Where Every Floor can be a Work of Art.

RT **Rainbow Tile**

POMPANO BEACH, FLOR1DA
TOLL FREE (800)900-8001
WWW.RAINBOWTILE.COM

SICIS

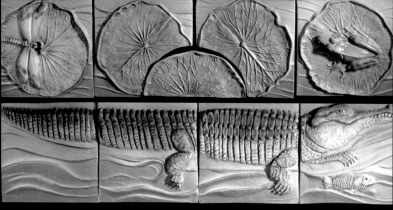

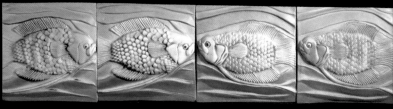

Serie 800

cattedrale

cattedrale

Molduras

by Hugo Bertora

Largest Selection of
Accent Tiles

Borders and Medallions

Italian, Spanish and Mexican Tiles

in Stock

Finest Selection of
Saturinia, Marble and Limestone

RUBEN SORHEGUI
TILE DISTRIBUTORS

Marble &
Granite

ACCEL ....**(561) 640-1003**
2140 Scott Avenue, Suite 2, West Palm Beach — Fax: (561) 640-0151
See Ad on Page: 551 — 800 Extension: 1005

ADVANCED STONE TECHNOLOGIES, INC............**(863) 467-8944**
2455 NW 16th Blvd., Okeechobee — Fax: (863) 467-5857
See Ad on Page: 566, 567 — 800 Extension: 1007
Website: www.advancedstonetechno.com
email: inquiry@advancedstonetechno.com
Additional Information: Creators of custom mosaic work in marble & granite. Unlimited design possibilities minimal delivery time. Created in the USA.

ANTHONY'S ....**(941) 594-5847**
1406 Rail Head Blvd., Naples — Fax: (941) 594-5178
See Ad on Page: 388, 389 — 800 Extension: 1016
Principal/Owner: D. Vichot

ARC STONE ....**(877) 263-5596**
3114 Tuxedo Avenue, West Palm Beach — Fax: (561) 478-8896
See Ad on Page: 547 — 800 Extension: 1019
Principal/Owner: Michael Coiro
Website: www.arc-stone.com
Additional Information: The largest natural stone supplier on the East coast. Slabs - Tiles - Cut to Size projects.   New Chicago location.

BELLISSIMO MARBLE DESIGN INC. ....**(954) 717-9985**
4792 W. Commercial Blvd, Tamarac — Fax: (954) 717-8464
See Ad on Page: 554, 555 — 800 Extension: 1032
Principal/Owner: Francis P. Esposito

FERAZZOLI IMPORTS INC. ....**(800) 523-1628**
2110 N. Andrews Avenue, Pompano Beach — Fax: (954) 977-1793
See Ad on Page: 563 — 800 Extension: 1098

continued on page **559**

546

Photo courtesy of Piedras

Specializing in European Limestone

Material Pictured: Senia LimeStone Anticnovo

Natural Stone ● *Marble* ● *French Limestone* ● *French Antique Pavers*
Granite ● *Jerusalem Stone* ● *Travertine* ● *Custom Fabrication*

Main Office & Showroom	South Miami Showroom
1155 NW 76th Ave.	4760 S.W. 72nd Ave.
Miami, Florida 33126	Miami, Florida 33155
Phone: (305) 513-0848	Phone: (305) 666-8555
Fax (305) 513-0828	Fax (305) 666-2113

http://www.piedras.com ● email: piedras@piedras.com

We Export Around the World

GRATE FIREPLACE & STONE SHOPPE
11000 METRO PARKWAY, SUITE #9
FORT MYERS, FLORIDA 33912
(941) 939-7187

GRANITE   MARBLE

INTERNATIONAL
STONE CONCEPTS
INCORPORATED

GRAMA BLEND
USA

2570 Forest Hill Blvd., Suite 101 ■ West Palm Beach, FL 33406
561.642.5808 ■ Fax 561.642.5075
www.intlstoneconcepts.com

ISC is a full service marble and granite corporation. When it comes to design, fabrication, and installation of conventional marble and our special lightweight natural stone, we are the leaders in high quality craftsmanship.

Recognized as a leader in natural lightweight stone panels, Grama Blend has an unrivaled advantage in weight-sensitive projects. Suitable applications include walls, ceilings, and wainscot-anywhere you have dreamed of installing stone, but could not! Imagine the luxury of covering multiple square footage with large formatted pieces (up to 4' x 8') without the liability of stress cracks. For the first time ever, envision cabinet doors inlaid with lightweight natural stone to match your countertops.

Mosaics Make a Comeback

Mosaic work has adorned buildings and dwellings from as far back as the 4th Century B.C. During these ancient times, mosaic artists would sketch a "cartoon picture" directly on the surface to be worked. The mosaic artist would come and lay the stones, or "tesserae," directly to the "cartoon" in mortar. Although the work is breathtaking to look at, it has not always been feasible to bring this art form to the mainstream public.

Mosaic today is enjoying a renewed comeback, with a slight difference. By combining modern technology with this ageless art, mosaic is making itself available to all those who wish to capture the everlasting beauty of a bygone era. New manufacturing and adhesive techniques are allowing for the piece to be created in the mosaic artist's studio and transported to the job site as a whole. Although every piece in a mosaic is still cut and placed by hand, this new technology has allowed mosaic work to become more popular than ever.

Homeowners are opting for the classical elegance of antiquity, while still incorporating personal style. Mosaic in itself portrays the feeling of ancient civilizations, yet is versatile enough to fit modern surroundings as well. Homeowners are adding mosaic touches in grand scale applications such as complete floors and walls, or incorporating small touches in their border and accent areas.

Regardless of how mosaic is used in modern society, a finished mosaic piece is surely to become as revered as the ancient art itself.

Lori Bozenbury, *Advanced Stone Technologies*

continued from page **546**

FINNISH GRANITE GROUP, INC. ....**(561) 274-8010**
1340 Neptune Drive, Boynton Beach
See Ad on Page: 560
Fax: (561) 274-8020
800 Extension: 1100
Principal/Owner: Tarik Saadetdin

GRATE FIREPLACE & STONE SHOPPE ....**(941) 939-7187**
11000 Metro Parkway, Suite 9, Fort Myers
See Ad on Page: 550
Fax: (941) 939-0394
800 Extension: 1112
Principal/Owner: Bill & Helen Stasko
Additional Information: We are a company specializing in fireplaces for existing and new construction and carry all fireplace related products from stoves- pipe- mantels- glass doors- electric fireplaces- stone- marble- brick- to a full line of fireplace accessories.

GULFCOAST MARBLE & GRANITE ....**(941) 566-7402**
6267 Lee Ann Lane, Naples
See Ad on Page: 557
Fax: (941) 566-3359
800 Extension: 1115
Principal/Owner: Servio Cortes
Additional Information: We specialize in countertops, tables and fireplace fabrication as well as floor installation and cut to size marble, granite, limestone & travertine.

IMPORTED STONES BY GILBRALTOR INC. ....**(954) 971-5000**
1771 N. Powerline Road, Pompano Beach
See Ad on Page: 564
Fax: (954) 971-2165
800 Extension: 1130

INTERNATIONAL STONE CONCEPTS, INC. ....**(561) 642-5808**
2570 Forest Hill Blvd, Suite 101, West Palm Beach
See Ad on Page: 556
Fax: (561) 642-5075
800 Extension: 1142
Principal/Owner: Lou Luzniak / Dennis Gelsomino
Website: www.intlstoneconcepts.com email: stoneconcepts@mindspring.com

MANTLE MAGIC & ARCHITECTURAL DETAILS INC................**(954) 776-7067**
Fort Lauderdale
See Ad on Page: 562
800 Extension: 1167
Principal/Owner: Victoria Digiulian
email: mantelmagic@msn.com
Additional Information: Fireplace mantels & surrounds, columns, ballustrades, custom pavers, concrete countertops, and stone accessories.

MARBLE OF THE WORLD ....**(954) 782-8000**
1216 S. Andrews Avenue, Pompano Beach
See Ad on Page: 552, 553
Fax: (954) 782-8809
800 Extension: 1168

PIEDRAS INTERNATIONAL..**(305) 666-8555**
4760 SW 72nd Avenue, Miami
See Ad on Page: 455, 548, 549
Fax: (305) 666-2113
800 Extension: 1206
Principal/Owner: Justo Parada
Website: www.piedras.com email: piedras@piedras.com

RUBEN SORHEGUI TILE DISTRIBUTORS ....**(941) 643-2882**
3876 Mercantile Avenue, Naples
See Ad on Page: 545
Fax: (941) 643-6285
800 Extension: 1229

559

RUBEN SORHEGUI
TILE DISTRIBUTORS

SP 026 Panel 80 cm x 80 cm / 32´ x 32´

Largest Selection of

Accent Tiles

Borders and Medallions

Italian, Spanish and

Mexican Tiles

in Stock

Finest Selection of

Saturinia, Marble and

Limestone

FERAZZOLI IMPORTS, INC.
WE IMPORT THE WORLD'S FINEST PRODUCTS

GRANITE, MARBLE & CERAMIC TILE

2110 N. Andrews Avenue
Pompano Beach, FL 33069-1417
    (954) 975-7775
    (800) 523-1628
Fax (954) 977-7193

3500 West 45th Street
WPB, FL 33407
    (561) 615-4000

www.ferazzoliimports.com

Marble of the Millenium
Voted Best Marble

Royal Oyster

Stone, Slate &
Concrete

ADVANCED STONE TECHNOLOGIES, INC...............................**(863) 467-8944**
2455 NW 16th Blvd., Okeechobee   Fax: (863) 467-5857
See Ad on Page: 566, 567   *800 Extension:* 1007
<u>Website:</u> www.advancedstonetechno.com
<u>email:</u> inquiry@advancedstonetechno.com
<u>Additional Information:</u> Creators of custom mosaic work in marble & granite.
Unlimited design possibilities minimal delivery time. Created in the USA.

"Nothing compares to the *artful elegance* of a carefully selected area rug placed on a hard surface."

MOSAICS
By
Boz Art

ARTISTIC MOSAICS IN M

Opus Sectile - Pebble -
Medallions - Inlays - Borders - W
Unlimited Design Possibil
CREATED

www.advancedstonetechno.com

RBLE, GRANITE & STONE

Finally...
South Florida's Own
Home & Design
Sourcebook

The SOUTH FLORIDA HOME BOOK, a comprehensive
hands-on Design Sourcebook to building, remodeling, decorating,
furnishing and landscaping a luxury home in South Florida is
a "must-have" reference for the South Florida homeowner.
At over 700 pages, this beautiful, full-color hard cover
volume is quite simply the most complete, well-organized
reference to the South Florida home industry. It covers all aspects
of the process, with hundreds of listings of local home industry
professionals, accompanied by hundreds of inspiring photographs.
You will also find articles to assist in planning and completing a
project. The SOUTH FLORIDA HOME BOOK tells you how to
find what you need when you need it.

Order your copy today!

SOUTH FLORIDA
HOME
BOOK

Published by
The Ashley Group
3440 Hollywood Blvd., Suite 460 • Hollywood, Florida 33021
Toll Free 888.458.1750   Fax 847.390.2902
E-mail: ashleybooksales@cahners.com

Photo courtesy of:
Inspiration Furniture

HOME FURNISHINGS & DECORATING

From Traditio

to
Conte

nal

LEATHER**design**STUDIO

mporary

“ One may do
whate'er one likes

In Art:
the only thing is,

to make sure
That one does
like it. ”

Robert Browning

Making Your House A Home

A beautifully designed, meticulously planned house becomes a home when the furnishings are set in place. Comfortably upholstered sofas and chairs in the family room, a unique faux-finished foyer, richly appointed windows in the dining room, all give a home its individual flair and welcoming livability.

Today's homeowners, whether they're in their first or final home, have the elevated taste that comes from exposure to good design. They know what quality furniture looks and feels like and they want it in their homes.

In the home furnishing industry, one item is more outrageously gorgeous than the next, and anything you can imagine can be yours. This freedom can be overwhelming, even intimidating, if you don't keep a sharp focus.

By visiting the finest stores, specialty shops, and artisans, like those presented in the following pages of the Home Book, you can be certain your desire for top quality is already understood and that knowledgeable people are ready to guide you. Enjoy.

MODERN IDEAS

With an evolutionary array of styles, contemporary furnishings add excitement, elegance and personality to a home. From Bauhaus, Retro, and Deco, to pure modern, these artful furnishings satisfy the desire for unique, individual expression.

KEEP IT ALIVE!

Regardless of your budget, you needn't sacrifice quality or style. Set your priorities and let your home take on a dynamic, ever-changing feel as you add or replace furnishings over a period of time.

574

ACCEPT ONLY THE BEST IN HOME FURNISHINGS

When you want only the best home furnishings, scout the stores offering top quality products and superlative service. These retail stores have knowledgeable staff, sometimes including trained and licensed interior designers, to help you make your selections. (Some may ask nominal fee, which is applied to later purchases, for the designer to help you develop thorough plans.) With a wealth of accumulated knowledge and an unwavering commitment to the highest level of customer service, these experts can advise you on combining optimum comfort with superior quality and fabulous style.

TAKE TIME TO CHOOSE FURNITURE

Your interior designer, or qualified store personnel, can direct your search and keep you within the scale of your floor plan. Their firsthand knowledge of pricing, products and features will help you find the best quality for your money.

To save time, take along your blueprint or a detailed drawing with measurements, door and window placements, and special architectural features. If your spouse or anyone else will be involved in the final decision, try to shop together to eliminate return trips. Most stores can deliver most furniture within eight weeks, but special custom pieces may take up to 16 weeks.

When furnishing a new room, concentrate on selecting one important piece to create a focus, like a Chinese Chippendale-style daybed or an original Arts & Crafts spindle table. Select around whatever special pieces you already own.

Ruthlessly assess your current interior. Clear out pieces that need to be replaced or no longer work with your lifestyle, even if you have no clear idea of what you'll be replacing them with. Sometimes empty space makes visualizing something new much easier.

Be open-minded and accept direction. Salespeople at top stores can help you find exactly what you're seeking, and, if you ask them, can guide you away from inappropriate decisions, towards more suitable alternatives.

THINKING ABOUT FURNISHINGS

Beautiful furnishings complete your vision of "home." If you've been working with an interior designer, kitchen and bath designer, or an architect, you're familiar with the process of defining your personal style. Nowhere is that ability more important than in the selection of furnishings, the most visible and functional contributors to your home interior. Continue to refine your own sense of style. In addition to the Home Book, there are dozens of shelter magazines that showcase beautiful interiors in many styles, and ways to mix them together. Visiting model homes, loft or condominium developments, designer showhouses, or house walks, will help you define your own style preference. By walking through these settings, you'll get a good idea of what furniture arrangements really feel like in a home environment. As you browse through the endless possibilities, keep these thoughts in mind:

• What are your priorities? Develop a list of "must have," "want to have," and "dreaming about."

• Do you want your furnishings to follow the architecture? This always proves a good starting point.

• What colors or styles are already established through the flooring, walls, windows, or cabinetry?

• Can you get the furnishings through the doorway, up the elevator, or down the stairs?

• Does the piece reflect your tastes? Don't be influenced too strongly by what looks great in a showroom or designer house.

• What major pieces will be with you for a long time? Allow a lion's share of your budget for these.

• Does the piece fit the overall decorating scheme? Although the days of strict adherence to one style per room are over it's still necessary to use coordinated styles.

• Do you have something (a lamp, antique candlesticks, a framed picture) you can put on the table you're considering? If not, choose accessories when you choose the table.

• Will a piece work for your family's lifestyle? Chose upholstery fabrics, colors and fixtures that will enhance, not hinder, your everyday life.

• Is the piece comfortable? Before you buy, sit on the chair, recline on the sofa, pull a chair up to the table.

THREE IS THE MAGIC NUMBER

In accessorizing a home, thinking in "threes" is a good rule of thumb: Three candlesticks with candles of three different heights. Three colors of pottery grouped together, one less vibrant to highlight the others. Three patterns in a room.

575

LOFT LIGHTING

Lofts do have large windows, but they're usually on one wall. That presents a lighting challenge that is often met with new low voltage systems. The transformer is hidden in a closet of soffit; decorative transformers are mounted on a wall. The halogen bulbs last thousands of hours – very important given the height of loft ceilings.

A BRIGHT IDEA

Buy a few clip-on lights with 50-watt bulbs and take them home with you to pinpoint your needs and favorite lighting looks. Experiment with them to create different effects. See if you like up- or downlights to highlight an architectural feature. Get an idea of how much light it takes to illuminate a room.

576

CONSIDERING CUSTOM FURNITURE

Our area is home to many talented, accessible furniture designers who can create whatever you need to fill a special space in your home, and to satisfy your desire for owning a unique, one-of-a-kind object.

Contacting a furniture designer is the first step toward attaining a fabulous piece of individualized art for your home. Some of the best known designers working here today are listed in the following pages of the Home Book. You can contact them directly, or through your interior designer.

The second step is an initial meeting, during which you'll see examples of the designer's work and answer questions like:

What kind of piece do you want? Free standing entertainment system, dining table, armoire?

What functions must it serve? It is a piece of art, but the furniture still must function in ways that make it practical and usable. Explain your needs clearly.

Do you have favorite woods, materials or colors? As with ordering custom woodwork, the possibilities are almost unlimited. Different woods can be painted or finished differently for all kinds of looks. Have some ideas in mind.

Are you open to new ideas and approaches? If you'd like the designer to suggest new ways of reaching your goal, let him or her know.

If the designer's portfolio excites you, the communication is good, and you trust him or her to deliver your project in a top quality, professional manner, then you're ready to begin. Ask the designer to create a couple of design options. Make sure you and the designer are in agreement regarding finishes, materials, stain or paint samples you want to see, and a completion date. Most charge a 50 percent deposit at the beginning with the balance due upon completion. If you decide not to go ahead with construction of a piece, expect to be billed a designer's fee. A commissioned piece of furniture requires a reasonable amount of time to get from start to finish. If you want an entertainment system for Super Bowl Sunday, make your final design decisions when you take down the Halloween decorations. Keep in mind that the process cannot be rushed.

FILL YOUR HOME WITH SPIRIT...ACCESSORIZE

It is through a table full of delightfully framed family photographs, treasured collectibles on the mantle, or stacks of favorite books in an armoire, that your personality will come shining through. Accessorizing is critical to successful furnishing, because it adds the special touches which make you feel truly at home.

Accessorizing often starts with collections or photographs. Take a handful of your favorite family photos to a fine accessory store, or to your interior designer, to get help in choosing interesting frames that will do justice to the pictures and add flair to any room. Add to an old collection or start a new one. It can be anything – quilts, candlesticks, antique books, or baseballs.

The best thing about accessories is their flexibility. By changing them, or simply moving them around the room or the house, you can create a fresh, new look anytime. By recognizing the great impact of the smaller items in your home, you'll have the ability to refresh and invigorate your interiors to reflect your changing interests and lifestyle.

THE LITTLE THINGS MEAN A LOT

A decor doesn't always start with rugs, furniture and lighting. Many area homeowners are making the decision to give their collections, their interests or their families priority when decorating the home. When a collection of turtles, a passion for music, or a love for flowers is allowed to take front and center in a decorating process, the result will always be intensely personal and fulfilling.

Accessorizing is artful, and an interior designer or salesperson at a fine store will help you establish ways to display your treasures in the most appropriate way. Some people love a 'cluttered' tabletop; others prefer a more ordered composition.

THE GLOBAL MARKETPLACE

There are so many exciting lighting designs available from all over the world, a lighting retailer can't possibly show you even half of them in the showroom. Allow yourself enough time to pour over the catalogs of beautiful chandeliers, luminaries (lamps), and other lighting fixtures available to you. A special order may take up to eight weeks, but it may net you the most beautiful piece of art in your room!

577

LIGHTING YOUR ENTERTAINMENT ROOM

One suggestion for properly lighting a 20-foot by 20-foot room to be used for watching television, listening to music and entertaining friends:
• General lighting provided by recessed fixtures
• A wall-mounted dimming package, with remote control
• A decorative ceiling fixture for more lighting when entertaining.

FABULOUS FABRICS!

You can design an entire room based on a fabulous fabric choice for a pillow, tableskirt, window treatment, or furniture. Evocative color and rich texture are added to any decor through the choices of fabrics and upholstery. Choose what you find enjoyable and comfortable. Always take a swatch home to test it in your light, with the rest of your decorative scheme.

SPOTLIGHT ON LIGHTING

Lighting can be the focal point of a room, or it can be so subtle that it's almost invisible. The trick is knowing what you want to accomplish.

Indeed, when we remember a place as cozy, elegant, or dramatic, or cold and uncomfortable, we're feeling the emotional power of illumination.

This is an exciting time to be choosing a lighting scheme for your home. You will be selecting from an array of imported and domestic products which, when properly used, enhance your furnishings and artwork as well as the comfort level of your daily life. It's critical to make correct lighting decisions.

The industry is filled with options and combinations, from fixtures and bulbs to dimmers and integrated systems. Top lighting retailers in the area employ in-house design consultants to guide you. Or you can employ a residential lighting designer.

To deliver a superior lighting scheme, a designer must know:

• What is your budget? One of the biggest mistakes custom home owners make is under budgeting for their lighting program.

• What are your needs? Lighting falls into three categories – general, task, and atmospheric. A study/work area, a cozy nook, and a kitchen each require different lighting.

• What feeling are you trying to create?

• What "givens" are you working with? Where are your windows or skylights? The use of artificial, indoor light depends to a great degree on the natural light coming in.

• What materials are on the floor and what colors are on the walls and ceiling? This affects reflectance.

• Where is your furniture placed, and how big are individual pieces? This is especially important when you're choosing a dining room chandelier.

• If you're replacing something, why are you replacing it? Know the wattage, for instance, if a current light source is no longer bright enough.

• Are there energy/environmental concerns? Lighting consumes 12 to 15 percent of the electricity used in the home. An expert can develop a plan that maximizes energy efficiency.

• Who lives in the house? Will footballs and frisbees be flying through the kitchen? Pass on the hanging fixture and choose recessed lighting instead.

Finally, try to shop together. The reason for almost all returns is that "my husband or wife didn't like it!" This can tack weeks on to the process of finishing a room. Special orders take up to eight weeks. Your builder will let you know at what point you need to supply fixtures for installation.

THE WELCOME LIVABILITY OF CASUAL FURNISHINGS

As more homeowners opt for a casual, yet elegant ambiance, casual furnishings continue to grow in popularity. In fact, the viability of the trend has recently been recognized within the industry, which has created a separate casual furnishings classification.

Casual furniture is simply less formal in style and function than traditional furniture and is usually found in the family room, sunroom, breakfast room, and bedroom. More often now, these pieces are in the living room. Iron and glass tables, Baker's Racks of pewter and wood, rattan dressers, wicker chairs, and futons are all examples of casual furniture. Sometimes found in traditional furniture stores as accent pieces, full lines of innovative, functional casual furnishings, including accessories, are available at casual furniture specialty stores like those presented in these pages.

"DECKED OUT" FOR OUTDOOR LIVING

As homeowners strive to expand comfortable living space into their yards, top quality outdoor furniture responds with new and innovative styles. Before you go looking at outdoor furniture, think about:

• What look do you like? The intricate patterns of wrought iron? The smooth and timeless beauty of silvery teak wood? The sleek design of sturdy aluminum, which comes with straps, slings or cushions?

• What pieces do you need? Furnishing larger decks and terraces requires careful planning. Area homeowners are buying more seating and end tables and phasing out umbrellas. Ask your landscape architect, deck contractor, or casual furniture store personnel for ideas.

• Can you store the furniture in the winter or will it stay outdoors under cover?

• Can you see the furniture from inside? Make sure the outdoor furnishings won't distract from established design inside or outside.

STAYING IN TUNE

Local piano dealers report that new pianos must be tuned three or four times within the first year. After that, once or twice a year is plenty.

579

'FAUX' FINISH" TROMP L'OEIL?

Any painting technique replicating another look is called a 'faux.' (fake) finish. There are many methods to achieve wonderful individual effects. Tromp l'oeil (fool the eye) is a mural painting that creates illusion through perspective. A wall becomes an arched entry to a garden.

• What is the level of maintenance? If you invest in a top quality product and maintain it well, you can expect it to last you at least 20 years.

THE SPECIAL QUALITY OF PIANOS

A new or professionally reconditioned piano makes an excellent contribution to the elegance and lifestyle of a growing number of area homes. Pianos add a dimension of personality that no ordinary piece of furniture can match. They are recognized for the beauty they add, visually and acoustically.

First time piano buyers may be astonished at the range of choices they have and the variables that will influence their eventual decision. Go to those showrooms that carry the best brand name pianos. Not only will you be offered superior quality instruments, but you'll also get the value of the sales staff's professional knowledge and experience. Questions that you need to answer will include:

• Who are the primary players of the instrument?

• What level of players are they (serious, beginners)?

• Who are their teachers?

• What is the size of the room the piano will placed in?

• What are your preferences in wood color or leg shape?

• Are you interested in software packages that convert your instrument into a player piano?

Pianos represent a significant financial investment, one that will not depreciate, and may actually appreciate over time. If a new piano is out of your financial range, ask about the store's selection of reconditioned instruments that they've acquired through trades. The best stores recondition these pieces to a uniformly high standard of excellence, and are good options for you to consider. These stores also hold occasional promotions, when special pricing will be in effect for a period of time.

FROM SONATA TO SYMPHONY

Even if you don't play a note, you can enjoy the rich sound of live piano music in your home today. Any good quality piano can be turned into a player piano with the installation of a state of the art software package. These packages offer high quality sound reproduction, including all nuances of live performance. You can also manipulate the performance - speeding it up or slowing it down - and even make your own discs. Upgrades include an orchestra attachment, so you can get the effect of an entire orchestra playing along with the piano - or with you - in perfect synchronicity.

ART–OUT OF THE FRAME

Through their travels, reading and exposure to art and design, sophisticated homeowners are aware of the beauty that can be added to their homes with specialty decorative painting. They see in walls, furniture, and fabrics the perfect canvases for unique works of art. The demand for beautiful art applied directly to walls, stairs or furniture has created a renaissance in decorative painting. Faux finishes, tromp l'oeil and murals have joined the traditional finishes of paint, wallpaper and stain for consideration in outstanding residential interiors.

Decorative painting is often applied in kitchens, entryways, and great rooms, where families and guests will get the most enjoyment from this special touch. Faux finishes on walls are intensely original and creative, an outlet for your desires for artistic expression in your own home. Completely custom in color and texture, it has no seams and is generally more durable than wallcovering.

Elegance, drama, whimsy – whatever your style, it's important to find an artist whose vision can translate your desire for something "fantastic" into reality. Specialty painters of the highest caliber, such as those on these pages, can help you fine-tune your idea, or develop a concept from scratch. At your initial meeting, discuss your ideas, whether they're crystal clear or barely there. Don't be apprehensive if you don't have a clear idea. Artists are by profession visually creative, and by asking you questions and showing you ideas, you can develop a concept together.

LIGHTBULB POWER

New and improved lightbulbs are hot news in the late 1990's. Newly engineered light sources now bring natural sunshine-quality light into area homes. Energy efficiency and life expectancy are both way up. Ask your lighting provider for information.

581

MARGAUX, A HOME COLLECTION
Pillow Collection:

By definition, the pillow is the most versatile accessory in any room. In this wonderful collection of unique, richly decorated pillows, each one is a work of art with trims from all over the world. Our natural silk embroidered pillows are adorned with beads and come from India and Thailand, while our richly woven tapestry pillows come to us from Italy, France and Spain.

Photo by Sweet Dreams, Inc.

STRAUSS & WASSNER, INC.
Armoire and Chest:

This armoire and chest are made of box-matched cherry veneers with a natural closed grain satin finish. The clean, crisp lines represent a move toward contemporary styling. This piece also is available in other exotic woods and finishes.

Photo by Grossman Photography

BERRY'S BARBELL & EQUIPMENT, INC.
Precor Elliptical Crosstrainer:

The no-impact motion of the Precor Elliptical Crosstrainer eliminates impact-related joint and muscle pain and injury. Precor's Elliptical Crosstrainers are now available in four different models.

Photo by Precor

SIPURE DESIGN
Lounge Chair:

Displayed is one item of the new collection from Dema "Le Foglie" by Claudio Silvestrin. It is a design combining extreme softness and sturdy

structures, and offers the pleasure of natural materials, pear wood, linen, cotton and cashmere.

Showroom

o see who and what everyone will be talking about.

AVAKIAN'S ORIENTAL RUGS

Bromley Hall Collection:
The luxurious wool pile of the Bromley Hall collection is painstakingly hand-knotted in Nepal. Available in a wide variety of colors and designs, Bromley Hall is our most exciting new addition for Fall 2000.

STEFEN JĀ STŪDĒOS

Reef Sculptures:
Oceans cover a vast majority of our planet and contain an incredibly diverse array of life. Vast forests of coral teaming with schools of fish and every imaginable size, shape and color of creature populate the warmer waters. Mirror Image is an original life-sized, hand-formed and painted sculpture made to reflect just a portion of an incredible creation.
Photo by Liz Ordoñez

583

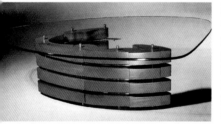

INTERNATIONAL INTERIORS

Tension Table:
Rich wood and stainless steel make this coffee table a working piece of art. This imported masterpiece can be used in many rooms to bring warmth and uniqueness to any setting.
Photo by Gonzalo Cano

Custom Furniture Portfolio

QUIET TIME INC.

Stuart Surfer:
"Defining the purpose of a perspective furniture concept, respect for the materials, attention to details and a rapport with the client are the major ingredients of good design. Design is a very structured process for me; function is the main element around which style, material selection and construction revolve. When the clients become partners in the design by expressing their needs and tastes, the end result is always a more rewarding experience."
Photo by Stuart Surfer

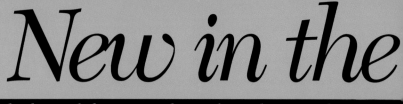

THE WORKSHOPS OF DAVID T. SMITH

Noah's Ark Chandelier:

This chandelier is hand-turned, carved and painted to create a bond of form and color unavailable from any other maker. The turned post creates the Ark and marching two by two along the forged tin arms are an amusing assortment of hand-carved animals. It measures 26 inches high with a diameter of 34 inches.

MOSAICA

Foyer Ensemble:

This mirror and console table with wrought-iron base uses the classic materials of marble and Venetian glass accents to create enduring beauty for any foyer. It was designed by Robyn Crosfield.

RESOURCEASIA

Balinese Judang:

This exquisitely carved teak judang was originally used in Bali to house hand-embroidered silks. Today it adds a touch of exotic functioning as a settee, side table or storage cache. It measures 40 inches long by 21 inches wide.
Photo by C. J. Walker

HOUSE OF HIGH FIDELITY

McIntosh Receiver:

The great American powerhouse is reintroducing this powerful receiver. It has A/V Dolby digital DTS in 6.1 at 100 watts x 6.

SHOWROOM 84

Palace Athene Collection:

SHOWROOM 84 is proud to announce this newest collection from Pavilion Furniture. It includes a love seat, arm chair, ottoman, dining table with both side and arm chairs, chaises, coffee tables, end tables, serving carts, bar tables, bar stools and consoles. Table tops are available in glass, faux stone or mosaic stone. There are 18 metal finishes to choose from.

PALMA BRAVA

Magical Palm Tree:

585

Stand in awe of the Magical Palm Tree, a royal combination of materials and finishes with nearly 1,000 glass leaves. Upward, built-in light fixtures create spectacular lighting effects. It stands 10 feet 6 inches tall with a 5-foot 6-inch diameter. It is available as a half palm design to allow for wall mounting. Also part of this family is the Magical Bamboo Tree.

KRISARTT

Suede Armchair:

Designed exclusively for the Krisartt Collection and manufactured in Brazil, this armchair exhibits a design sensitivity that appeals to your comfort level as well as to your eye. Shown in golden suede, this 27-inch wide, 24-inch deep and 28-inch high armchair is available in 10 colors to harmonize with any décor.

RAINBOW TILE

Gold Byzantium Stone Mosiacs:

For the discerning buyer looking for an Old World look with the flexibility to be combined with new innovations, this line of stone and glass mosaics provides diverse solutions. With a wide range of colors and patterns, the design possibilities are endless. Pictured are Gold Byzantium staggered stone mosaics outlined with the Fern 4 Murano Glass mosaics.

SOUTH DADE LIGHTING, INC.

Chandelier:

This Empire-inspired chandelier finds enrichment in ancient classical and Italian Renaissance details. A cartouche motif that would have signified an Italian family name or its heraldic bearings adorns the cups that support the small, creamy alabaster bowls. Important to many decors, the bronze patina finish paired with the warmness of the alabaster imparts a romantic feeling.

INTERIOR MARKETPLACE

1988 Grand Piano:

We are finding that the requests for interior consignment pieces is expanding from furniture and accessories to items such as pianos, bars, pool tables and architectural fixtures. Featured is a 1988 Kimball professional grand piano in the polyester ebony finish. It features an imported Schwander Roller grand piano action and is a perfect instrument for use in concert halls, conservatories, schools or homes.

PALM BEACH POTTERY

Alex Vale Sofa:

A decorator has to be able to envision a room with style and distinction. Alex Vale influences concept and creativity from color blend to the latest trend. Let your imagination give you a unique look. What you see can be modified to get what you want.

Showroom

o see who and what everyone will be talking about.

GLOBAL FURNITURE

Living Room Group:

Exotic bamboo…so right for Florida! Exterior big pole bamboo is the basis of our exclusive multi-pillow-back sofa and loveseat living room group, and is richly accented with tightly woven rattan peel from Far East Rattan. The living room group is available in more than 75 fabrics and has guaranteed delivery within 15 working days.

HANSEN L.C.

Custom Library Unit:

This custom-made library room wall was handcrafted in a traditional style from natural American cherry wood veneer. The client chooses the veneer and finish suited to the project, as well as the overall design of the room or units being made. The wall unit shown can be utilized as an entire library, or part of a study, family room, master bedroom or den.

Photo by Robert Brantly

587

ABC CARPET AND HOME

Fine Oriental Carpets

An exciting and extensive collection of spectacular handmade oriental carpets awaits you in our showroom. From tribal and traditional to the most innovative designs, our internationally famous, rich wool carpeting beautifully completes any room.

Finally...
South Florida's Own
Home & Design
Sourcebook

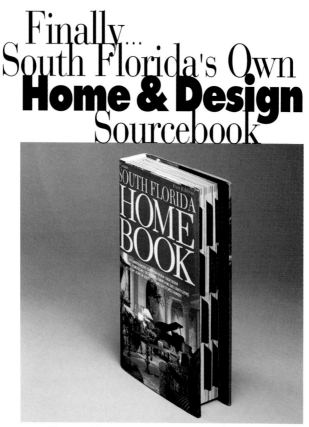

Call Toll Free at 888-458-1750

The South Florida Home Book, www.floridahomebook.com, is your final destination when searching for home improvement services. This comprehensive, hands-on-guide to building, remodeling, decorating, furnishing, and landscaping a home, is required reading for the serious and discriminating homeowner. With over 700 full-color, beautiful pages, this hard cover volume is the most complete and well-organized reference to the home industry. The Home Book covers all aspects of the process, including listings of hundreds of industry professionals, accompanied by informative and valuable editorial discussing the most recent trends. Ordering your copy of ***The South Florida Home Book,*** now, can ensure that you have the blueprints to your dream home, in your hand, today.

Order your copy today!

O R D E R   F O R M

THE SOUTH FLORIDA HOME BOOK

☐ YES, please send me _____ copies of the SOUTH FLORIDA HOME BOOK at $39.95 per book, plus $3 postage & handling per book.

Total amount sent: $_____   Please charge my: ☐ VISA   ☐ MasterCard   ☐ American Express

Card # _____ Exp. Date_____

Signature _____

Name _____ Phone ( ) _____

Address _____

City _____ State _____ Zip Code _____

Send order to: Attn: Book Sales–Marketing Dept., The Ashley Group, 1350 E. Touhy Ave., Suite 1E, Des Plaines, Illinois 60018
Or Call Toll Free at: 1-888-458-1750   Or E-mail ashleybooksales@cahners.com

All orders must be accompanied by check, money order or credit card # for full amount.

Home
Furnishings

ABC CARPET & HOME...**(561) 279-7777**
   777 S. Congress (between Linton & Atlantic), Del Ray Beach   Fax: (561) 279-4920
   See Ad on Page: 530, 531, 590, 591   800 Extension: 1003
   <u>Principal/Owner:</u> J. Weinrib
   <u>Website:</u> www.abchome.com
   <u>Additional Information:</u> The New York home furnishing legend, now in DelRay
   Beach. Oriental rugs, wall-to-wall antiques, linens and more.

COLETTE DESIGN, INC....**(561) 367-9626**
   2142-2150 N. Federal Highway, Boca Raton   Fax: (561) 367-9606
   See Ad on Page: 441, 596   800 Extension: 1060
   <u>Principal/Owner:</u> Jurgen Muller, MBA
   <u>Website:</u> www.colettedesign.com
   <u>Additional Information:</u> Designers and direct importers of fine German brand
   names.

DÉCOR HOUSE FURNITURE ....**(305) 448-8500**
   4420 Ponce de Leon Blvd., Coral Gables   Fax: (305) 448-3537
   See Ad on Page: 604, 605   800 Extension: 1068

FIRST IMPRESSIONS CUSTOM
FURNITURE COMPANY, INC. ....**(954) 969-7963**
   2250 NW 30th Place, Pompano Beach   Fax: (954) 969-1647
   See Ad on Page: 618   800 Extension: 1102
   <u>Principal/Owner:</u> Robert Pacillo
   <u>Website:</u> www.yourfirstimpression.net <u>email:</u> yourfirstimp@aol.com
   <u>Additional Information:</u> We innovate the utmost in custom elegance!

589

continued on page **598**

Photo courtesy of International Interiors Association

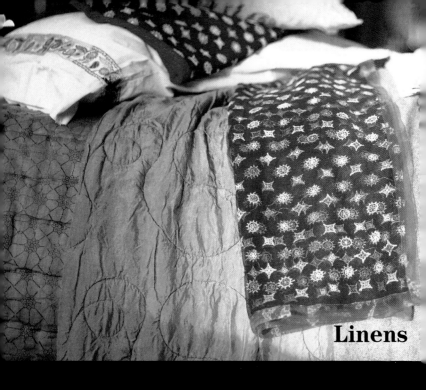

Linens

Pictured: Karastan

Broadloom

ABC Carpet & Home in Manhattan is the ultimate destination for those seeking unique and eclectic home furnishings. ABC's Florida store epitomizes the same style, originality and value. Find an exciting collection of handmade oriental carpets, innovative design rugs, rich wool carpeting, antiques and furniture, linens for bed and bath, and a wide range of decorative accessories. Open seven days a week. American Express, MasterCard, Visa accepted.

Orientals & Design Rugs

Furniture

inspiration

by cattelan italia

furniture
by scan design

Florida's largest selection of European contemporary furniture.

*we export

Global Furniture
GROUP

Manufacturer & Distributor of Custom Upholstery, Rattan and Stone

Famous Makers As: Grand Bay, Far East Rattan and Kent

CORPORATE OFFICE: 1200 N. W. 167 Street, Bay 1 Miami, FL 33169
Tel 305.627.9127 Fax 305.627.9122 Toll Free 800.471.9739

FLORIDA: *Ft Lauderdale, Far East Rattan* 2533 E. Sunrise Blvd. 954.630.0303
Ormond Beach, Modernage Galleries, 445 S. Yonge St. 904.615.7520

N. CAROLINA: *Highpoint,* Medallion at the Atrium Mall, 336.889.3432
Hickory, Medallion at Catawba Mall 828.267.0228

www.medallion-furniture.com

**Good living does not result by chance... whether it is a
21st Century, Classical Period or International design...**

Come and visit with **colette design, inc.**

importers of fine German furniture
2142-2150 North Federal Highway
Boca Raton, FL 33431
Phone 561-367-9626 Fax 561-367-9606
www.colettedesign.com

Living means to take possession of your site. Living is individuality.
Come and visit our showroom and let us help you develop your own ideas
that suit your requirements.

Truggelmann, **hülsta**, *wellmann*, ALNO, **gruco**, omnia, Brinkmann

continued from page **589**

GLOBAL FURNITURE GROUP ....**(800) 471-9739**
1200 NW 167th Street, Bay 1, Miami
See Ad on Page: 595
Principal/Owner: Larry Glanber
email: globalfg@bellsouth.net

Fax: (305) 627-9122
800 Extension: 1110

Additional Information: Considered one of Florida's leading sources for rattan, wicker and stone furniture, Global Furniture has set itself apart by offering exclusive designs that reflect exceptional quality and value.

IN ART & FURNITURE GALLERY/ IN GALLERY ....**(305) 377-3222**
625 SW 1st Avenue, Miami
See Ad on Page: 616, 617

Fax: (305) 377-4919
800 Extension: 1131

INSPIRATION FURNITURE ....**(305) 944-8080**
3025 NE 163 Street, North Miami Beach
See Ad on Page: 592, 593
Principal/Owner: Peter Knudsen
Website: www.inspirationfurniture.com

Fax: (305) 944-7666
800 Extension: 1134

Additional Information: Inspiration Furniture by Scan Design has been serving Florida for 31 years; specializing in high end home furnishing.

INTERIOR MARKETPLACE, INC. ....**(561) 743-2944**
243 South US One, Tequesta
See Ad on Page: 614, 615
Principal/Owner: Rusty LaScala

Fax: (561) 743-7167
800 Extension: 1137

Website: www.palmbeachconsignments.com email: impl@earthlink.net

KRATON GALLERY USA, INC....**(561) 447-7171**
139 NW 11 Street, Boca Raton
See Ad on Page: 611
Principal/Owner: Jacquie Macleod

Fax: (561) 447-7171
800 Extension: 1154

Website: www.kraton-gallery.com email: jacquie@kraton-gallery.com

LEATHER DESIGN STUDIO ....**(305) 572-0788**
101 N.E. 40th Street, Miami
See Ad on Page: 570, 571, 612
Principal/Owner: William Chepp

Fax: (305) 572-0782
800 Extension: 1163

Additional Information: South Florida's premier showcase of fine leather furniture.

LIGNE ROSET ....**(314) 965-1991**
12412 Powerscourt Drive, Suite 175, St. Louis, MO
See Ad on Page: 601
Principal/Owner: Jon Panullo

Fax: (314) 965-8848
800 Extension: 1164

LIGNE ROSET ....**(312) 867-1207**
56 E. Walton Street, Chicago
See Ad on Page: 601
Principal/Owner: Jon Panullo

800 Extension: 1165

LUMINAIRE ....**(305) 448-7367**
2331 Ponce De Leon Blvd., Coral Gables
See Ad on Page: 609
Principal/Owner: Nasir Kassamali

Fax: (305) 448-9447
800 Extension: 1166

Website: www.luminaire.com email: info@luminaire.com

MARGAUX..**(305) 662-2663**
5805 Sunset Drive, South Miami
See Ad on Page: 600
Principal/Owner: Margarita Courtney

Fax: (305) 662-2664
800 Extension: 1171

continued on page **608**

Strauss & Wassel

3200 S. Congress Ave.
Boynton Beach, FL 33426
(561) 736-7800

509 N.E. 20th St.
Boca Raton, FL 33431
(561) 395-6447

Margaux
a world collection

A Collection of Fine Furniture, Accessories, Fabrics, Bedding
& Gifts for your Home.
Visual Coordination and Design Services Available.

5805 Sunset Drive
South Miami, FL 33143
305.662.2663 ▪ Fax 305.662.2664

LE STYLE

ligne roset ®

DE VIE.

Distinctive, understated furniture, lighting, and
home accessories crafted in France.

Rose de Paris

and Provence

4330 Gulf Shore Blvd. North
The Village on Venetian Bay #304
Naples, FL 34103
941.430.0155

Decor House Furniture

4119 Ponce de Leon Boulevard
Coral Gables, Florida 33146
Tel: (305) 448-8500
Fax: (305) 448-3537

Opus 2.000

Home Furnishing &
Custom Made Sofas

201 Bird Road   •   Coral Gables, Florida 33146

Tel. (305) 448-4819   •   Fax (305) 448-9048

continued from page **598**

MARIE ANTOINETTE'S FURNITURE & ACCESSORIES ....(561) 575-1095
Gallery Square North- 363 Tequesta Drive, Tequesta
See Ad on Page: 613
800 Extension: 1173

MARIE ANTOINETTE'S FURNITURE & ACCESSORIES ....(561) 841-2313
Oaks Plaza- 9339 Alt. A1A, Suite 7A, Lake Park
See Ad on Page: 613
800 Extension: 1174

MARIE ANTOINETTE'S FURNITURE & ACCESSORIES ....(561) 841-2313
9339 Alt. A1A, Suite 7A, Lake Park
See Ad on Page: 613
800 Extension: 1175

MAURICE'S ANTIQUE PINE ....(561) 742-4528
2532 W. Indiantown Rd., Jupiter
See Ad on Page: 597, 666, 667
Fax: (561) 575-1558
800 Extension: 1178
Principal/Owner: Maurice Jonker
Website: www.mauricepine.com email: mauricepine@aol.com
Additional Information: Imports of European antique pine furniture, we offer our own unique line of European inspired reproductions, reminiscent of old world charm.

OPUS 2000 HOME FURNISHINGS ....(305) 448-4819
201 Bird Road, Coral Gables
See Ad on Page: 607
Fax: (305) 448-9048
800 Extension: 1196

PALMA BRAVA, INC. ....(561) 451-1099
20665 Lyons Road, Boca Raton
See Ad on Page: 603
Fax: (561) 451-3721
800 Extension: 1201
Principal/Owner: Winston Lee / The Lee Family
Website: www.palmabrava.com email: palmabrava@aol.com
Additional Information: Palma Brava, Inc. is the designer & manufacturer of its exclusive collection of hand made home furnishings.

RESOURCE ASIA ....(561) 659-6597
500 Palm Street, Suite 24, West Palm Beach
See Ad on Page: 594
Fax: (561) 659-3693
800 Extension: 1222
Principal/Owner: Susan Retz
Website: www.resourceasia.net email: sretz@resourceasia.net
Additional Information: Furnishings that embody the best of nature. The finest in teak, for indoors or out.

ROSE DE PARIS & PROVENCE ....(941) 430-0155
4330 Gulfshore Blvd. N., Suite 304, Naples
See Ad on Page: 602
800 Extension: 1225

SIPURE DESIGN, INC. ....(305) 576-2277
135 NE 40th Street, Miami
See Ad on Page: 610
Fax: (305) 576-2275
800 Extension: 1237
Principal/Owner: Michelle Billet
Website: www.sipuredesign.com email: info@sipuredesign.com

STRAUSS & WASSNER, INC. ....(561) 736-7800
3200 S. Congress, Boynton Beach
See Ad on Page: 599
Fax: (561) 369-7135
800 Extension: 1250
Principal/Owner: Madelyn Strauss
email: strausswassner@aol.com

VIA SOLFERINO ITALIAN FURNITURE ....(305) 572-1182
3930 NE 2nd Avenue, Suite 105, Miami
See Ad on Page: 606
Fax: (305) 572-0017
800 Extension: 1269
Principal/Owner: Simona Ciancetta
email: viasolferino@aol.com

608

What is Luminaire?

enduring
functional
accessible
classic
adaptive
innovative

sofas
chairs
tables
lighting
office furniture
accessories
books
shelving
beds

Agape
B&B Italia
Cappellini
Driade
Ingo Maurer
Montis
Porro
Vitra

Starck
Citterio
Lissoni
Morrison
Wright
Le Corbusier
Gray
Lovegrove

Living
Eating
Working
Sleeping
Dreaming

Come visit Luminaire to experience our entire collection of furnishings, accessories, and the knowledge of our informed staff. Let Luminaire's timeless design be a part of your lifestyle, today and tomorrow.

LUMINAIRE®

Brilliant European Design. At Home. At Work.

"Le Foglie" - DEMA - Designer Claudio Silvestrin

"M" - MODENATURE - Paris
Designer Jean Paul Marzais

"Sitting Bed" - MODENATURE - Paris - Designer Henry Becq

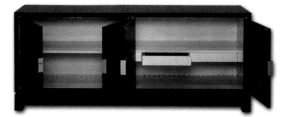

"Ba-Li" - MODENATURE - Paris - Designer Henry Becq

"Slow" - DIX HEURES DIX - Paris
Designer Fabrice Berrux

Exclusively at

Sipure
design

Sipure design - Miami Design District - 135 N.E. 40th Street - Miami, Fl 33137
Tel 305.576.2277 - Fax 305.576.2275 - www.sipuredesign.com
e-mail: info@sipuredesign.com

LEATHERdesignSTUDIO

Casual Living & Lifestyles

101 NE 40th Street ▪ Miami, FL 33137
Ph. (305) 572-0788   Fax: (305) 572-0782

Marie Antoinette's
FURNITURE ACCESSORIES

GALLERY SQUARE NORTH
363 TEQUESTA DRIVE
TEQUESTA, FL 33469
561.575.1095

OAKS PLAZA
9339 ALT. A1A, SUITE 7A
LAKE PARK, FL 33403
561.841.2313

Interior
MARKETPLACE

Consignments of Fine Furnishings, Art and Accessories

VILLAGE SQUARE • 243 SOUTH U.S. ONE • TEQUESTA, FLORIDA 33469
PHONE: 561-743-2944
www.palmbeachconsignments.com

gallery

Miami Downtown/Bricknell
625 SW 1st Avenue
Miami, FL 33130
(307)377-3222

DCOTA
1855 Griffin Road, C230
Dania Beach, FL 33004
(954)926-5613

www.ingallery.org

First Impressions
CUSTOM FURNITURE COMPANY, INC.

Libraries • Wall Units
Entertainment Centers
Home Theatres

Decorators &
Consultants

DISTINCTIVE INTERIORS OF MIAMI, INC. ....**(305) 571-5016**
4141 NE 2nd Avenue, Suite 102, Miami   Fax: (305) 571-4091
See Ad on Page: 620   800 Extension: 1074
<u>Principal/Owner:</u> Gary Thomas Kelly
<u>email:</u> gary@distinctiveinteriorsfl.com

Photo courtesy of Distinctive Interiors of Miami

619

Distinctive Interiors of Miami, Inc.

Gary Thomas Kelly

4141 N.E. 2 Avenue, Suite 102
Miami, Florida 33137
Tel: 305-571-5016   Fax: 305-571-4091

Custom
Furniture

ARCHITECTURAL WOOD WORKING CONCEPTS, INC...........(941) 596-2070
2090 Elsa Street, Naples
See Ad on Page: 626, 627
Principal/Owner: Nelson Badillo
Fax: (941) 596-2072
800 Extension: 1021

AREAS & SPACES ....(305) 674-8027
533 West Avenue, Miami Beach
See Ad on Page: 624
Fax: (305) 674-0693
800 Extension: 1022

ELEGANT HOUSE INTERNATIONAL ....(954) 457-8836
1960-A SW 30th Ave, Hallandale
See Ad on Page: 622, 623
Principal/Owner: Alan Nadar / John Hennassy
Website: eleganthouseusa.com
Fax: (954) 457-7838
800 Extension: 1080

**FIRST IMPRESSIONS CUSTOM
FURNITURE COMPANY, INC. ....(954) 969-7963**
2250 NW 30th Place, Pompano Beach
See Ad on Page: 618
Principal/Owner: Robert Pacillo
Website: www.yourfirstimpression.net email: yourfirstimp@aol.com
Additional Information: We innovate the utmost in custom elegance!
Fax: (954) 969-1647
800 Extension: 1102

INTERNATIONAL INTERIORS ASSOCIATES...........(954) 922-8223
DCOTA- Suite B-200- 1855 Griffin Rd., Dania
See Ad on Page: 272, 273, 625
Principal/Owner: Rebecca Tedder
Website: www.interiors-inc.com email: info@interiors-inc.com
Additional Information: Award winning designs & services for over 4 decades.
Full service interior design & architectural renovations with an eclectic array of
unique handcrafted furnishings from around the globe achieves the utmost in
creation, values and client satisfaction.
Fax: (954) 825-2454
800 Extension: 1140

621

ISTRA METALCRAFT INC. ....(941) 597-6445
6089 Lee Ann Lane, Naples
See Ad on Page: 628
Principal/Owner: Mark Houdasheldt
Fax: (941) 597-6230
800 Extension: 1146

KRISARTT..(305) 567-8930
300 Aragon Avenue, Suite 120, Coral Gables
See Ad on Page: 629
Fax: (305) 567-8932
800 Extension: 1155

THE WORKSHOPS OF DAVID T. SMITH ....(941) 649-0901
330 13th Avenue South, Naples
See Ad on Page: 630
Principal/Owner: John Mankiewcz
Website: www.dtsworkshops.com email: dtsnaples@aol.com
Additional Information: The Workshops specializes in custom furniture & cabi-
netry, handmade in hard to fine woods. The custom kitchens, baths & libraries
are built like furniture, with solid wood and traditional joinery.
Fax: (941) 649-0701
800 Extension: 1265

English custom size bookcase

Louis XV hand-carved table, 144" L x 50½" W x 31½" H open to 192"

Presidential hand carved desk, 82" L x 45" W x 31½" H

Sectional custom size sofa

Wave custom size sofa

Kidney custom size sofa

Areas & Spaces

Showroom
533 West Avenue
Miami Beach, FL 33139
305 535 0086

Showroom
1624 Alton Road
Miami Beach, FL 33139
305 674 8027

ARCHITECTURAL WOODWORKING CONCEPTS, INC.

2090 Elsa Street
Naples, Florida 34109
Tel: 941-596-2070 Fax: 941-596-2072

Istra Metalcraft, Inc.

UNIQUE POLISHING, RESTORATION AND METAL DESIGNS.

We SPECIALIZE in polishing brass, sterling, copper, bronze, and even plated pieces. SPECIALIZING in the RESTORATION of bronze and other metals. We are PROFOUNDLY COMMITTED to fabricating UNIQUE

and EXCITING pieces. Like furnishings, accessories, railings, gates, mailbox stands and architectural elements and even toilet paper holders. You can be ASSURED that when we custom design a table base or use a designers drawings to hold granite or glass, it will be SOLID. We work close with designers, builders, and even with you the public. We take great PRIDE in each piece, providing the HIGHEST level of personal services to our clients with QUALITY. CREATIVITY is seeing something that doesn't yet exist. And then finding the right company to CREATE it.

Istra Metalcraft

6089 Lee Ann Lane
Naples, FL 34109
office: 941-597-6445
fax: 941-597-6230

Fine Furniture & Accessories

*This photo is from our showroom.

- *Exclusive Collection*
- *Interior Design Services*
- *Bridal Registry*
- *Gift Certificates*

**Our products
are available for
immediate delivery!**

Krisartt

S h o w r o o m
300 Aragon Ave. # 120
(corner of Salzedo)
Coral Gables, FL 33134
Tel.: (305) 567.8930
Fax: (305) 567.8932
info@krisartt.com

www.krisartt.com

Hand-made furniture crafted in hard-to-find woods or painted finishes.

Custom kitchens

Cabinetry for the bath, library, office or fireplace

Fine crafts and accessories

THE
WORKSHOPS
OF
DAVID T. SMITH

330 13th Avenue South
Naples, FL 34102
Phone 941-649-0901   Fax 941-649-0701
E-mail dtsnaples@aol.com

Lifestyle &
Casual Furniture

SHOWROOM 84 INC. ....**(954) 925-8400**
1855 Griffin Road, #B-228, Dania Beach
See Ad on Page: 632, 633

Fax: (954) 925-1617
800 Extension: 1236

Photo courtesy of Showroom 84

631

Lacquered Resi

Wood

Aluminum

Accessories

SHOWROOM 84
CASUAL LIFESTYLE FURNITURE

DCOTA
1855 Griffin Road Suite B228
Dania Beach, Florida 33004
(954) 925-8400 Voice
(954) 925-1617 Fax
Email: showroom84@aol.com
Hours: 9-5 Monday Friday

MIAMI
3901 NE 2nd Avenue
Miami, Florida 33137
(305) 573-5114
(305) 576-1326 Fax
Email: showroom84@aol.com
Hours: 9-5 Monday Friday

Accessories

ANDREA'S LAS OLAS LINENS & BATH......................................**(954) 467-7396**
2426 Las Olas Blvd., Fort Lauderdale   Fax: (954) 523-6957
See Ad on Page: 635   800 Extension: 1015
Principal/Owner: Richard Owen
Additional Information: Specialize in exquisite Custom Linens for your home or yacht. Fort Lauderdale's most distinctive bed and bath shop.

ARTE CERAMICA..**(561) 820-0032**
256 Worth Avenue, Palm Beach   Fax: (561) 659-0530
See Ad on Page: 640   800 Extension: 1026
Principal/Owner: John Fariello
Website: www.arteceramica.com

MOSAICA..**(954) 923-7006**
2029 Harrison Street #4, Hollywood   Fax: (954) 923-7046
See Ad on Page: 638   800 Extension: 1187
Principal/Owner: James Crosfield
Website: email: mosaicaintl.com
Additional Information: We specialize in custom made mosaics for residential or commercial applications. Designed by award winning Robyn Crosfield.

PALM BEACH POTTERY & SILKS ....**(561) 845-7900**
1120 10th Street, Lake Park   Fax: (561) 844-6972
See Ad on Page: 636, 637   800 Extension: 1200
Principal/Owner: Harley Eagar

STEFAN JA STUDEOS ....**(561) 775-0080**
10 Governors Court, Palm Beach Gardens   Fax: (561) 630-4521
See Ad on Page: 641   800 Extension: 1248
Principal/Owner: Stephen Gerhart

634

Photo courtesy of Andrea's Las Olas Lines & Bath

Specializing
in elegant
accessories for
your home
or yacht.

PALM BEACH POTTE[RY]
~home & garden~

Your source for all your fine decorating needs.
We offer a great showroom, filled with unique furniture,
accessories, pots and permanent botanicals presented to you
by friendly and courteous professionals.

RY

- ◆ Permanent Botanicals
  - Custom Silk Arrangements
  - Custom Trees
  - Floor Plants
  - Greenery

- ◆ Imported Pottery
  - Hand Made Greek
  - Italian Terracotta
  - Glazed Fishbowls

- ◆ Accessories
  - Artwork
  - Mirrors
  - Lamps
  - Containers
  - Sculptures

- ◆ Furniture
  - Unique Antiques
  - Classic Reproductions
  - Custom Designs
  - Traditional
  - Contemporary

Photography © Peter Morpurgo

1220 Tenth Street
Lake Park, FL 33403
Tel: 561-845-7900
Fax: 561-844-6972
E-mail: pbpots@digital.net
Web: www.palmbeachpottery.com

Custom mosaics in marble, ceramic, china & glass made in our studio since 1988 Furniture, mirrors, floor inlays & accessories

MOSAICA STUDIO & GALLERY

2029 Harrison Street #4   Hollywood, FL 33020
Tel: 954.923.7006   Fax: 954.923.7046
www.mosaicaintl.com

Finally...
South Florida's Own
Home & Design
Sourcebook

The SOUTH FLORIDA HOME BOOK, a comprehensive hands-on Design Sourcebook to building, remodeling, decorating, furnishing and landscaping a luxury home in South Florida is a "must-have" reference for the South Florida homeowner. At over 700 pages, this beautiful, full-color hard cover volume is quite simply the most complete, well-organized reference to the South Florida home industry. It covers all aspects of the process, with hundreds of listings of local home industry professionals, accompanied by hundreds of inspiring photographs. You will also find articles to assist in planning and completing a project. The SOUTH FLORIDA HOME BOOK tells you how to find what you need when you need it.

Order your copy today!

Published by

The Ashley Group

3440 Hollywood Blvd., Suite 460 • Hollywood, Florida 33021

Toll Free 888.458.1750   Fax 847.390.2902

E-mail: ashleybooksales@cahners.com

ARTE CERAMICA

Spanish Imports & Tile Murals

256 Worth Avenue Via Gucci Palm Beach, Florida 33480
Tel 561.820.0032 Fax 561.650.0530
www.arteceramica.com

Photography: Liz Ordoñez

▲ Aquarium Art
90" W x 50" H x 10" D

▲ Table Base
50" L x 30" W x 17" H

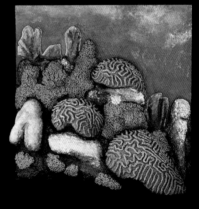

▲ The Wall
68" W x 80" H x 21" D

▲ Tubes & Brains
48" W x 48" H x 21" D

Stefen Jā Stüdēoṣ

Palm Beach Gardens
Florida
ph: (561) 630-6621
fax: (561) 630-4521
www.reefsculpture.com

Lighting

FARREY'S LIGHTING & BATH..**(305) 947-5451**
1850 NE 146 Street, North Miami   Fax: (305) 947-0157
See Ad on Page: 410, 458, 511, 643   800 Extension: 1092
<u>Principal/Owner:</u> Bud Farrey
<u>Website:</u> www.farreys.com <u>email:</u> info@farreys.com
<u>Additional Information:</u> Largest selection of lighting, decorative hardware,
plumbing, furniture and accessories. Branch location at 4101 Ponce de Leon
Blvd in Coral Gables.

LAMP HOUSE & SHADE CENTER ....**(954) 561-0408**
4150 N. Federal Highway, Ft. Lauderdale   Fax: (954) 561-8847
See Ad on Page: 646   800 Extension: 1160

PAUL MORGAN LIGHTING DESIGN, INC................................**(954) 566-0951**
2050 E Oakland Park Blvd, Suite 204, Ft Lauderdale   Fax: (954) 566-1875
See Ad on Page: 648   800 Extension: 1204
<u>Principal/Owner:</u> Paul Morgan
<u>email:</u> pmltng@aol.com
<u>Additional Information:</u> Independent lighting design and consultants, over 20
years experience — residential, commercial, and landscape.

PALM BEACH LIGHTING & FAN CO., INC. ....**(561) 575-6878**
880 Jupiter Park Drive, Suite 12, Jupiter   Fax: (561) 744-8551
See Ad on Page: 412, 644, 645   800 Extension: 1199
<u>Principal/Owner:</u> Walter Miller

SOUTH DADE LIGHTING INC...**(305) 233-8020**
13006 SW 87th Ave, Miami   Fax: (305) 233-4295
See Ad on Page: 647   800 Extension: 1244
<u>Principal/Owner:</u> Kathy Held
<u>Website:</u> www.south-dade.com <u>email:</u> sdl@south-dade.com

Photo courtesy of Farrey's Lightng and Bath

Lighting & Bath
Since 1924

*Your complete source of lighting, decorative
hardware, plumbing, furniture and accessories.*

131,000 SQ. FT. MAIN LOCATION:
1850 N.E. 146th Street • North Miami, FL 33181 • 1-800-377-5483

CORAL GABLES BRANCH:
4101 Ponce de Leon Blvd. • Coral Gables, FL 33146 • 305-445-2244

CALL 305-919-0125 FOR A FREE VIDEO
www.farreys.com • E-mail: info@farreys.com

Island Fans

by
Palm Beach Lighting & Fan
Ph (561) 575-6878

Barbados blades
21" X 12" X 1/2"

Jamaican blades
30" X 12" X 1/2"

Bahama bent bla
36" X 6" X 3/16"

All blades are hand crafted, custom carving is availabl

ALL BLADES ARE BALANCED AND MOVE MORE AIR THAN STANDARD BLADES

* Patent Pending

* All blades are offered
unfinished or stained

* Shown above and to the
left a walnut stain

* Below white pickled

* All blades are signed by
artist and made in U.S.A.

Palm Beach
Lighting & Fan Co.
Professional Custom Lighting Consultants

PMLD

Paul Morgan
Lighting Design, Inc.
I.E.S.N.A., I.A.L.D.

ARCHITECTURAL LIGHTING DESIGN

2050 E. Oakland Park Blvd.
Suite 201
Fort Lauderdale, FL 33306
Tel: (954) 566-0951
Fax: (954) 566-1875
pmltng@aol.com

Pianos

HALE PIANO, INC. ....**(954) 942-1400**
880 SW 10th Avenue #4, Pompano Beach
See Ad on Page: 650   800 Extension: 1119
<u>Principal/Owner:</u> Charles K. Hale

649

Bösendorfer

Can you afford not to buy a Bösendorfer?

CONSERVATORY SERIES · CS · BÖSENDORFER

Why settle for the second best when you can afford a handmade, genuine Bösendofer grand piano for the same price?

Since the early days of the Bösendorfer Piano Company the greatest named composers such as Franz Liszt, Johannes Brahms, Antonin Dvorak, Leonard Bernstein and many of the greatest artists such as André Previn, András Schiff, Garrick Ohlsson, Oscar Peterson or Tori Amos, have trusted Bösendorfer.

...handmade precision since 1828

Hale Piano Inc.

Exclusive Dealer

Window Coverings
& Fabric

MODERN VENETIAN BLIND CORP..**(561) 585-2561**
417 Bunker Road, West Palm Beach   Fax: (561) 585-6170
See Ad on Page: 652   800 Extension: 1185
Principal/Owner: Cynthia Hall Othus
Website: www.modernvenetianblind.com email: modernvenetianblind@msn.com
Additional Information: Family owned and operated since 1946. Serving the
Palm Beaches for 54 years.
TOTAL WINDOW ....**(305) 921-0109**
PO Box 17388, West Palm Beach
See Ad on Page: 653   800 Extension: 1266
Principal/Owner: Stephen Stolow

651

Photo courtesy of Modern Venetian Blind Corp.

PHOTO BY JOHN STILLMAN

SHOWN ABOVE:
SOLARWEAVE Cascade Roman Shade

Circle Response 004

TOTAL WINDOW
CUSTOM WINDOW TREATMENTS

P.O. BOX 17388
WEST PALM BEACH, FL 33416
(800) 344-4558
www.totalwindow.com

1855 GRIFFIN ROAD
SUITE B-486 DANIA BCH, FL 33004
(954) 921-0109
FAX: (954) 921-0302

Custom Hand-Woven Vertical and Roman Blinds, Shutters, Shoji Screens,
Branch Covered Screens, Solarweave Window Shades, Architectural and Motarized Systems.

Specialty
Wall Finishes

AESTHETIXX ....**(407) 466-4544**
670 N. Orlando Avenue, Suite 1001, Orlando   Fax: (407) 539-0973
See Ad on Page: 657   800 Extension: 1008
Principal/Owner: Patrick Daly

MULDOON STUDIO'S ....**(800) 436-8332**
P.O. Box 664, Marco Island   Fax: (941) 642-0807
See Ad on Page: 655   800 Extension: 1188
Principal/Owner: Stephen Muldoon
Website: www.muldoonart.com

SWEET ART & DESIGN, INC. ....**(941) 597-2110**
1813 J&C Blvd, Naples   Fax: (941) 597-4205
See Ad on Page: 656   800 Extension: 1256
Principal/Owner: Dede Sweet / Brad Conrad
Website: www.sweetartstudios.com
Additional Information: Sweet Art & Design, Inc. offering museum quality faux finishing, venetian plaster, murals & trompe l'oeil. Creating artful environments for distinctive residential and commercial clients.

"As more homeowners opt
for a *casual, yet elegant ambience,*
furnishings continue to
in popularity."

Sweet Art & Design, Inc. featuring Museum quality faux finishing, Venetian plaster, Murals and Trompe l'oeil. Creating artful environments for distintive residential and commercial clientele.

Sweet Art & Design Studios

1813 J & C Blvd.
Naples, FL 34109
Tel: 941-597-2110
Fax: 941-597-4205

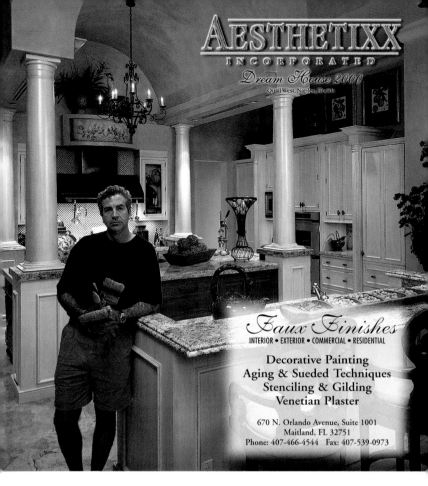

"EVERY TIME
WE SAY LET THERE BE!
IN ANY FORM,
SOMETHING HAPPENS."

Stella Terrill Mann

The
Ashley
Group

Publishers of Fine Visual Reference for the Discerning Connoisseur
1350 Touhy Ave. • Des Plaines, Illinois 60018
888.458.1750 • FAX 847.390.2902
ashleygroup@cahners.com

Home Office,
Closet & Garage

212 DESIGN ....**(786) 425-0032**
1110 Brickell Avenue, Suite 430, Miami — Fax: (786) 425-1050
See Ad on Page: 660 — 800 Extension: 1000
Principal/Owner: Louis Mesa

THE CLOSET COMPANY ....**(941) 434-6655**
3605 Tamiami Trail, Naples — Fax: (941) 434-8514
See Ad on Page: 659 — 800 Extension: 1263
Principal/Owner: Robert King
Website: www.naplesnetnews.com/closetcom.htm email: theclosets@aol.com

DESIGNER CLOSETS, INC....**(941) 596-8700**
1410 Railhead Blvd, Naples — Fax: (941) 596-8702
See Ad on Page: 661 — 800 Extension: 1071
Principal/Owner: Nancy Meesig

Photo courtesy of Closte Company\Photo by Warner Photography

thinkwood®

wood solutions at plastic melamine prices™

888-207-1418
www.thinkwood.com

Miami • Ft. Lauderdale • Boca Raton • Orlando

"THE BEAUTIFUL
RESTS
ON THE
FOUNDATIONS
OF THE
Emerson # NECESSARY "

The
Ashley
Group

Publishers of Fine Visual Reference for the Discerning Connoisseur

1350 Touhy Ave. • Des Plaines, Illinois 60018
888.458.1750 • FAX 847.390.2902
ashleygroup@cahners.com

Home Gyms &
Entertainment

BERRY'S BARBELL AND EQUIPMENT CO..............................**(941) 432-0800**
14041 South Tamiami Trail, Fort Myers   Fax: (941) 432-9034
See Ad on Page: 664   800 Extension: 1034
FORTRESS RECREATIONAL PRODUCTS, INC..........................**(561) 334-9733**
1298 NE Business Park Place, Jensen Beach   Fax: (561) 334-9731
See Ad on Page: 663   800 Extension: 1105
<u>Additional Information:</u> The world's premiere hand carved billiard tables. Made of the finest mahogany and other exotic wood and burls. Each table is a true masterpiece.

Photo courtesy of Barry's Barbell & Equipment

Photo courtesy of:
The America's Collection

ART&
ANTIQUES

Maurice is Florida's premier importer of the finest quality European antique and reproduction pine furniture.

We offer our own unique line of European inspired reproductions, reminiscent of the old world charm. Available in our hand-rubbed natural wax finish, custom colors and crackle paint.

"**Art** does not reproduce the *visible;* it makes visible. "

Paul Klee

Something Old Something New

photo courtesy of:
Bonin Ashley

The fine art and antiques scene is as dynamic as ever. From cutting-edge modern galleries to showrooms of stately antiques, few places in the world offer more choice for bringing truly unique works of art into the home.

Beloved one-of-a-kind items give a home personality in a way that other purchases can't match. Fine art must speak to the soul of the owner. Antique furnishings tell their story through the generations.

Art and antiques, unlike so many other pieces purchased for the home, have the potential to become a family's heirlooms. Even an inexpensive "find" may someday become a most treasured item because of the warm memories it rekindles. Truly, these choices should be made with the care and the guidance of an experienced professional who understands their significance in your home.

LEARN ABOUT ART & ANTIQUES

Part of the pleasure of collecting art or antiques is learning about them. Many homeowners buy a particular painting or sculpture they love, and find that following the art form or the artists becomes a lifetime passion.

The best place to start to familiarize yourself with art is a wander through historic homes in the different historic neighborhoods and get an idea of what the art feels like in a home environment. Go to auctions. Buy the catalog and attend the viewing. At the sale, you'll begin to get an idea of the values of different types of items. Finally, get to know a dealer. Most are pleased to help you learn and want to see more people develop a lifetime love affair with art, similar to their own. If a dealer seems too busy or isn't genuinely interested in helping you, then go to another dealer.

Haunt the local bookstores and newsstands. There are many publications dedicated to these fields.

THE WORLD OF ANTIQUES

Homeowners find their way to antiques by many different paths. Some are adding to an inherited collection that connects them with past generations of family or with the location of their birth. Some are passionate about pottery or porcelain, clocks or dolls, and want to expand their knowledge while building a life-time collection.

Antique furniture, artwork and collectibles also can be used to make a singular statement in an interior. Through a 19th Century English chest, or an American Arts & Crafts table, homeowners put a personal signature stamp on their interior design.

Making the right selection is as much a matter of taste and personal aesthetic as it is knowledge and experience. An interior designer or gallery owner will be a good guide to making a choice.

As top quality antique paintings, photographs and other desirable items become more and more difficult to find, getting expert guidance in identifying good and worthwhile investments is crucial. Top galleries in the area are operated and staffed by knowledgeable professionals who will do just that.

When you enter a store or gallery, be prepared to seriously consider what type of investment you wish to make and how it will work in a given interior. If someone besides yourself will be involved in the final decision-making process, try to have them with you.

If you're pursuing pieces to add to an existing collection, do your research to determine which galleries in town cater to your interests. Or, check with a favorite gallery for information.

Be open to ideas and suggestions, especially when you're just beginning a collection, or a search for a special antique. The best galleries are gold mines of information and ideas. There is so much to know about so many different objects, time periods, and design, that it truly does take a lifetime to develop an expertise. The owners of these establishments are first and foremost interested in finding you an antique that will impress and delight today, and in the future, and usually prefer to have you invest in one or two good pieces, than in a handful of items that won't bring you as much pleasure in the long run.

VISITING THE GALLERIES

More than anything else, choosing to make beautiful and distinctive art objects a part of your home brings the joy of living with beautiful things into the daily life of yourself, your family and your guests.

The most important rule to know as your begin or continue to add art to your home is that there truly are no "rights or wrongs." Find what reaches you on an emotional level, and then begin to learn about it.

Use your eyes and react with your heart. Look at art magazines and books. There are many, many beautiful periodicals, and just as many books published on artists and art genres. Visit the museums in town, and those in other cities as you travel. Go to the galleries. Visit many of them for the widest exposure to different possibilities. Let only your sense of beauty and aesthetics guide you at this point. Consider other constraints after you've identified the objects of your desire.

When you've found what really speaks to you on a personal level, start learning more about who creates art in that style, where it's available locally, and if it's within your budget. The more information you can take with you when you begin your shopping, the more help a gallery can be to you in your search.

EXPERT ADVICE

The most reputable art gallery owners and dealers have earned their reputation by establishing an expertise in their field, and serving their clients well.

Buying from these established and respected professionals offers many benefits. Their considerable knowledge of and exposure to art translates into opinions that mean a great deal. You can put stock in the advice and education they offer you. They've done considerable research and evaluation before any item gets placed in their gallery, and determined that it's a good quality item, both in terms of artistic merit and market value. You'll also enjoy a sense of security when you patronize these businesses. They will stand behind the authenticity of what they present in their galleries. Most offer free consultations, trade-back arrangements, and installation, and will help you with selling your art at some point in the future as your collection grows, you change residences, or your tastes change.

Don't expect a gallery to be an expert in categories outside of those they specialize in.

VALUE JUDGEMENTS

Buy for love, not money. This is the advice we heard time and again from the best art galleries. Not all art appreciates financially – often it fluctuates over the years according to the artist's career, consumer tastes, and the state of the overall economy. If you love what you own and have been advised well by a knowledgeable professional, you'll be happiest with your investment.

THE FALL SEASON

Fall signals the beginning of the art season. Galleries will open exhibits and the excitement is contagious. Ask to get on gallery mailing lists to stay informed of fall openings.

SEE THE SHOWS

The South Florida area abounds with arts, antiques, and collectibles shows and festivals. These are great places to browse for and learn about thousands of items –

671

from jewelry to pop culture collectibles. Local newspapers and magazines run announcements for these kinds of events, or ask your favorite gallery owner for information.

MATCHING ART TO ARCHITECTURE

If you're renovating an historic or old home of distinction, ask your favorite gallery owner or renovation specialist for guidance in choosing art that will fit your home.

There is no upper limit on what you can spend on an art collection, or a single artwork, and there are no set standards for pricing. Gallery owners set prices according to their own standards, evaluations and experience, to represent a fair market value. Set a working budget (possibly a per-piece budget) and let the gallery know upfront what the guidelines are. This saves both you and the gallery time and energy. You'll be able to focus on items that are comfortably within the range of your budget. Buy the best quality possible in whatever category you like. You will appreciate the quality for years. Don't hesitate to do some comparison shopping. Although each art object is unique in itself, you may find another piece in the same style that you enjoy equally as well.

The best dealers understand budgets, and respect your desire to get good quality at a fair price. They are happy to work with enthusiastic clients who want to incorporate beautiful art into their lives. Ask if the dealer offers terms, if you're interested in making your purchases on a payment plan. Also inquire about return or exchange policies, consignment plans, consultations and trade-up policies.

Only deal with dealers who are helpful and present their art fairly. If you feel intimidated in a gallery, or feel the dealer isn't giving you the time and information you deserve to make intelligent choices, visit another gallery. Never buy art under pressure from a dealer, or to meet an imposed deadline in your home interior timetable.

GO TO AN AUCTION HOUSE

Attending an auction is an excellent way to learn about decorative arts, develop and add to a collection, and simply have a good time. Whether you attend as a buyer, seller, or observer, an auction is an experience that will enrich your understanding and enjoyment of the art and antiques world.

If you're a novice, it's important to choose a well established auction house with a reputation for reliability. Try to be a patient observer and learn about the process as well as the value of items you may be interested in later on.

Buy a copy of the catalog and attend the viewing prior to the beginning of the auction itself. Each item, or "lot," that will be available for sale at the auction will be listed, and a professional estimate of selling price will be included. Professionals will be available during the viewing to answer questions and help you become familiar with the art objects as well as the process. Once bidding starts, it is done by "paddle," small numbered placards used to signal a bid, which are obtained before or during the auction.

CHOOSING AN AUCTION

Find out about interesting auctions from the proprietors of galleries you like, or ask to be added to the mailing list of a reputable auction house. With these sources of information, you'll be informed of events that will feature quality items that interest you. Local newspapers and magazines also print upcoming auction dates and locations. The established auction houses that have earned a reputation for reliability and expertise generally have a single location where they hold their auctions. Sometimes an auction will be held at an estate site, or a seller's location.

Before attending the auction, spend some time researching the art or antique you're interested in bidding on, so you'll be informed about its value and can make an informed decision. Talk to people at the galleries. There also are books available that publish recent auction sales to help you get an idea of price and availability. Check your library or book seller for publications like Gordon's Price Annual.

There is an air of mystery and sophistication that surrounds the auction experience, but don't let that discourage you from discovering the auction experience. Auctions are enjoyable and educational for anyone who is interested in obtaining or learning about art and antiques.

BE REALISTIC

For many of us, an auction might seem an opportunity to pick up an item at a bargain price. Realize that there may be bargains to be found, but in general, auctioned items are sold for a fair price. There may be a "reserve price," which is a private agreement between the seller and the auctioneer on a minimum bid.

If you educate yourself about the category you're interested in, you'll be in better stead at an auction. It's equally important to research the market value of any lot you may be considering. Remember that there is an auctioneer's commission of 10 to 15 percent of the hammer price, to be paid on top of the purchase price, as well as applicable sales taxes.

Auctions are essentially competitive in nature, with potential buyers bidding against one another. Until you've attended enough auctions to feel confident in your own knowledge, as well as in your understanding of the auction process, don't become an active participant. It's easy to get swept up in the fast pace and excitement. While you won't end up making the top bid simply by tugging your ear, it's important to pay attention when you're bidding. Be aware of the way the auctioneer communicates with the bidders and always listen for the auctioneer's "fair warning" announcement just before the gavel falls. ■

VISIT OUR MUSEUMS

As you develop your passion for art and items of antiquity, take advantage of the collections and public education opportunities at some of Florida's distinguished art museums, like:

Norton Museum of Art
1451 S. Olive Ave.
West Palm
Beach, FL 33401
(561) 659-4689

Historical Museum of Southern Florida
101 W. Flagler St.
Miami, FL 33130
(305) 375-1492

Miami Art Museum
101 W. Flagler St.
Miami, FL 33130
(305) 375-1700

Museum of Art
1 Las Olas Blvd.
Fort Lauderdale, FL
(954) 525-5500

673

Antiques

BONNIN ASHLEY ANTIQUES..**(305) 667-0969**
4707 SW 72 Avenue, Miami — Fax: (305) 665-9212
See Ad on Page: 678, 679 — 800 Extension: 1039

CHRISTA'S SOUTH ANTIQUES & SEASHELLS ....**(561) 655-4650**
3737 S. Dixie Highway, West Palm Beach — Fax: (561) 659-0055
See Ad on Page: 681 — 800 Extension: 1055
Principal/Owner: Christa Wilm
Website: csseashell.com email: ckwantique@aol.com

CORINTHIAN ANTIQUES..**(305) 854-6068**
2741 SW 27th Avenue, Coconut Grove — Fax: (305) 854-6068
See Ad on Page: 682 — 800 Extension: 1061
Principal/Owner: Roland Castro
Additional Information: In business over 15 years providing designers with some of the best and most stylish pieces to be found anywhere.

THE ELEPHANT'S FOOT ....**(561) 832-0170**
3800 South Dixie Highway, West Palm Beach — Fax: (561) 832-0186
See Ad on Page: 680 — 800 Extension: 1264

FIORELLI ANTIQUES ....**(305) 441-2203**
323 Aragon Avenue, Coral Gables — Fax: (305) 441-1146
See Ad on Page: 683 — 800 Extension: 1101
Principal/Owner: Nino Pernetti
Website: www.fiorelliart.com email: info@fiorelliart.com
Additional Information: Specializing in Art Nourveau, Art Deco and Venetian glass originals.

674

MAURICE'S ANTIQUE PINE ....**(561) 742-4528**
2532 W. Indiantown Rd., Jupiter — Fax: (561) 575-1558
See Ad on Page: 597, 666, 667 — 800 Extension: 1178
Principal/Owner: Maurice Jonker
Website: www.mauricepine.com email: mauricepine@aol.com
Additional Information: Imports of European antique pine furniture, we offer our own unique line of European inspired reproductions, reminiscent of old world charm.

EVELYN S. POOLE, LTD ANTIQUES GALLERY ....**(305) 573-7463**
3925 North Miami Avenue, Miami — Fax: (305) 573-7409
See Ad on Page: 685 — 800 Extension: 1087
Principal/Owner: Evelyn S. Poole
Website: www.evelynpooleltd.com email: evelynpoole@evelynpooleltd.com

JOHN PRINSTER ART DECO-MODERNE ....**(561) 835-1512**
3735 S Dixie Highway, West Palm Beach — Fax: (561) 833-8322
See Ad on Page: 675 — 800 Extension: 1149
Principal/Owner: John Prinster
Additional Information: Fine furniture, lighting, sculpture and ceramics created by the leading designers and artisans fo the 1920's, 1930's and 1940's.

SOUTH DIXIE ANTIQUE ROW ASSOCIATION ....**(561) 588-3119**
PO Box 6815, West Palm Beach — Fax: (561) 588-3122
See Ad on Page: 684 — 800 Extension: 1245
Principal/Owner: Nancy Nauman
Website: www.westpalmbeachantiques.com

BERNARD BARUCH STEINITZ..**(014) 289-4050**
9, rue du Cirque, Paris — Fax: (014) 289-4060
See Ad on Page: 676, 677 — 800 Extension: 1033
Principal/Owner: Bernard Baruch Steinitz

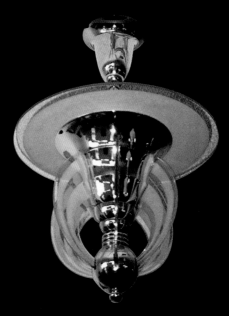

JOHN PRINSTER

ART DECO • MODERNE

Fine furniture, lighting, sculpture, ceramics,
and accessories created by the leading designers
and artisans of the 1920s and 1930s.

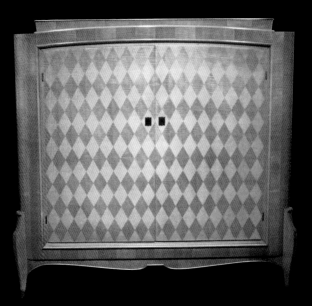

3735 South Dixie Highway • West Palm Beach, FL 33405
561-835-1512

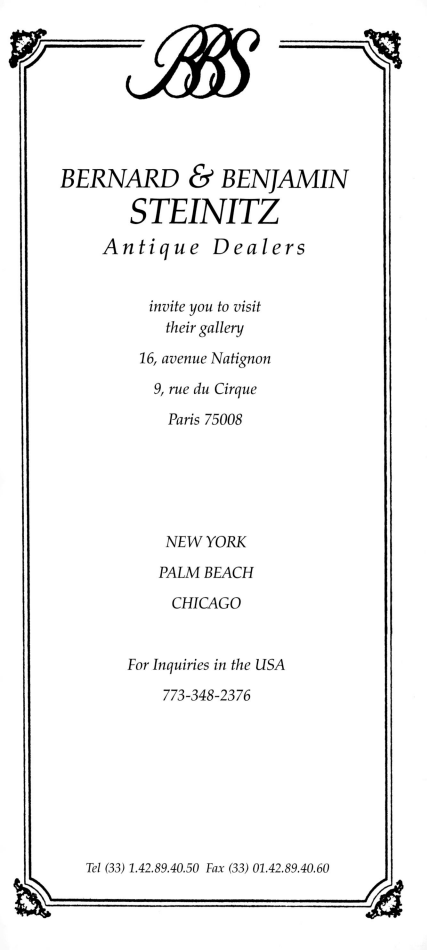

BBS

BERNARD & BENJAMIN
STEINITZ
Antique Dealers

invite you to visit
their gallery

16, avenue Natignon

9, rue du Cirque

Paris 75008

NEW YORK

PALM BEACH

CHICAGO

For Inquiries in the USA

773-348-2376

Tel (33) 1.42.89.40.50 Fax (33) 01.42.89.40.60

BONNIN ASHLEY ANTIQUES

4707 Southwest 72nd Avenue • Miami

305-667-0969

Monday – Friday 9:30 – 5:30

Saturday 10:00 – 5:30

Over 25,000 square feet to select from

*O*ffering the finest & most extensive
selection of 18th & 19th Century
European and American furniture,
hand-finished to the most exacting
standards for over fifteen years.

The Elephant's Foot

Antiques • Consignments • Estate Liquidation
3800 South Dixie Highway
West Palm Beach, Florida 33405
Phone: 561-832-0170   Fax: 561-832-0186

CHRISTA'S SOUTH SEASHELLS

Christa's South Antiques & Seashells
3737 S. Dixie Highway
West Palm Beach, FL 33405
Phone: 561-655-4650
Fax: 561-659-0055
www.csseashells.com

**"Christa's South Seashells features exotic seashell creations
from waters around the world."**

INVEST IN HISTORY

You may already be aware that antiques are the best investment to consider when choosing fine furnishings for your home. Many times they are less expensive than quality reproductions. With over 20 years of experience, Corinthian Antiques provides one of the finest collections of 18th and 19th century period furnishings and accessories available in South Florida.

CORINTHIAN ANTIQUES

2741 SW 27th Avenue, Coconut Grove, FL 33133

305.854.6068

At your service since 1979.

"THE BEAUTIFUL RESTS ON THE FOUNDATIONS OF THE NECESSARY"

Emerson

The
Ashley
Group

Publishers of Fine Visual Reference for the Discerning Connoisseur
1350 Touhy Ave. • Des Plaines, Illinois 60018
888.458.1750 • FAX 847.390.2902
ashleygroup@cahners.com

Evelyn S. Poole, Ltd.

ANTIQUES GALLERY

www.evelynpooleltd.com

Art Galleries

THE AMERICAS COLLECTION ....**(305) 446-5578**
2440 Ponce de Leon Blvd., Coral Gables   Fax: (305) 446-1148
See Ad on Page: 691   800 Extension: 1262

PATRICIA CLOUTIER ART GALLERY ....**(561) 744-5427**
375 Tequesta Drive, Tequesta   Fax: (561) 745-0645
See Ad on Page: 693   800 Extension: 1203
Principal/Owner: Patricia Cloutier

ROBERT CORDISCO STUDIO ....**(561) 744-3611**
See Ad on Page: 688   800 Extension: 1223
Principal/Owner: Robert Cordisco

FLORENCE GALLERY ....**(561) 833-6660**
309 Worth Ave, Palm Beach   Fax: (561) 833-6149
See Ad on Page: 687   800 Extension: 1104
Principal/Owner: Alio Gasborro
Website: www.florencegallery.com
Additional Information: Museum quality hand painted oil recreations.

MARSH..**(561) 994-9119**
6560 W. Rogers Circle, Suite 25, Boca Raton   Fax: (561) 994-8811
See Ad on Page: 689   800 Extension: 1177

STUDIO GALLLERY NAPP, INC. ....**(305) 365-3690**
260 Crandon Blvd., Key Biscayne   Fax: (305) 365-3690
See Ad on Page: 692   800 Extension: 1251
Principal/Owner: Gudrun Napp
Website: studiogallerynapp.com email: art1100@aol.com
Additional Information: The Gallery takes commisions on custom handpainted pillows, mosaic tables and mosaic work on location, handtufted area rugs and photography.

Photo courtesy of Florence Gallery

Recreations of the Masters
OIL ON CANVAS WATERCOLORS DRAWINGS

Hand Painted Oil Recreations

Each of our Recreations is hand painted by a living
master's artist on the finest Belgium linen canvas to our
specifications and mounted in a beautiful custom frame.
Choose from our large inventory or custom order the piece
you need in the dimensions and frame desired.
The art you want at a price you will love.

FLORENCE GALLERY
309 Worth Avenue
Palm Beach, Florida 33480
(561) 833-6660
http://www.florencegallery.com

ROBERT CORDISCO

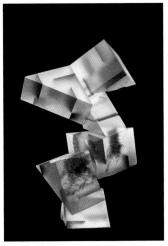

Marsh

6560 W. Rogers Circle, Ste. 25
Boca Raton, FL 33487
561.994.9119
fax 561.994.8811
www.rgarrettdesigns.com

The Importance of Art in the House

From prehistoric man's first cave paintings, art has been essential to human existence. In the 21st Century, all dwellings, from the most traditional to the most contemporary, require some form of artistic expression to be complete. It is important, then, to understand the importance of art in reflecting the personalities of those who live in a home. Art should be one of the most enjoyable and satisfying of the decisions involved in creating the atmosphere of a home.

Decisions about art should be made with three general factors in mind. First and foremost, the artwork should reach the sensibility of the prospective owner, enhancing client enjoyment and appreciation of life. In other words, "you should love it."

The second factor to consider is that the piece should be appropriate to its space, keeping in mind the image, the scale of the piece, the color, and the general environment. The last factor is a thorough understanding of the value of the work based on an analysis of the artist's career, his curriculum, and his position within the art market. These three factors provide a guideline to the process of acquisition of work for the home. Shaped on an anvil when hot, 'wrought' is cold iron bent into the required shape. 'Cast iron' is heated liquid iron poured into a mold.

Dora Valdes Fauli, *The Americans Collection*

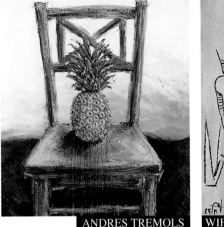

ANDRES TREMOLS

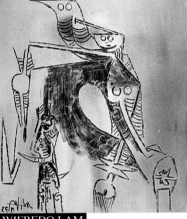

WIFREDO LAM

LINA BINKELE

SEBASTIAN SPRENG

THE AMERICAS COLLECTION

Private and Corporate Fine Art Dealers

2440 Ponce de Leon Boulevard, Coral Gables, FL 33134 ■ (305) 446-5578

Please Visit Our Website For More Information:

www.americascollection.com

Studio Gallery Napp

At **STUDIO GALLERY NAPP**
you will find **Fine Art,** large **Corporate Art**
and **Accessories** for the home. Custom design
commission may also include **Mosaic Work,**
Hand Tufted Area Rugs, Hand Painted Pillows.

Studio Gallery Napp at the Square
260 Crandon Blvd, Ste 18
Key Biscayne, FL 33149
by appointment:
Ph & Fax 305-365-3690 • E-mail ART1100@aol.com
Web. www.studiogallerynapp.com

The Ashley Group Luxury Home Resource Collection

Call Toll Free at 888-458-1750

The Ashley Group is pleased to offer as your final destination when searching for home improvement and luxury resources the following Home Books in your local market: Chicago, Washington DC, South Florida and the Los Angeles area. These comprehensive, hands-on design source books to building, remodeling, decorating, furnishing, and landscaping luxury a home, is required reading for the serious and selective homeowners. With over 600 full-color, beautiful pages per market, these hard cover volumes are the most complete and well-organized reference to the home industry. The Home Books in each market, cover all aspects of the building and remodeling and design process, including listings of hundreds of industry professionals, accompanied by informative and valuable editorial discussing the most recent trends. Ordering your copy of any of the *Home Books* now can ensure that you have the blueprints to your dream home, in your hand, today.

Order your copies today and make your dreams come true!

O R D E R F O R M

Photo courtesy of:
South Eastern Sound

HOME
THEATER

TECHNOLOGY

SOUND
COMPONENTS

For over 27 years, Sound Components has offered

Home Cinemas

Music Systems

Lighting Control

Home Automation

the finest music and film systems available.

1533 Madruga Avenue
Coral Gables, Florida 33146
305-665-4299
Fax 305-663-4138
www.soundcomponents.com

"There is *music* wherever there is

harmony, order and proportion. "

Sir Thomas Browne

photo courtesy of:
Designer Audio
photo by:
Laurence Taylor

Living the Tech Life

Home theaters just keep getting better and better. Technology wizards continue to deliver bigger and better products less obtrusively, and more affordably, into our homes. What was once a rare home luxury has become a top priority item in new custom homes, and in home additions and renovations.

Sophisticated Florida area homeowners have had their level of appreciation for quality in sight and sound elevated through years of experience in concert halls, movie theaters and sports arenas. As they gravitate toward making the home the focus of their lifestyle, and strive to incorporate that high level of performance into their leisure time at home, home theater becomes a more desirable and practical investment. Systems are used for viewing commercial movies, home videos, live concerts and sport events, playing games, and accessing interactive technology. Media or entertainment rooms, custom-sized and designed to deliver concert hall sound and a big, sharp picture, are frequently specified in new construction and remodeling projects. Interest in upscale prefabricated home theaters, which are far more luxurious than some of today's movie theaters, continues to increase. "Hey, kids, let's go to the movies!"

THE IMPORTANCE OF A HOME THEATER DESIGN SPECIALIST

Home theater is widely specified as a custom home feature today. The sophisticated homeowner with a well-developed eye (and ear) for quality demands the latest technology in a home entertainment system that will provide pleasure for many years. Because of the fluid marketplace, the vast possibilities of the future, and the complexity of the products, it's crucial to employ an established professional to design and install your home theater.

The experts presented on the following pages can advise you on the best system for your home. They can find an appropriate cabinet (or direct you to expert custom cabinet makers), expertly install your system, and teach you to use it. Their expertise will make the difference.

THE HOME THEATER DESIGN PROCESS

Tell your builder or remodeling specialist early if you want a home theater, especially if built-in speakers, a large screen or a ceiling-mounted video projection unit are part of the plan.

Inform the interior designer so proper design elements can be incorporated. Window treatments to block out light and help boost sound quality, furnishings or fabrics to hide or drape speakers, and comfortable seating to enhance the media experience should be considered. If you plan to control the window treatments by remote control, these decisions will have to be coordinated.

Visit one of the following showrroms. Be ready to answer these questions:

• What is your budget? There is no upper limit on what you can spend.

• Do you want a television tube or projection video system? A DVD player or hi-fi VCR? Built-in or free-standing speakers?

• Do you want Internet access?

• What style of cabinetry and lighting do you want? Do you want lighting or a built-in bar? How much storage is needed?

• What are the seating requirements? Seating should be at least seven feet from the screen.

• Do you want whole-house control capability so you can distribute and control the system from different rooms of the house?

• How will you incorporate the system with the rest of the room? Must the home theater room meet other needs?

• Do you want extra luxuries, like multiple screens, or a remote control system that allows you to dim the lights and close the draperies? Ask your salesperson for ideas.

• Will this room function in the future? As technology continues to change our lifestyle, plan for this room to grow and change as well. Ask your salesperson for advice.

Take your blueprints or pictures to a specialty store where an "experience room" is set up for firsthand testing of different components and knowledgeable consultants can answer your questions. Electronics is a complex subject, but a good consultant will educate, not mystify you.

An in-home consultation with the designer should take place early in the planning stages. You can discuss issues like speaker placement and location of wall control panels.

Before hiring a designer, make sure your service needs will be met in a timely and expert manner. Ask for the names of former and repeat clients for references.

Experienced audio-video or media consultants can astutely determine your needs. They can design and install an end product that is properly sized for your room, satisfies your desire for quality, and meets the terms of your budget. They respect cabinetry requirements and the decorating elements that must be addressed in the deliverance of a top quality home theater.

The media consultant should be willing to work with the architect, builder and interior designer to make sure your requirements will be met.

Home theaters are installed at the same time as the security and phone systems, before insulation and drywall. In new construction or remodeling, start making decisions at least two months before the drywall is hung. Allow four weeks for delivery and installation scheduling.

CREATING A HOME THEATER

For the best seat in the house, you'll need:

• A large screen television and/or projection video system (from 32-inch direct view up to 200-inches, depending on the size of the room). New, compact products are available now.

• A surround-sound receiver to direct sound to the appropriate speaker with proper channel separation

• A surround-sound speaker system, with front, rear, and center channel speakers and a sub-woofer for powerful bass response

• A hi-fi stereo VCR or DVD (digital video) player for ultimate audio and video quality

• Appropriate cabinetry, properly vented

• A comfortable environment, ideally a rectangular room with extra drywall to block out distractions.

PLAN AHEAD

Even if you aren't installing a home theater system right away, have a room designed to serve that purpose later. Get the wiring done and build the room an appropriate shape and size. Get the right antenna. Ask for double drywall for noise control.

BEST TIP:

Have phone lines pulled to every TV outlet in the house for Internet access and satellite reception.

701

Home Theater
Design

AUDIO-VIDEO CREATIONS ....**(954) 321-5548**
300 NW 70 Street, Suite 103, Plantation   Fax: (954) 452-8592
See Ad on Page: 715   800 Extension: 1027
Principal/Owner: Brad Gibson

CINEMA SOUND UNLIMITED ....**(954) 255-8786**
7381 W. Sample Road, Coral Springs   Fax: (954) 255-8726
See Ad on Page: 711   800 Extension: 1057

DESIGNER AUDIO ....**(941) 514-4904**
2011 Trade Center Way, Naples   Fax: (941) 514-4905
See Ad on Page: 704, 705   800 Extension: 1070
Principal/Owner: Denise Novack
Website: www.designeraudio.com email: sales@designeraudio.com

EXCEL AUDIO VIDEO...**(941) 643-0154**
3920-A Progress Ave., Naples   Fax: (941) 643-6159
See Ad on Page: 714   800 Extension: 1088
Principal/Owner: Robert W. McManus
Website: www.excelav.com email: rmcmanus@excelav.com

HOUSE OF HIGH FIDELITY...**(941) 262-0100**
5187 Tamiami Trail N.,   Fax: (941) 262-3743
See Ad on Page: 706, 707   800 Extension: 1125
Principal/Owner: Pamela Futch

702

INTERNATIONAL AUDIO VISUAL, INC ....**(954) 630-9797**
3215 NW 10th TCE #206, Fort Lauderdale   Fax: (954) 630-9775
See Ad on Page: 712, 713   800 Extension: 1139
Principal/Owner: Wade Gilbert
Website: www.iavi.com email: info@iavi.com
Additional Information: For the latest in home theater products and installation.

SOUND COMPONENTS ....**(305) 665-7299**
1533 Madruga Ave, Coral Gables   Fax: (305) 663-4138
See Ad on Page: 696, 697, 710   800 Extension: 1241
Principal/Owner: Mark Goldman

SOUND PERFORMANCE ....**(305) 446-8055**
4030 Aurora Street, Coral Gables
See Ad on Page: 708, 709   800 Extension: 1242

SOUTH EASTERN SOUND & COMMUNICATIONS ....**(561) 998-2010**
7630 NW 6th Avenue, Boca Raton   Fax: (561) 998-2007
See Ad on Page: 703   800 Extension: 1246
Principal/Owner: Robert Fields
Website: www.sesound.com

Photo courtesy of Sound Plus Wood

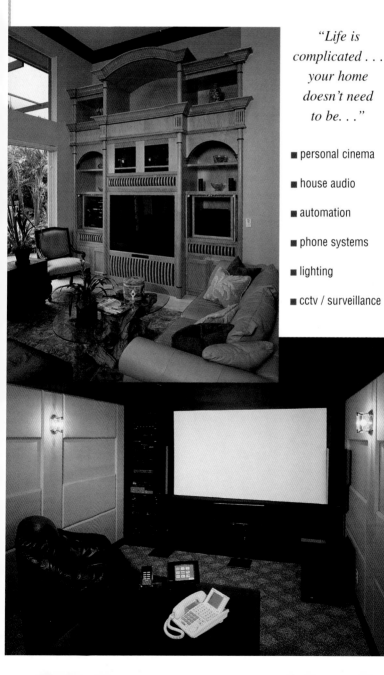

DESIGNER audio

Let us show you what a "push of a button"

Audio Video

Home Theatres

Security Systems

Lighting Control

Automation Systems

can really do…

2011 Trade Center Way
Naples, FL 34109
Off.　(941) 514-4904
Fax.　(941) 514-4905
Sales@designeraudio.com
www.designeraudio.com

**Authorized Sales
and Service**

Sony
Macintosh
Mitsubishi
Lexicon
AMX
Sonance
Sony ES
Marantz
Snell
Tannoy
Velodyne
Energy

5187 North Tamiami Trail, Naples, Florida 34103
941.262.0100 800.300.0693 Fax 941.262.3743
houseofhighfi@worldnet.att.com

Retail Showroom
Full Home Theater
A/V Automation
Custom Cabinetry

Member of
Para Cedia
Naples Chamber of Commerce

high end hifi equipment

home theater systems

hotels and resorts

the ultimate in sound and video

AUDIO, VIDEO AND LIGHTING EXPERTS FOR OVER 25 YEARS
Specialized in custom engineering and installation.
Working with state of the art manufacturers.
Serving hotels, resorts, luxury homes, yachts and aircraft.

Whatever your environment we custom tailor your video and sound experience

- *Home Theater / Media Rooms
  Experience Sharpvision*

- *Multi-room Audio*

- *Home Automation*

- *Satellite Systems*

- *Home Security*

- *Digital Audio and Video*

- *Lighting Systems*

- *Yachts*

- *Phone Systems*

7381 West Sample Road, Coral Springs
Call **(954) 255-8786** Fax **(954) 255-8726**

HOME THEATRE SYSTEMS

Audio-Video Creations and **AVC Woodcraft**
combine to provide you with the theatre of
your dreams. We build dedicated theatres or
custom home entertainment systems. Whether you
need equipment, custom furniture, or a turnkey
theatre system, we can provide it
for you. Call us today for an appointment.

954.321.5548
300 NW 70 Ave, Suite 103
Plantation FL 33317

Intergrated
Home Systems

ENVIRONMENTAL TECHNOLOGY CONTROL............................(561) 881-8118
2921 Australian Avenue, West Palm Beach   Fax: (561) 882-0110
See Ad on Page: 719   800 Extension: 1083
Principal/Owner: William G. Maronet
email: etc2921@msn.com
Additional Information: Recognized as one of the top 50 Home Integration
Companies nationally.

INTERNATIONAL AUDIO VISUAL, INC ....(954) 630-9797
3215 NW 10th TCE #206, Fort Lauderdale   Fax: (954) 630-9775
See Ad on Page: 712, 713   800 Extension: 1139
Principal/Owner: Wade Gilbert
Website: www.iavi.com email: info@iavi.com
Additional Information: For the latest in home theater products and installation.

ISR
1701 West Quincy, Suite 10, Naperville, IL
See Ad on Page: 717   800 Extension: 1145

SOUND PLUS WOOD ....(561) 243-1843
1055 SW 15th Avenue, Delray beach   Fax: (561) 243-9555
See Ad on Page: 718   800 Extension: 1243
Principal/Owner: Mike Moran
email: msmoran@bellsouth.net

SOUTH EASTERN SOUND & COMMUNICATIONS ....(561) 998-2010
7630 NW 6th Avenue, Boca Raton   Fax: (561) 998-2007
See Ad on Page: 703   800 Extension: 1246
Principal/Owner: Robert Fields
Website: www.sesound.com

Photo courtesy of Sound Plus Wood

What's in a name?

Pictures are nice, but they say little about what a **systems specialist** actually does.

Our name, Integrated Systems by Rich, reflects our "Rich" **tradition** and our systems approach. Rich Inc., our predecessor, changed the way stock market information was obtained and used with the innovative CIS system. ISR continues that tradition with the **revolutionary open architecture** TRONARCH Home Management system. We are more than just audio, video or electrical specialists branching out into other systems. We're more than just a dealer, we're a leader working directly with **partners** like Microsoft, Sony, Vantage, EPA/Energy Star and the AIA to deliver solutions for today & tomorrow. We address the entire systems process for **unified solutions** from start to finish, saving up to 30% by avoiding common problems others miss.

Our clients and counterparts take our name seriously also:

"It's really awesome. It makes this large home really manageable"

> Missy Butcher, ISR client
> – as featured on The Oprah Winfrey Show

"I'd have to hire 10 separate people to do what they do, and then make sure they're all coordinated with each other."

> Grey Marker, Miller Construction
> – as featured in Robb Report

"Homes over 10,000 square feet are complex and should have a management system, ISR is the leader in home management systems."

> Paul Morgan – Paul Morgan Lighting Design

"There is only one ISR." John Oleson, Vantage

Call today to see for yourself or check our references.

A Rich Tradition in Systems Technology Solutions

www.isr-usa.com

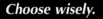

Choose wisely.

TRONARCH

For more information on how we can help you, call (800) 451-4370 for your personal consultation.

Aspen I Austin I Chicago I Palm Beach I San Francisco

- **Fine Custom Cabinetry**
- **Kitchens and Baths**
- **Home Theaters**
- **Smart Homes**
- **Audio Video Systems**

Sound P·L·U·S WOOD

Serving Discriminating Consumers since

By Appointment only
561-243-1843

Delray Beach • Florida

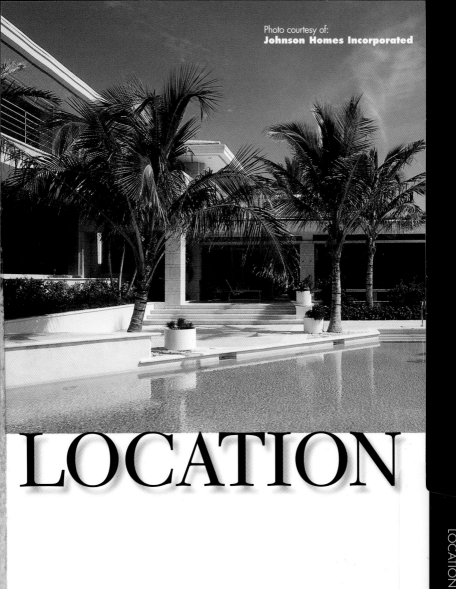

LOCATION

WCI. Creating

THAT MAKE

**Deering Bay
Yacht & Country Club,
Coral Gables**
Golf Course &
Yachting Community
From the $600s
to nearly $2 Million

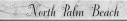

North Palm Beach

Jupiter

Harbour Isles
Exclusive Waterfront Living
From $1.6 Million

Jupiter Yacht Club
Luxury Mid-Rise Intracoastal Living
From the $400s to over $1 Million

Exceptional Lifestyles

DREAMS COME TRUE

WCI's (Watermark Communities Inc.) award-winning communities are home to nearly 150,000 residents and include 351 holes of golf currently open for public and private play; eight miles of beach-front and waterfront property; boat slips at five deep-water marinas accommodating more than 1,000 boats; plus several restaurants and commercial sites. WCI builds single-family and multi-family homes, as well as luxury condominiums, ranging from the $100s to more than $10 million. When your name is on the door of a WCI residence, you can be confident that you've chosen the best. WCI has solid, unparalleled experience. For over 50 years, we have been developing excellence in Florida with a commitment to lasting value, location and lifestyle.

East Coast Communities

HARBOUR ISLES
561-776-1991 OR
888-688-6687

JUPITER YACHT CLUB
561-575-5224 OR
800-268-5701

HERON BAY
954-346-5532 OR
800-290-8053

PARKLAND ISLES
954-757-2918 OR
800-290-8053

DEERING BAY YACHT AND COUNTRY CLUB
305-254-2100

And Watch For These Other Communities Coming Soon!

ONE WATERMARK PLACE
561-775-2120

EVERGRENE
561-775-2120

Visit Our Website:
www.wcicommunities.com

Prices and availability are subject to change without notice.
Broker participation encouraged.

WCI

Watermark Communities Inc.

Where Florida Lives

Coral Springs

Heron Bay
Luxury Single-Family & Townhomes
From the $200s to over $1 Million

Parkland

Parkland Isles
Single-Family "Island" Community
From the mid $200s to over $600,000

"Must I leave thee,
Paradise?
Thus leave thee,
native soil,
these happy walks
&
shades. "

John Milton

photo courtesy of:
SRD Building Corp.

Home Sweet Home

One of the most endearing charms of this area is the wide diversity and individuality of its neighborhoods. Whether your fantasy is to live in a stately, traditional home surrounded by lush sweeping lawns, or an ultra-modern custom built home overlooking a golf course, you are sure to find a neighborhood to call you home. To savvy homeowners, location is the most valuable of assets, and has long been their mantra.

Today's state-of-the-art homebuilders have given life to new communities in masterfully planned environments. Visually delightful and diverse, yet cohesive in architectural style and landscape, these communities address with impeccable taste the needs of their residents: proximity to excellent schools, shops, restaurants, favored leisure pursuits, the workplace. Safe havens, often in country or golf course settings, these developments cater to the homeowners' active lifestyles. Artistically designed for ease, these gracious homes welcome family and guests; they are sanctuaries in which to entertain, relax and nourish the spirit.

Location

THE COMMUNITY SPIRIT

Enclave neighborhoods built in luxury locations have the benefit of being part of two communities. The neighborhood identity is strong and so is the larger community spirit. It's the best of both worlds.

THE MASTER PLAN

Homes and landscapes in "master plan" locations are as unique and customized as anywhere in the South Florida area. However, they are established according to a well-defined overall plan, which gives the homeowners the security of knowing that the high quality look of their neighborhood will be rigorously upheld.

THE ULTIMATE IN LUXURY LIVING

The builders and developers of custom homes in upscale locations throughout the city and the suburbs realize the value of simplicity and strive to deliver it.

Simplicity is one of the qualities we most desire in our lives. By offering a community designed and built on the philosophy that homeowners deserve a beautiful environment, peaceful surroundings and luxurious amenities to enhance their lives, locations like those featured in the following pages deliver simplicity on a luxury scale.

Homeowners who live in these kinds of communities and locations know what they want. They want an environment where architecture and nature exist in harmony. Where builders have proven dedication to protecting the natural surroundings. They want recreation, like golf, swimming, lakes, walk and biking paths, or tennis courts. They want to live where there is a sense of community, and the convenience of close-by shopping and transportation. Finally, they want the conveniences of a well-planned community – guidelines on buildings and landscaping, strong community identity, and commitment to quality.

FINDING THE PERFECT LOCATION

Think about what kind of location would enhance the lifestyle of yourself and your family:

Do you need to be near transportation?

Do you want the security of a gated community?

What kind of recreational amenities do you want? Golf, tennis or pool? Paths, fishing lakes, or horse trails? Party facilities, restaurants?

What kind of natural environment do you prefer? Wildlife sanctuary, urban elegance, club luxury?

What kind of home do you want to build? Determine if your dream house fits the overall essence of a particular community. Some planned communities allow only certain builders at their locations. Find out if these builders create homes that would satisfy your desires.

THE VALUE OF A LUXURY LOCATION

The availability of building sites diminishes with every passing year, and the builders and developers of our finest residential locations know that quality must be established to attract custom home owners. Their commitment to building top quality homes is apparent in the designs and materials used in their projects and in the reputations their locations enjoy.

The demand for homes built in these locations is growing. Their benefits, plus the unique opportunity to build a new custom home in a totally fresh, and new environment, are very enticing. ■

WCI COMMUNITIES LTD. PARTNERSHIP ....**(954) 752-1100**
11575 Heron Bay Blvd., Coral Springs
See Ad on Page: 722, 723, 728

Fax: (954) 755-1885
800 Extension: 1270

"Homeowners want an *environment* where nature and harmony exist in *harmony.*"

... another growing WCI *luxury condominium.*

One seed to mark the start of man;

One brick to start a building

Both score a miracle so grand;

It's an awesome world we're guilding.

WCI
Watermark Communities Inc.

Please Contact Elaine Edwards **(877) 659-MARK**

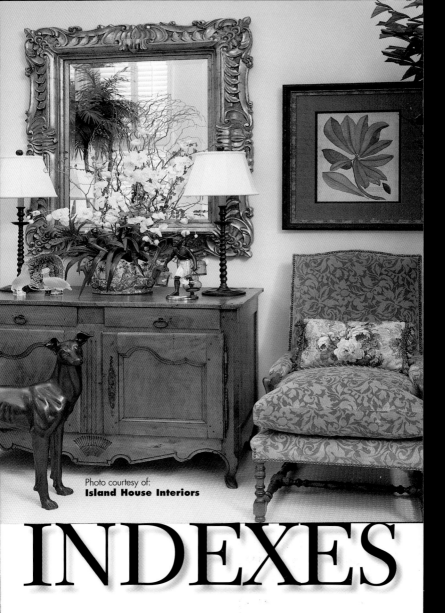

Photo courtesy of:
Island House Interiors

INDEXES

Simply the Best!

Even in 120 mile per hour winds.

The Legacy that began almost a century ago continues today.
Zeluck's timeless design is combined with precision craftsmanship
to produce what are simply the best windows and doors
money can buy.

New York

Alphabetical Index

733

Alphabetical Index

T

U

V

W

Z

ARCHITECTS

738

739

HOME FURNISHING & DECORATING

Accessories

American Traditional

Art Deco

Professional Index

743

747

748

749

750

751

752

753

754